Rise and Shine!

A Southern Son's Treasury of Food, Family, and Friends

Advance Praise for *Rise and Shine!*

With seven generations of Georgia heritage to draw upon, Johnathon Scott Barrett has mastered the Southern food memoir in *Rise and Shine!* The reader can't help but become charmed with his love of food, family, and friends—all of which are showcased in each and every chapter. It is both a delightful read and a scrumptious cookbook.

—Nathalie Dupree, James Beard winning
cookbook author and television host

Being drawn into the vivid stories told in Barrett's new memoir is a foregone conclusion—the cadence, rituals and even the fragrances of Georgia come to life in these pages—but it's the recipes that will bind you, stitch you into his world with the effectiveness of the best cookbooks. *Rise and Shine!* is a joy to read, and it's truly a rare thrill to cook alongside Mama and JB.

—Matt Lee and Ted Lee, authors of
The Lee Bros. Charleston Kitchen

If you are a cook, Johnathon Scott Barrett's new food memoir will have you searching for your grandmama's black iron skillet and a nice meaty hambone, but if you just prefer to devour memoirs of a forgotten time way down south in Georgia, you will simply reach for a glass of sweet tea and head to the porch swing, even if that is a place you inhabit only in sweet memory. Either way, yes, ma'am! If you have this book in your hand, you are in for a rare treat.

—Mary Kay Andrews, *New York Times* bestselling author of
Beach Town, *Summer Rental* and *Hissy Fit*

Johnathon Scott Barrett is the very model of that rare breed, the true Southern Gentleman—charming, thoughtful, kind, and generous—yet always ready and willing to laugh at himself. *Rise and Shine! A Southern Son's Treasury of Food, Family, and Friends* is a charming love song to all the best things about growing up, not to mention eating, in the South.

—Damon Lee Fowler, author of *Essentials of
Southern Cooking* and *Beans, Greens, & Sweet Georgia Peaches*

Johnathon Scott Barrett is a part of the Savannah, Georgia, food scene. We all love food, love cooking, and love everyone else who loves food and cooking. In this beautifully written book, Barrett takes us on a sentimental journey as he charts his joy of cooking from birth to the present. We visit with the people and the places that shaped his palate. We visit the farms, the farmers' markets, the islands, and the big cities. With wit and wisdom, Barrett writes lovingly about the family and friends who have encouraged him to both cook and write. After reading his memoir, I can't decide if I want to go cook something, or write a love letter to my Mother. You will love this book!

—Martha Giddens Nesbit, author of *Savannah Collection: Favorite Recipes
from Savannah Cooks*, *Savannah Entertains*, and *Savannah Celebrations*.

Johnathon Scott Barrett understands that food tastes better when there is a story behind it. *Rise and Shine!* is a family memoir, a culinary travelogue, and a rich collection of inherited and invented recipes. Barrett celebrates chili dogs served in a pool hall, meringue-topped banana pudding, and the joy of having breakfast at suppertime. Aunts, uncles, parents, and grandparents populate these pages, sharing memories of bread-and-butter pickles, barbecue on the beach, and soul-satisfying slices of coconut cake.

—Fred Sauceman, author of *Buttermilk & Bible Burgers:*
More Stories from the Kitchens of Appalachia

Johnathon Scott Barrett's life has been filled with warm family relationships and savory food. His book about both subjects leaves you hungering for more from this talented writer and memoirist.

—Jackie K. Cooper, author of *Memory's Mist*

Food in the South is created with a blend of family, local color, history, and celebration. In his cooking memoir, Johnathon Scott Barrett richly captures these elements. As a food history of Georgia, Barrett recounts the traditional culinary resources of Middle Georgia and how members of his family utilized this bounty for their entertainment and feast. As Barrett's career took him to cities and countries far from his roots, he managed to hold homage to the past while adding new cultural elements to his table and festive gatherings. Barrett's storytelling makes *Rise and Shine!* feel like an evening on the porch sharing stories after a good meal—one that lingers with sighs and smiles.

—Joyce Dixon, SouthernScribe.com

Filled with fishing tales and blue-ribbon recipes, *Rise and Shine!* creates a kinship with his Southern stories that delight the soul and are a feast for the heart. Keep your eye on Johnathon Scott Barrett—he is a Southern Gentleman, an eloquent storyteller, a phenomenal cook. An excellent book worthy of high praise!

—Renea Winchester, award-winning author of
Farming, Friends, and Fried Bologna Sandwiches

(continued)

As a fellow "Perrysian," I immediately identified with Johnathon Scott Barrett's new book. From "It Started on Ball Street" to the folks and places I too have known and loved, each page was a reminder of the adage "it takes a village to raise a child." Barrett's village is the same as mine—an agrarian, rural, small Southern town with pecan groves and peach orchards and a cast of characters.

A village like Perry, Georgia, gives its children a place to love and be loved—a place of security and confidence and nostalgia and wonderful memories of our childhood and families. Barrett seizes upon the nostalgia of a place like our hometown, and further evokes emotion and candor through Southern food and our fondness for family meals, celebrations, and our heritage. I love that Barrett's work is as if he's telling us all a story on the porch on the farm—having to turn the page, more so, than to await the next vocalized word. I hope y'all enjoy *Rise and Shine!* in the same manner as I did—and it leaves you hungry for home!

—James T. Farmer III, editor-at-large, *Southern Living*
and author of *A Time to Plant, A Time to Cook* and *Dinner on the Grounds*

Johnathon Scott Barrett's valentine to the South, *Rise and Shine!* reads as much memoir as it does cookbook, tapping into the universal truth that food memories are often our strongest. They are wrapped in family lore, celebration, and destinations that mark turning points in our lives. With this book, he has welcomed us to his table—and it is a feast, not just for the belly, but also for the soul.

—Amy Paige Condon, *Savannah Magazine*

Rise and Shine!

A Southern Son's Treasury of Food, Family, and Friends

To Karen —
Happy Cooking!

JOHNATHON SCOTT BARRETT

J Barrett

MERCER UNIVERSITY PRESS | Macon, Georgia

MUP/H907

© 2015 by Mercer University Press
Published by Mercer University Press
1501 Mercer University Drive
Macon, Georgia 31207
All rights reserved

9 8 7 6 5 4 3 2 1

Books published by Mercer University Press are printed on acid-free paper that meets the requirements of the American National Standard for Information Sciences—Permanence of Paper for Printed Library Materials.

ISBN   978-0-88146-542-6

Cataloging-in-Publication Data is available from the Library of Congress

Contents

Preface

People begin writing at different times in their lives and for different reasons. Some seem to be born with a pen and paper in hand. While I was always an avid reader, it was after my fortieth year before I began putting my thoughts into the written word.

A few months after my mom passed away, I was asked by my friend Monica to host the members of her supper club, "The Girls on the Grill," in my home and present some favorite recipes and menus as a part of the party. These "girls" are all past the ingénue stage of life as well as excellent and renowned Savannah hostesses, meaning I had to take this task seriously in terms of what I would present.

As I began to put together my ideas, which included menus inspired by trips abroad and dinners in a variety of restaurants, my mind kept straying back to years growing up and the delicious food prepared by my mom and family members. The loss of my mother, who died just a few months before the supper club meeting, was absolutely heart-wrenching for me, and it came right on the heels of the death of her baby sister, Beatrice, who was like my second mother. As long as Mama was here, it was almost as if all the other relatives who had died, including my sport of a dad, his gentle sister, Aunt Lil, and my vivacious aunt Martha, were still with us. Mama told stories about them in daily conversation, keeping them alive in our hearts and minds. When she was gone, it was as if I had lost them all over, yet again.

As the project progressed, though, I began to realize how fortunate I'd been over my lifetime to have had such loving relatives; as A. A. Milne wrote, "How lucky I am to have something that makes saying goodbye so hard." I wrote of the years I was a tow-headed child fishing on Big Indian Creek, of the laughter and jokes I've shared during a countless array of dinners and parties, and my adventures on trips both here as well as those far outside the land of Dixie. With all these stories and recipes, a book was born. As Janis Owens, the incredible Southern novelist, said to me about my inspiration for these writings, "It's wonderful what the power of love—right at the painful intersection of grief and loss—can do."

I appreciate each of you taking the time to visit with me with *Rise and Shine!* Sit back and sip a little bourbon, or have a glass of iced tea, and hear some of the tales I have about being Southern, my love of great food and family, and my warm circle of friends. I hope you enjoy...JSB

Foreword

I met my friend Johnathon Barrett at the Savannah Book Festival in 2008 when he introduced me before I spoke. I was there with my recently released cookbook, *The Cracker Kitchen*, which was a paean to all things rustic, porcine, and backwater, Florida Cracker style. I couldn't imagine how it would go over in beautiful, inclusive Savannah, a jewel of the Old Confederacy, where dinner parties are themed, set in china, and complete with asparagus forks, and if so much as an inch of burlap is in evidence, it's a rustic bow in a centerpiece, with no history whatever with humble conveyances like potato sacks.

So I was taking the podium at a considerable disadvantage and was delighted and surprised when Johnathon approached and introduced himself as my escort, his face alight with excitement, for, like me, he was also a Cracker—a Georgia Cracker, raised on butterbeans and fried chicken in Perry, Georgia, where his family still lived. I must have looked unbelieving, as he was dressed then (and always) like a Dorothy Sayer bon vivant in a striped bow tie and blazer. But as we walked to the auditorium where I was to speak, he backed up his claim of Cracker kinship by expounding on purple-hulls versus zipper peas, and whether fatback was really preferable to ham, then made a sidetrack into explaining his family tree's migration to Middle Georgia in some detail, including ways our joint trees might have intersected, oh, a hundred years ago. All this, without missing a step or getting lost or failing to open every door before me.

I knew then that I was in the presence of a Cracker Prince of some caliber. We not only enjoyed a merry visit but became long-distance friends who enjoyed a lively correspondence via email, exchanging mama-stories, jelly-stories, what's-for-dinner stories, and the occasional vintage photograph—the kind you find tucked away in a Bible, of a certain time and place and relatives that needs no explanation; that says it all. In Johnathon, I found a kindred spirit who'd grown up deeply rooted in the small-town, Waffle House splendor of the New Old South, where interstates and pecan orchards coexist peacefully, and our greatest private passion is exiting to take a nostalgic road trip to some little-known speck on a blue highway.

These were the places that brought to mind the homes and cafés and church suppers of our childhoods—the land of fat pigs and stewed hens and produce stands on every corner, where our passion for a well-set table was born. Johnathon's devotion is plainly shown in his memoir, in his deep and abiding love for his darling aunts, his rattle-snake killing father, and his wonderful diva of a mother, Joyce, a matriarch of such unwavering confidence in her jellies and jam recipes that she withheld from entering them in the national fair so as to give the other contestants a chance at a ribbon.

This bright birthright launched him into a successful career as a CPA and nonprofit business executive that took him far beyond the city limits of Perry and established his influence at tables all over the South. Being a good Southern Son, he never forgot the early lessons he learned at his family table of generosity and hospitality and welcome. He brought them with him when he made his move to town, to become a well-loved host and epicurean in America's supper club paradises of Savannah and the Golden Isles. Both professionally and privately he has hosted a gamut of storied celebrations, from humble home suppers to magnificent fundraiser fetes, making his invitations sought-after and highly prized. So nuanced is his palate that he was a James Beard judge for many years. He has tested and critiqued the best food in America, but his roots and heart remain in the simplicity of the farm-raised, handed-down recipes of his youth.

I don't recommend his charming memoir as a cookbook only, but as a dear companion to sit and read and savor. The stories, the history, and the family photos that tell the tale of Johnathon's Bilbo-Baggins-like here-and-back journey to and from his youth in Perry and his adulthood beyond will touch your heart with their humility and cast of oh-so-familiar characters. When you incorporate his recipes in your own parties or dinners, you can honestly say, as I do, that they were passed on from a friend of yours, a gentleman named Johnathon, from Georgia.

—Janis Owens,
author of *American Ghost* and *The Cracker Kitchen*

Mama and Daddy, shortly after they were married, Clinchfield, Georgia, 1949.
In their heaven, the fish are always biting and the fried chicken is always hot.

*This book is dedicated in loving memory of my
mother and father,
Joyce Nipper Barrett and John F. Barrett*

With Daddy, Linda Faye (Sissie), and Mama, 1966

Introduction

It Started on Ball Street

Ever since I was a young fellow, I have had a close relationship with good food. I received my first exposure to cooking and meal preparations as a youngster in my family's kitchen in the small town of Perry, Georgia. A surprise baby who came along twelve years after my sister, I was the only one around the house a good bit of the time and often left alone with my nanny, Carrie Rumph. Carrie was also the cook for our family, and I spent many a day at the kitchen table watching her magic, gleaning cooking techniques and recipes that I'd remember and use as an adult. Those were some wonderful afternoons spent together, and I learned not only about cooking, but life lessons as well. Her mantra was "graciousness," and I hope a bit of it rubbed off on me.

As I grew older, I also learned a number of things from my mother, who was a very talented cook. She was known particularly for her ability to make some of the best preserves, jams, and jellies known in Middle Georgia and brought home top honors from the National Fair for these dishes. People also raved about her homemade biscuits, and on Sundays, our dinner table would be full of a variety of fresh vegetables, roasted meats, and homemade desserts.

While I am waxing fondly on these times, let me admit that I was not always so happy with the sheer labor it took to produce our bounty of harvest. Mind you, I grew up in a small Southern town, and back in the '60s and '70s, my family still had strong ties to farming with a number of our relatives who kept extensive vegetable gardens and orchards. My father built a "little house" in our backyard where he had an upright *and* a flatbed freezer to hold our frozen goods, shelves for the jars of canned items, and exposed rafters for Vidalia onions, which hung in knotted cloth sacks. As a child and into my teen years, it was a family outing to pick these fruits and vegetables each summer, and before you get misty-eyed and murmur, "How sweet," let me tell you: stoop labor is no picnic.

Most of our harvest was in summertime, and the heat in Georgia is sweltering. My father would wake us all up before dawn to start the day off, going through the house slinging open bedroom doors and singing at the top of his baritone voice the old spiritual "This Train is Bound for Glory" or maybe a few lines of "Jubilee!" a song made famous by the Florida Boys and the Happy Goodman Family, two of his favorite gospel groups. He might also try to inspire us with trumpeting out a portion of Isaiah 60:1, "Rise and shine for your light has come!" Rise and shine indeed. He would walk away snickering, knowing how aggravating it was for this lazy teenage boy. I found absolutely no pleasure in getting hauled out of bed at 5 a.m. to be led over the countryside to handpick hairy and itchy things—okra, corn, peaches, figs—all in the scalding heat.

So while I retained a love of fried chicken and would go to an occasional fish fry, I was finished with Southern vegetables by the time I left for Georgia Southern University in 1982. I knocked the red clay dust off my penny loafers and moved from Perry and pretty much vowed never to allow another butter bean or spoonful of stewed squash to pass through the lips of JSB, budding Esquire.

The bright lights of Washington, DC, and Atlanta caught my eye, and further travel to cities that were only read about as a boy introduced me to an array of foods and cultures that eventually took the place of, at least for a while, those traditional dishes I grew up with.

Over the years, I have been fortunate to dine in some of the best restaurants from New York to Paris, and many places in between, sampling exotic items that would have been totally foreign in our kitchen on Ball Street. I mean, whoever heard of eating a piece of eel wrapped in rice? Growing up, I never would have considered for a moment that those creatures could be delicacies. I remember catching them from time to time while fishing on a slow-moving creek, and I'd cut the line and throw those slithering, prehistoric creatures right back into the muddy water from whence they came. Eat them? Please, not even if they were fried. And shaved truffles? Someone would actually *want* to eat an odiferous subterranean fungus? As Carrie would have said, "Pray tell!"

But people change, and I expanded my food horizons to things I'd never dreamed of eating as a teenager, and I've loved every mouthful. (Except the eel; never could do eel.)

And as I've grown into adulthood, I have found that I have a real passion and joy for making people happy with food. I'm very much a social creature who loves to entertain, and I was born into a family and culture that honors good food as a way of relating and interacting with people. In Perry, as in other small towns in the South, food was the common denominator in life for all reasons. A gift of a cake or a basket of fried chicken could express empathy, joy, grief, friendship, love; it just depended on the occasion for which it was given. Food was how we socialized, and your favorite dishes were prepared for birthdays, funerals, holidays, or any other special time in life. This practice was not limited to just ladies; men were involved as well. I recall on several occasions my father frying a big pan of fish to take to a shut-in or delivering a churn of his homemade peach ice cream to an elderly couple who were in need of company and friendship.

This inherited affinity for good eating and close association with fresh food has helped lead to my current career as a professional fundraiser. I started my corporate life in the beautiful coastal city of Savannah, where I became a Certified Public Accountant. Not knowing anyone when I arrived, at the tender age of twenty-three, my mom encouraged me to volunteer and devote time to good causes; she said that was the best way to meet nice people in a new city. I became involved with a score of charities and soon found myself sitting on a number of boards of directors. In the course of my volunteer work, people learned I was very good at putting my financial acumen together with my fondness for parties and food and so was asked to chair several high-profile fundraisers, such as Savannah's Festival of Trees, Historic Savannah Foundation's Annual Gala, and the Georgia Historical Society's Antique Show and Sale. After enjoying many rewarding years donating my time, I changed career paths when I turned thirty-five and moved into nonprofit management, specializing in major-donor fundraising. The biggest part of my job is relationship building, and that involves making people feel comfortable and at ease. I often employ food and entertaining to cement those key partnerships, from presenting small, informal dinners to smart cocktail receptions and large, over-the-top black-tie affairs.

Entertaining is also a large part of my personal life, and there is nothing I love more than being in the midst of a warm group of friends. My dinners and parties have been varied and extensive in terms of what was hosted: black-tie cocktail parties with someone crooning out Johnny Mercer tunes next to the baby grand, seated dinners for thirty folks for a landmark birthday, or maybe just four of us sitting in the bar, enjoying a very casual summer supper in our shorts and sports shirts.

Because of my love of good food and the fact that I was an experienced diner who frequented various restaurants, particularly in the Southeast, I was approached several years ago to become a restaurant judge for the James Beard Foundation. I was flattered to have been asked, and I used the designation to find excuses to dine out even more. It can prove to be expensive, though; you pay for your own food, there is no stipend, and under no circumstances can you let the restaurant staff know of your position. However, I fully enjoyed the volunteer task and undertook the duties very seriously, as a James Beard designation for a chef is an honor that is coveted like no other in the field of culinary arts. Each year, as balloting began, I would take out my travel log and pore for hours over whom to vote for in which category.

So for many years into later life, my food choices and dining experiences were those quite a long way from our dining room back in Perry. But as I started writing this book, more and more memories of food and family kept arising from my childhood, along with those fun times I've hosted as an adult. It dawned on me that I had come full circle in terms of my thoughts on the food I enjoy eating and serving to my friends. Over the last decade, as my mom's health declined and I became her caregiver, things changed. She would have me drive her to the farmers' market and local farms to buy produce, and I then would help her prep and cook these Southern staples she had never tired of eating. Slowly, I started coming back around to realizing how good a bowl of fresh creamed corn really can be, especially when served with a hot-buttered biscuit, and how delicious a baby pod of okra is when battered lightly with cornmeal and fried up hot just out of the cast-iron skillet.

Looking back, I realize now that food to my family was much more than just what we ate; what we had on the dining table brought us together in bonding and loving traditions that we have enjoyed for generations. My mother, father, and aunts all shared with us children the stories of their meals from childhood, and why things were cooked and served to our family's way of liking. The reasons why we farmed or grew gardens, or how we canned and prepared our own food, were important parts of our combined heritage. This love and appreciation of food seems a part of my birthright, and I place a very high value on this good fortune, particularly as

I get older. I use my grandmother Nipper's wooden mixing spoon and bowl, along with her iron skillet, to make hoecakes or pancakes. At Christmastime each year, the candies and sweet treats that are placed on old family platters are from recipes that Daddy's sisters made with their mother back before World War I. And even though our ranks have diminished with loved ones gone, our family still fishes and churns ice cream together in the summers, although not as often as I'd like.

Getting back to the basics of these Southern dishes holds a great deal of nostalgia for me; serving these foods brings back memories of relatives long since having moved on to their final rewards—and as I've gotten older, and so many of my loved ones have gone "over the River Jordan," a good peach pie can put me right back on the doorsteps of my childhood home.

So a number of the menus I prepare now and the dishes I serve are a balance of the new techniques and recipes I've learned from Julia and Jacques and the old wooden mixing bowl that was my grandmother's to make a pan of homemade biscuits. This intersection of traditional, Deep South food-ways and those discovered from contemporary inspirations has provided a life filled with wonderful culinary experiences. And it all started with Mama, Daddy, Sissie, and Carrie, in our corner cottage on Ball Street, in a town called Perry.

With Carrie in our front yard in Perry, February 1968

Part I

Memories of a Tow-Headed Boy

The Barrett girls, Gladys (front) with Pauline (left) and Lillie, amidst the limbs of a pecan tree on the family farm. Aunt Lil had written on the back of the photograph "July 1, 1924 Lillie, Pauline & Gladys Barrett our last picture together." Gladys passed away the following year from a fever.

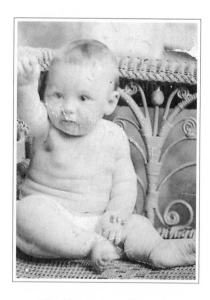

Daddy, one year old, 1919

1

Daddy's Sisters

My grandfather moved his family to Middle Georgia when he bought a farm in Pulaski County in 1916. The Barretts, Trotters, and Allisons had been in north Georgia in the Cleveland and Clarkesville communities since the early 1800s. My great-grandfather was sheriff of White County, and a number of our relatives still live in the area. But farming was not an easy way of life in the Georgia mountains, and my grandfather, John Frank, believed he could make a better living with more land that was easier to cultivate. When he had the chance, he moved the family south. However, my grandmother, Mattie Louise, missed her family very much, and you can read in some of her letters how she wished she were again back in the cool of Appalachia. She sadly passed away in 1920 when my father was just two years old. With a farm to run, my grandfather turned the care of Daddy over to his two daughters, my father's sisters, Lillie and Polly.

Aunt Lil, who was eighteen at the time, had been living with relatives in Gainesville where she studying to be a teacher. She moved back home, and besides helping care for Daddy, taught children in the proverbial one-room schoolhouse in the tiny town of Grovania, Georgia. Aunt Polly, who was a few years younger, was living at home, and over the years Daddy began to consider them his mothers. They doted on him as a child, and while there was no money to spoil him with in terms of material things, they showered him with love and affection just as they would their own children later in life. He adored his sisters and kept a very close relationship with each of them until he died.

As Daddy grew older he helped out on the family farm until his father passed away in the early '30s. Afterward, he lived alternately with Aunt Lillie and Aunt Polly, who had both since married. Interestingly, the two Barrett girls married two of the Owens brothers of nearby Hawkinsville, and my cousins have the distinction of being "double-firsts." Daddy stayed with them, working as a farmer, until he went off to serve in World War II.

I have letters from Father during the war that he sent to Aunt Polly and Aunt Lil, from the time he was in boot camp in Wyoming through his service in North Africa and Italy. These letters are a testament to Daddy's affection for his sisters. He was never one to talk too much, much less write, but the notes he wrote, mostly in pencil and on lined paper, give great insight to how he missed and loved them.

The letters changed some in content as the war came to a close, and Daddy tarried for a couple of years in Italy. His notes began asking his sisters to send him lipstick, hosiery, and other feminine items. I surmise, as did the rest of our relatives, that he had a girlfriend in Capri and that these gifts were for her. I'm not sure what happened to their courtship, but Daddy returned back home to the states in 1947. He met my mother one summer afternoon in 1948 at his brother Roy's general store in rural Clinchfield, Georgia. They married a year later.

Growing up, Aunt Polly and Aunt Lil were constant figures in my life as well. My maternal grandmother had also passed away before I was born, and these two sweet ladies were loving stand-ins for my grandmothers. Reflecting back over the years, I was so blessed to have had their close influence on my life. There have been many times when I've been met with a difficult situation and thought to myself that I needed to face the problem as Aunt Lil or Aunt Polly would have done. I never, ever in all my years heard them swear or say an unkind word about another person or even raise their voices. They could quote Scripture as well as any preacher, and they lived their lives, as proscribed by their faith, with gentleness and kindness.

Aunt Lil lived across the street from us in Perry, and I would see her on a daily basis. Some of my favorite memories of childhood are the picnics she prepared for just the two of us, served underneath the arms of a big mimosa tree in our side yard. We always had the same things—fresh-squeezed lemonade she'd made a pastel shade of pink with a little red food dye, slices of cheddar cheese, soda crackers, and either homemade sugar cookies or cupcakes. After I left home and went to college, we stayed in constant touch with one another. I remember once receiving a letter from her while I was living in Washington, DC. It contained a bright gold dogwood leaf from her yard that she had pressed. Her note said that it was a glorious fall back home and she missed me. You know, of course, that I will never part with either the leaf or the note.

While Aunt Polly lived a half hour away in Hawkinsville, going for weekend visits to her house was a regular trip for us. She and Uncle Ed had a wonderful place in town with a big wooden front porch where we'd sit and

Aunt Polly, left—born in 1906—is still with us at this writing in 2015.
Aunt Lil, on the right, was ninety-eight when she passed away in 2000.
Note the cake pan in my hand; they always showed up
at family functions with a cake.

Daddy and Aunt Lil in our front yard, 1995.
She loved the running rose Daddy had planted on the side fence.
You can see her house across the street in the background.

Aunt Polly, around 1985, with a big catfish she had caught
at one of the ponds at their farm

Daddy with his sisters at Aunt Polly's house for a birthday dinner, 1996

swing in the shade of an ivy trellis. Along with their son, Ed Jr., they also had a sizeable farm in the country; it was covered in acres and acres of pastureland where their cows roamed, and had two fishing ponds stocked with bream, bass, and catfish. Aunt Polly dearly loved to "wet a hook," and some of my best weekends were spent with her on the banks of those ponds, pulling in the fish. The afternoons always ended with a fish fry or a barbecue, which would include some of Aunt Polly's incredible cakes or cookies.

My aunts were great cooks, particularly when it came to sweets and baked goods, though they prepared them in moderation. Both ladies were slim throughout their lives; their diets were the same farm-to-table items I grew up on, and the occasional sweets, which were more prevalent during the holidays and on occasions such as birthdays.

My father's birthday was always a special time for my aunts, and each and every year that I can remember from the time I was a little boy until my father passed away, Aunt Polly would present Daddy with a multilayered fresh coconut cake and Aunt Lil would give him her favorite, a lemon Jell-O cake. This tradition was as promising as the sunrise and the sunset. As I write these lines, I can smell the sweet aroma of freshly grated coconut, and my mouth puckers remembering the tartness of wonderful lemon icing.

I've included here some of the recipes that were my aunts'. My sister and I treasure these heirlooms, and preparing them always brings back our memories of holidays and childhood celebrations. They include, of course, the coconut cake and the lemon cake, along with such treats as apple tarts, lemon meringue pie, chocolate macaroons, and icebox cookies.

Lemon Jell-O Cake

I was totally surprised when I received the recipe for this cake from my cousin, Aunt Lil's daughter. She said her mother had used a boxed cake mix since the 1960s, and I had assumed all along it was made from scratch. I thought about trying to adapt the recipe without the aid of Duncan Hines, but in the end figured it would be a waste of time; it is delicious and has been one of my family's favorites for decades.

Ingredients
Cake
1 box Lemon Supreme cake mix
¾ cup vegetable oil
1 teaspoon finely grated lemon zest
4 large eggs, beaten well
1 3-ounce package lemon Jell-O, dissolved in 1 cup hot water
Lemon Confection Icing (recipe follows)

Lemon Confection Icing
2 cups confectioner's sugar
4 tablespoons fresh-squeezed lemon juice, with pulp

Instructions
Cake:
1. Preheat oven to 275 degrees F.
2. Combine the cake mix, oil, zest, and eggs; with an electric mixer, beat over low speed until smooth.
3. Add dissolved Jell-O; beat for a minute or two until thoroughly incorporated.
4. Pour into a greased and floured Bundt pan or tube pan.
5. Bake for 1 hour and 10 minutes.
6. Remove from oven and allow to cool; unmold onto a cake plate and spread the icing on the top and sides.

Icing:
1. Mix ingredients with a whisk until smooth.
2. Immediately spread over the cooled cake.

Servings
Serves 10 to 12

* * *

Apples grow in profusion in north Georgia. My great-aunt Carrie Barrett, who lived outside of Cleveland in the Mt. Yonah area, had three huge apple trees that produced a much smaller variety of fruit than we see in stores today, but the taste was much more intense. Apples are now grown to look appealing, but often lose their taste in the process. It is the same with roses; the hybrids are stunning to look at, but the fragrance is minimal compared to the old-growth varieties that carry a heady perfume.

Aunt Lil brought an affinity for apples to Middle Georgia with her, and she was known for her wonderful apple tarts. These delicacies are simple, but delicious. Without a great deal of sugar or spice, you really taste the flavor of the fruit. She, of course, made her own crusts, which were rolled out by hand. However, baking is not my strong point, and this step is time-consuming. Instead, I use commercially prepared pie dough that is sold at the grocer's.

I found this recipe also makes an excellent apple cobbler. Aunt Lil's recipe was written out in very general terms, and I was trying to replicate the tarts to get all amounts and steps precise. On that first batch, no matter how hard I tried, I continually put too much apple onto the dough, so that filling spilled out and the edges would not adhere. After I had unsuccessfully worked through all the dough, I was pretty annoyed with myself. If you were to measure my patience on a scale of one to ten, I'd hover somewhere around two or three. The tarts were a raw disaster—and I hated wasting all that money and time. Improvising, I put together what turned out to be a very good deep-dish pie. I took the dough and placed a layer on the bottom of a thoroughly buttered deep Pyrex dish and then filled it with half the apple filling. I added another layer of dough scrap and then more apples, ending with the last of the dough on top. I brushed on some melted butter, sprinkled it with a little sugar, and then baked it in a 350-degree oven for about 45 minutes. So if you want the taste of the tarts and don't want to spend the time cutting them out, the cobbler is a great alternative. But the individual pies are a special and personal sweet treat.

Aunt Lil's Apple Tarts

Ingredients

6 cups (about 6 medium-sized) baking apples, such as Granny Smith, Jonagold, Rome Beauty, or Winesap, peeled, cored and cut into 1-inch to 2-inch cubes

3 cups water

2/3 cup sugar (or a bit more depending on the sweetness of the apples)

½ teaspoon ground cinnamon

2 teaspoons all-purpose flour

2 dashes salt

2 16-ounce packages rolled piecrust (4 crusts)

2 tablespoons unsalted butter, melted

Instructions

1. Preheat oven to 350 degrees F.
2. Place the apples in a pot and cover with the water. Bring to a gentle boil; decrease heat to a steady simmer, stirring occasionally. Cook for 20 minutes.
3. Drain the apples, and place back into the boiler.
4. With a potato masher, crush the apples until a thick consistency. Leave some small lumps.
5. Add sugar, cinnamon, flour, and salt; stir and mix thoroughly. Place in the refrigerator and chill for 20 to 30 minutes (if the filling is hot, the dough will be difficult to manage).
6. Unroll the crusts and cut into 16 4-inch to 5-inch rounds.
7. Spread 2 scant tablespoons of apple filling onto the middle of each circle; fold one side over the top and seal the tart's edges creating a half circle.
8. Press the sealed edges down with the tines of a fork. With the fork, gently pierce several holes in the top of each tart.
9. Place tarts on a large nonstick cookie sheet and brush on the butter.
10. Bake for 20 minutes or until the tarts start to slightly brown. Remove from oven and place on a wire rack to cool. May be stored in an airtight container for 2 to 3 days.

Servings
Makes 16 tarts

* * *

Besides Aunt Lil's lemon cake, she also made a wonderful lemon meringue pie; this recipe is not as rich as some I've sampled, where the filling is more of a curd. Her recipe does not call for butter and uses only three egg yolks; however, it is full of citrus flavor and is a nice, light dessert.

Lemon Meringue Pie

Ingredients
1 cup sugar
6 tablespoons cornstarch
2 cups water
3 large egg yolks, slightly beaten
2 teaspoons finely grated lemon zest
½ cup freshly squeezed lemon juice
3 large egg whites
¼ teaspoon cream of tartar
6 tablespoons sugar
1 prebaked deep-dish pie shell

Instructions
1. Preheat oven to 350 degrees F.
2. Mix sugar and cornstarch in a medium-sized saucepan.
3. Stir in water; cook over medium-high heat, whisking, until the mixture thickens, about 5 minutes.
4. Remove from heat; while continuously whisking, slowly drizzle the egg yolks into the mixture.
5. Return to medium-low heat, whisking until the filling becomes very thick, another 5 minutes or so.
6. Whisk in lemon zest and juice. Remove from heat and set aside.
7. Prepare the meringue by adding the egg whites and cream of tartar to a mixing bowl; beat over high speed until soft peaks form. While

continuing to beat, add sugar 1 tablespoon at a time, and mix until stiff peaks form.

8. Pour the filling into the pie shell and cover with the meringue, gently spreading the topping all the way across so that it covers the crust as well as the filling (this will prevent the meringue from shrinking away from the shell).

9. Bake 12 to 15 minutes until the meringue begins to brown. Remove from oven.

10. Chill the pie thoroughly in the refrigerator before serving.

Servings
Serves 6

* * *

My Aunt Polly, named Ida Pauline, was a great inspiration to my mother in terms of cooking, especially when it came to candies and cakes. I loved her kitchen, which was large, bright, and painted a cheery, pale yellow with windows that let in the Georgia sunshine. I was always fascinated by the smiling black Kit-Cat clock she had on the wall in that room, with its swishing tail and rolling eyes.

Her coconut cake was one of Aunt Polly's signature dishes, and we all clamored for it when it arrived through our doors. Mama would divvy it out so that we each got a portion and then would slice the remainder and freeze it so that we would have it for another day.

The cake here is a simple Southern 1–2–3–4 with a basic 7-minute frosting. It is a classic recipe similar to that of Mrs. S. R. Dull, the famous food columnist with the *Atlanta Journal*. When Mrs. Dull passed away in 1964, the newspaper printed that her cookbook, *Southern Cooking*, "was the standard by which regional cooks have been measured since 1928."

Coconut Cake

Ingredients
1 cup unsalted butter
2 cups sugar
4 large eggs, separated
3 cups all-purpose flour
2 teaspoons baking powder
1 cup whole milk
½ teaspoon vanilla extract
¼ teaspoon lemon extract

Fresh Coconut 7-minute Frosting
Instructions
1. Preheat oven to 350 degrees F.
2. Grease and flour three cake pans; line bottoms of each pan with lightly greased parchment paper.
3. In a large bowl, cream together the butter, sugar, and egg yolks with an electric mixer.
4. In a separate bowl, sift together the flour and baking powder.
5. Mix the extracts with the milk in a small bowl.
6. To the creamed butter, sugar, and eggs, add the flour mixture and the milk mixture alternately. Start and end with the flour, mixing continuously. Set aside.
7. In another bowl, beat the egg whites until gentle peaks form.
8. Gently fold the beaten egg whites into the cake batter.
9. Pour the batter into the prepared cake pans.
10. Bake for 25 to 30 minutes until done.
11. Remove the layers from the oven and cool on a wire rack. Cool completely before frosting.

Before making your icing, prepare your fresh coconut. You'll need one that is large. Pierce both ends with an ice pick and crack the outer shell with a hammer. Reserve the milk, if possible, for other uses. Scoop out the flesh with a knife or wedge and cut away any brown parts. Finely grate the white part of the coconut either with a hand grater, using the larger grates, or in a food processor. You should have about two cups. If you cannot grate your own, purchase a well-regarded brand at the grocer's.

7-Minute Frosting for a 3-Layer Cake
Ingredients
2¼ cup sugar
3 large egg whites
3/8 cup cold water
1½ tablespoons white corn syrup
3/8 teaspoon cream of tartar
1 teaspoon vanilla extract

Instructions
1. In the bottom of a double boiler, bring about 3 inches of water to a steady simmer over medium-high heat.
2. In the top of the double boiler, beat together the sugar, egg whites, water, syrup, and cream of tartar for 1 minute, until well incorporated.
3. Place the frosting base onto the simmering water, and beat at high speed for 7 minutes. Remove from heat, and add vanilla. Continue to beat until the icing is thick and forms firm peaks. This may take an additional several minutes.
4. Spread between layers and on the cake; sprinkle the grated coconut evenly on the tops and sides of the frosted cake.

Servings
Serves 10 to 12

* * *

Christmas always meant chocolate macaroons from Aunt Polly. They are my favorite holiday candy; the richness of the cocoa, coconut, and peanut butter combine to create a wonderful morsel. Many people think when they hear the word "macaroon" it means a frothy, sweet, egg-white confection. However, my French niece-in-law, Caroline, says that the proper word for those types of sweets is actually "*macaron*."

Aunt Polly's Chocolate Macaroons

Ingredients
1 cup sugar
¼ cup cocoa
¼ cup milk
¼ cup unsalted butter, melted
¼ cup creamy peanut butter
1½ cup quick oats
½ cup shredded coconut
½ teaspoon vanilla flavoring

Instructions
1. Place sugar, cocoa, milk, and butter in a saucepan; stir to mix; bring to a gentle boil and cook over steady heat, stirring, for 2 minutes.
2. Stir in the peanut butter and remove from heat.
3. Pour into a mixing bowl and add in the oats, coconut, and vanilla, mixing well.
4. Drop by the tablespoonful onto wax paper. Allow to cool and harden.

Servings
Makes about 2 dozen macaroons

My aunt's recipe was double the one I wrote above, but I found it difficult for me to get all the macaroon mix out of the bowl and onto the wax paper before the candy started to harden. But if you're a little more adept with a spoon and mounding out candy than I am, the recipe can certainly be increased twofold.

* * *

When I was a little boy, I thought that icebox cookies really meant that that you made them in the freezer; when I later learned that they were just chilled in the icebox, I wondered why they would be referred to in such a way. Regardless of their name, the cookies are delicious served with a glass of cold milk in the summer or a cup of hot tea in the cool of the winter.

Icebox Cookies

Ingredients

1 cup unsalted butter, at room temperature
2 cups dark brown sugar
1 cup finely chopped pecans
3½ cups all-purpose flour
1 teaspoon baking soda
¼ teaspoon salt
2 large eggs, beaten
1 teaspoon vanilla

Instructions

1. In a large bowl, cream the butter and sugar with an electric mixer.
2. Add the pecans and stir to mix.
3. Add the flour, baking powder, and salt; mix until thoroughly incorporated.
4. Add the eggs and vanilla; stir to mix well together.
5. Roll into logs about 2 inches in diameter on wax paper that has been sprinkled with a little flour.
6. Wrap the logs in aluminum foil and freeze for 2 to 4 hours or longer.

To bake:

1. Preheat oven to 350 degrees F.
2. Remove the foil and wax paper and cut the frozen dough into ¼-inch slices; place on a nonstick cookie sheet.
3. Bake for 10 to 12 minutes until just beginning to brown; watch the oven carefully as the edges of the cookies can burn quickly.
4. When done, use a spatula and remove to a wire rack to cool.

Servings

Makes 6 dozen

2

Mama during the War

My mother was the last surviving child of Charles Cleveland Nipper and Eunice Florence Musselwhite. Both the Nippers and Musselwhites were of Scottish descent, and members of each family were some of the first settlers of Middle Georgia, having received lottery land grants in the Pulaski County area dating back into the early 1800s. The Musselwhites were in the logging business, and the Nippers were mostly farmers.

Mama was born during the Great Depression in Clinchfield, Georgia, which is about halfway between Perry and Hawkinsville. Life in the little unincorporated town centered around the quarry plant, Penn-Dixie. Most all the men who lived in the area worked for the company, which manufactured cement from the limestone deposited there eons ago when the ocean's edge met what is now Middle Georgia. My grandparent's house was on the ridge called the fault line, a geographical expression given to where the coastal plain meets the piedmont, right where the Atlantic used to reach. On a clear night you could see the twinkling lights of Perry in the distance.

My grandfather was a crane operator for Penn-Dixie and farmed a small plot of land as a way to help keep his family healthy and fed. Mama was very close with her parents and siblings, and she often spoke and told stories of her childhood. She described her father as a very loving man but strict with his children, and her mother as an easygoing, sweet lady who suffered from a heart condition caused by rheumatic fever.

Charlie, as Papa was called by his friends, was known for his extensive garden. Each year he cultivated a large acre plot that grew a variety of vegetables, from string beans to beets, as well as harvested crab apples, pears, and figs from the trees on his property. His specialty was tomatoes; Mama said that one slice of his Big Boy variety was wide enough to cover a whole slice of bread. He also kept livestock, such as pigs, chickens, and cows, and made sure he had guineas hens on the property to eat snakes, which were prevalent in the area. My grandmother, known affectionately as Ninnie, loved to garden as well. Her yard was full of a variety of roses, from the trailing Seven Sisters with their tight blooms to a vast selection of fragrant tea roses. According to Mama, Ninnie could plant a cutting off any rose bush into the soil and make it grow; she also said that her mother felt that the best plants were "borrowed" or gifted ones from a friend's garden.

Life was not easy during the Depression for the Nippers, and maybe even less so during the war, but Mama never carried on about it. Things were what they were, as she said, and they made the best of it. She and her family were made of sturdy, Scottish blood, and held a work ethic and attitude of life that allowed them to cope even through the most difficult of situations. It was always fascinating to hear her and my aunts talking about life during those times, which was far from what we know today in terms of just simple comforts, such as air conditioning or a microwave oven.

It seems, through what I gleaned from Mama's stories, that their love for one another and determined resolve kept them together as a family as time marched on. Besides Ninnie being in chronic bad health, my grandparents also had a son, Charles Dewey, called Beau, who was an invalid; he was thrown from a school bus in an accident at age twelve and paralyzed. Coping with all this before health insurance existed, Papa struggled trying to keep his wife and son properly treated. Fortunately, the area doctors thought a great deal of Mama's family and would take produce and livestock for payment of their medicines and treatments.

At the outbreak of WWII, Mama's other brother, William Columbus, who was referred to as Buddy, joined the Army and was sent to France. He served his country with distinction there as a staff sergeant on the French front. Papa had depended on his eldest son to help with the farming, and without his assistance, it made things difficult to manage. Buddy's absence left Papa at home with a sick wife, an invalid son, the family baby, Shirley Beatrice, Mama, age nine, and my aunt Hazel Grace, who was seven years older. When Hazel married her sweetheart after graduating from high school in 1942, Mama started taking on responsibilities around the house. She soon learned to cook at Ninnie's direction, standing on a stool Papa had made so she could reach the kitchen counter and table. By the time the war ended, Mama said she could fry a chicken or bake a cake as well as any grown woman in Clinchfield.

Mama also had to help with the farm chores; it was not an option otherwise. There wasn't any money to hire a laborer, and so she learned to milk a cow, collect the eggs, weed the garden, pick vegetables, and do

Mama in her school photograph, age twelve, 1944

Ninnie and Papa, around 1918

William Columbus Nipper

whatever was needed as best she could. She would laugh with Aunt Bea later in life about how my aunt tried to learn to milk the heifer, but her hands were so small—Aunt Bea was just under 5-feet tall—that her fingers would not fit around the teats. Mama said Aunt Bea would do anything to get out of helping with the chores, which included making sure she had stumpy fingers.

I think the only thing I did hear Mama complain about from those years and times was having to go outside to work on winter mornings. Papa reported to the plant at 6 a.m. during the week, and Mama had to catch the school bus for the ten-mile ride into town, so the two of them had to be up very early. She was extremely cold natured, and she said it was torture having to get up before daylight to do the milking, collect the eggs, and feed the livestock.

When the war finally did come to an end, there was a steady stream of soldiers returning home to Middle and South Georgia. The veterans would leave the train terminals in Atlanta and Macon and make their way south. The service was very limited, and those who couldn't afford bus fare traveled on foot. Since there were few motels or hotels in our rural part of the state, the GI's were left to fend for themselves at night, camping out under a bridge or hopefully finding some hospitable family to give them shelter. My grandparents were some of those folks who willingly opened their home to these young men.

During this time just after the war, Buddy was trying to make his way back home to Middle Georgia. During a battle on the French front, he was critically wounded, and it took him quite a while to recover. The doctors were not able to remove all the shrapnel, and this complication haunted him for the rest of his short life. His health kept him from traveling for long periods of time, and the trip from the former front lines to Paris was arduous and difficult.

Ninnie and Papa waited anxiously for their son to return to the States, and in the meantime made certain that any soldier who came by their house was welcomed to spend the night on their wrap-around porch or in the barn. And with their home just off the major traffic artery from Atlanta to the coast, US Highway 341, hundreds of soldier walked by their farm. They also made sure that the men were fed. It was always simple fare, according to Mama, such as vegetable soup with a piece of cornbread for supper and maybe a biscuit and gravy with some sausage for breakfast. However modest, these soldiers went to sleep with something to eat and were sent on their way without being hungry.

Mama said that Ninnie was determined to do what she could for these young men. My grandmother's attitude was that her Buddy was trying his best to get home, and hopefully some French family was feeding him and giving him a place to rest. She felt she should do the same for the fellows who passed by her door who needed comfort and care.

I wanted to include a few of the dishes here that Ninnie would have cooked and kept on the "back of the stove" during that period. Like the French favorites we have today that foodies refer to as "plats du terroir," or peasant food, these were simple recipes using ingredients that were in season or easily available. The resulting dishes would be hearty and what I call good comfort food. Her vegetable soup, Brunswick stew, and white bean soup were all things that could be made in quantity and were healthy and inexpensive. I've also included what Mama said was Ninnie's favorite dessert, and which would often be found in her icebox, a buttermilk chess pie.

These dishes apparently were nostalgic for Mama, as so many of the things I cook today are for me. She served these items ever since I was a child, and up until she passed away, you could look in her freezer and find packages of these soups in marked containers. You can make a full meal off a bowl of these stews; just add a slice of cornbread and a green salad, or maybe, instead, a thick grilled cheese sandwich.

The white bean soup is very simply made but very hearty and nutritious. Mama would put the soaked beans, water, a ham bone, a couple of onions, and some black pepper in a big pot and cook the ingredients until the liquid was thick and opaque and the beans very tender. It is particularly good on a cold, winter night.

It was to my young, small-town surprise to have a very similar dish served to me when I was seated in the Senate dining room in 1983. I had the privilege and honor of working for the Honorable Sam Nunn as an intern during that fall, and it was in his company at lunch that I had a bowl of the famous Senate Bean Soup. It never occurred to me that such a simple soup would be served in such an august setting, but it has been a staple there now for a century.

White Bean Soup

Ingredients
1 pound navy beans or northern beans
1 gallon water
2 tablespoons vegetable oil
3 cups chopped onions
1 ham bone, or 1 pound ham cut into 3-inch cubes
½ teaspoon salt or more to taste, depending on the saltiness of the ham
½ teaspoon black pepper or to taste

Instructions
1. Place the beans and water into a large stockpot; bring to a boil. Cover and remove from heat; allow to sit for 2 hours.
2. Drain the beans in a colander and rinse; pick out and discard any pieces of loose shell.
3. Place the stockpot back on the stove on medium-high heat, and add the oil. When hot, add the onions and stir occasionally, cooking until tender, about 5 to 7 minutes.
4. Add the beans back to the stockpot, and fill with water to cover the beans by 2 inches.
5. Add the ham bone, salt, and black pepper. Bring to a boil.
6. Reduce heat to a steady simmer and cook, uncovered, stirring occasionally, adding more water if needed, until the beans are soft and the broth a nice opaque color, an hour-and-a-half to 2 hours. Adjust seasonings of salt and pepper to taste, and serve.

Servings
Serves 8

* * *

Ninnie's vegetable soup was loaded with tomatoes—again, Papa grew a profusion of them, and even out of season they were available in jars that had been canned over the summer. Ninnie was heavy-handed with the onions, but she loved the taste and they were cheap, easy to grow, and flavorful. Here is the recipe as best as I can remember Mama making it, with some small adaptions translating it for today's stores and kitchens. If you can find all fresh ingredients, that is wonderful. If not, the frozen varieties make fine substitutes. I used here fresh snap beans and corn, because regardless of the season, stores usually carry them. If you can't find fresh snap beans, use frozen English peas instead. I don't care how you cook them, commercially frozen snap beans are just not good.

Ninnie's Garden Vegetable Soup

Ingredients
3 tablespoons vegetable oil
3 cups chopped onions
2 quarts low-sodium chicken stock
2 cups black-eyed, crowder, or other Southern field peas
2 cups petite baby butter beans (I prefer McKenzie's Petite Deluxe)
2 cups fresh green beans, snapped into 2-inch pieces
2 cups fresh okra, cut into ½-inch slices
6 ears of fresh corn (or 3 cups frozen small kernel corn)
5 cups fresh tomatoes, chopped into 2-inch pieces, or 2 14.5-ounce
 cans diced tomatoes (no salt added or low sodium)
1 teaspoon black pepper or to taste
Salt to taste

Instructions
1. In a large pot or Dutch oven heat the oil over medium-high; add the onions and sauté for about 7 to 8 minutes until tender and beginning to just lightly brown.
2. Add stock and peas; bring to boil. Reduce heat to simmer, cover and cook for 10 minutes.
3. Add butter beans and green beans. Bring back to a boil and reduce heat to a steady simmer. Cover and cook another 10 minutes, stirring occasionally.
4. Stir in the okra, corn, and tomatoes; bring again to a boil, then reduce heat and simmer, covered, for 15 additional minutes.
5. Add black pepper and season to taste, adding salt if needed. Stir, cover pot, remove from heat, and let sit for an hour.

Note: if substituting English peas for the green beans, add these in step
4 above.

Servings
Serves 8

* * *

Mama loved Brunswick stew, particularly in the fall and winter. Various
places lay claim for the origin of this Southern dish, such as Brunswick,
Georgia, and Brunswick, North Carolina. There are also a number of ways
people cook theirs—some with beef, some not; some with mashed
vegetables, some that leave them whole. Basically, it is a thick, one-dish
smorgasbord of meats and vegetables, usually with a tomato base. Ninnie's
contained mostly pork and chicken and a scattering of corn, English peas,
and butter beans. When you ate her dish, you did not need a barbecue
sandwich on the side, like most people are accustomed to pairing. She and
Mama both would cook a whole pork roast and an entire hen when making
a stew; there would be enough to feed a dozen folks and still have some left
to store in the freezer for a later meal.

I've taken her recipe and slimmed it down by increasing the vegetables.
I also use beef stock as my liquid instead of the chicken stock or water that
most recipes call for. The heartier flavor of the beef gives an added depth to
the end result of the dish. You'll note also that I roast my potatoes before
adding them to the pot to prevent the stew from becoming starchy.

I use chopped, smoked barbecue in this recipe to save time trying to
cook a pork roast; the result is actually better to me because the barbecue
gives the stew a smoky taste. I use "dry" barbecue in which no sauce has been
added; however, if your local 'cue joint only does it wet, just adjust the
amount of barbecue sauce you add when making the stew.

The recipe here is more than enough for eight people as a main course.
Pair it with a slice of hot cornbread and a salad, and it is a great winter
night's meal. Many folks enjoy it as a side dish, along with coleslaw, pickles,
sliced bread, and barbecue. I had it served to me in a very unique way one
night at the Blackwater Grille on St. Simons Island. They called it a
Brunswick Stew Sundae, and presented it in alternating layers of stew, slaw,

and crumbled hush puppies, along with a cherry tomato on top, all set in a sundae glass. It was delicious.

Ninnie and Mama's Brunswick Stew

Ingredients
4 tablespoons vegetable oil, divided
1 pound lean ground beef, lightly seasoned with salt and black pepper
3 cups chopped onions
2 quarts low-sodium beef stock
1½ pounds chicken thighs (about 4 large ones)
1 pound chopped smoked pork barbecue (preferably dry)*, purchased
   from your favorite barbecue joint
1 14.5-ounce can no-salt-added diced tomatoes
1 8-ounce can no-salt-added tomato sauce
3 cups frozen baby butter beans
1 large (1 pound) baking potato, peeled, and cut into ¼-inch dice
3 cups of your favorite barbecue sauce
3 cups corn kernels (use fresh if you can, if not, I recommend the small
   kernel shoepeg)
2 cups frozen English peas
1 teaspoon black pepper
½ teaspoon hot sauce
*If the smoked pork you purchased is wet, or rather has sauce already
   mixed in, you may want to modify the amount of barbecue sauce you
   add to the dish at the end; instead of 3 cups, you may want to reduce
   it to 2½.

Instructions
1. Preheat oven to 425 degrees F.
2. In a very large Dutch oven, heat 2 tablespoons of the oil over
   medium-high heat. Add the ground beef and cook for about 6
   minutes until just done, stirring occasionally.
3. Transfer the meat to a colander and drain, leaving about 2
   tablespoons of the fat in the pan.

4. Return the pan to the stove, add the onions, and sauté, stirring occasionally, over medium-high heat until tender, about 5 minutes or so.
5. Add the meat back to the pot and pour in the stock. Add the chicken. Bring to a boil, reduce heat, and simmer for 20 minutes or so, until the chicken is cooked through.
6. Remove chicken from the stock, set aside, and allow the chicken to cool.
7. Add to the pot the barbecue, tomatoes, tomato sauce, and butter beans. Bring to a boil; stir and reduce heat to a steady simmer. Cook uncovered for 20 minutes, stirring occasionally.
8. While the stew is cooking, peel the potato, cut it into ¼-inch cubes, and place in a mixing bowl. Using a paper towel, pat dry the cubes, turning them over in the towel for a moment or two to absorb any liquid. Lightly season with salt and black pepper and add the remaining two tablespoons of oil; toss.
9. Place potatoes on a nonstick cookie sheet and cook until done and beginning to brown, about 18 to 20 minutes. Stir two or three times for even browning. Remove from oven.
10. Shred or chop the cooled chicken thighs. Add to the stew.
11. Add the barbecue sauce (I would recommend one that is neither too sweet nor too mustardy, such as Johnny Harris's) along with the corn, English peas, black pepper, and hot sauce. Bring to a boil, stir, and remove from heat.
12. Stir in the potatoes, cover, and allow the stew to sit a few hours before serving, or refrigerate overnight so that the flavors will develop.
13. To serve, bring the stew to a slow simmer over medium-low heat.
Note: some people like a stew with a creamy consistency. To get this result, allow to cool, and then puree batches of the stew (for a total of about half the total volume) in your food processor; add back to the stew and stir. You'll still have whole vegetables, but the base will now be smooth and thick.

Servings
Serves 8 to 10

* * *

I've also added here one of Ninnie and Papa's favorite desserts. Mama talked fondly about how Ninnie would make the most wonderful chess pies, using fresh cream buttermilk from their cows. Mama said you had to be certain and use whole milk buttermilk when preparing this dish; the reduced fat variety will result in a pie that is not as rich as it should be. Mama never wrote down her recipe, but the one I have here tastes just like hers. It is from my friend Ron Anderson, and he received it from his grandmother, Lillian, a wonderful cook from Morganton, North Carolina. Ron noted on his card to me that "as a child, we would get our buttermilk from the milkman; it was thick and tangy with bits of butter in it." When we host potluck suppers, I always ask Ron to bring not one, but two of these wonderful pies.

Buttermilk Chess Pie

Ingredients
3 large eggs, at room temperature
½ cup unsalted butter, melted
1½ cups sugar
3 tablespoons all-purpose flour
1 cup whole-milk buttermilk, at room temperature
1 teaspoon vanilla extract
1/8 teaspoon freshly ground nutmeg
1 9-inch unbaked pie shell

Instructions
1. Preheat oven to 350 degrees F.
2. Beat eggs until foamy; add butter, sugar, and flour and mix well.
3. Stir in buttermilk, vanilla extract, and nutmeg.
4. Pour the filling into the pie shell and bake in the upper third of your oven for 50 minutes.
5. Chill thoroughly before serving.

Servings
Serves 6

3

Trying Mama's Patience

"It's the merry-hearted boys that make the best men."
—Irish proverb

While I was growing up, my parents and I had a very clear understanding of how things worked: I did what they told me and all was good in the world. If, however, I stepped out of those boundaries, there would be consequences (or in Daddy's words, hell to pay). Actually Mama and Daddy weren't all that strict with either my sister or me, but the lines were in the sand. We at all times had to be respectful to our elders; the words "ma'am" and "sir" along with "please" and "thank you" were a major part of our vocabulary. We had to keep our rooms clean, do chores around the house, pick those darn vegetables and fruits each summer, and keep the yard mowed and raked. These were typical expectations of parents in our hometown, and while we followed along, the sailing was smooth.

When the seas got rough, though, which was not often, we knew Daddy could whip his belt off faster than a gunslinger could draw his six-shooter. Mama's favorite instruments of demonstrating her displeasure was either a flyswatter or a switch she'd get from a huge spirea that was planted in the side yard.

Both of us were good kids, though, and rarely did it come to a spanking. And the times I did run afoul of the parental law, it wasn't because of mean-spirited actions. My troubles were caused by my mouth operating before the synaptic vesicles could operate properly, and due to my deep sense of curiosity (or just plain nosiness, as Carrie would have said).

One of the most comical memories of my childhood, which was not funny to me at all when it happened, occurred because of my poor speaking filter. I was about six years old and sitting on the living room floor watching television. Carrie and I were faithful viewers of *The Secret Storm*, *Edge of Night*, and *Dark Shadows*, but I was watching the TV by myself that day; for some reason, Carrie was off for the afternoon.

At some point Mama came into the room while I was entranced by a scene at Collinwood Mansion and asked me a question.

Without taking my eyes off the screen, I told her in an exasperated tone and with the flip of a hand to "Hush! I can't hear Barnabas." I had a hard time as it was, being a little Cracker from Middle Georgia, understanding the English accent Barnabas spoke with, and here I had Mama interrupting in the middle of the episode.

As soon as the words left my mouth, though, the survival instinct of prehistoric ancestors kicked in—where the hair on the back of your neck stands up because you sense there is a saber-toothed tiger just behind you. I jumped up and was out the screen door in a flash. I ran into the middle of our fenced yard jumping up and down, spinning in all directions, looking for a place to escape.

And here comes the tiger, out the door just behind me.

The only cover accessible was a hedge of large Formosa azaleas by the front of the house. I ran over to the bushes and wiggled through a little opening that our dog, Hobo, had made coming and going from underneath the shade. I squeezed my way to the brick foundation of the house next to the sweet old mutt, who looked up from the hole she'd dug and thumped her tail a few times in greeting. It would be the only friendly face I would see for a number of hours.

Mama, meanwhile, had already broken off a switch from the bridal wreath bush. Its long, arching branches were perfect for wrapping around a little pair of skinny legs. And there she stood, just outside that opening. All I could see were pink capri pants and a pair of white espadrilles. "Come out of there right now, Mister!" she hissed at me through the bushes.

I naively thought it might be possible to sweet-talk my way out of the predicament, something Daddy would try from time to time. "No, thank you, ma'am, I think I'll just stay here with Hobo and visit for a while."

"I said get out of there this instant! DO NOT make me come in there after you!" She was mad, mad, mad.

I realize now what I was thinking at the time, I just don't know that my six-year-old brain processed it to mean *You must be bat-crazy, lady. No way in hell am I willingly going to give you and that switch access to my backside.*

"Well, Mama, you go on back in the house and take a rest. I'll just pet Hobo some more and I'll be out die-reckly." If people think I have a Southern accent as an adult, they should have heard my dialect as a child.

At Rigdon's fish ponds with my cane pole, spring of 1970

Mama at the King and Prince, 1968, with big hair and Ray-Bans

Aunt Hazel (left) and Mama, Christmas 1969

The next thing I knew—to my horror—my mother had dropped down on her hands and knees and started crawling toward me, switch still in hand.

I could not believe it; Mama was fastidious about her appearance, and she had just gotten her hair fixed that morning at Miss Kathy's Beauty Shop. It was just like a scene in the movies when the evil dragon is outside and has someone cornered in a cave.

Mama's hair in those days was done in a large, round bouffant that encircled her head; before she went to bed at night, she wrapped it in a crown of toilet paper, secured with bobby pins, so to help the hairdo stay in place. When she tried to maneuver her way into the bushes, Miss Kathy's helmet creation, shellacked with Adorn hairspray, got snagged on one of the azalea limbs. She was caught tight, with a large branch sticking right into the top of her hair, and that just threw fuel on the fire. She used some extremely colorful language as she tried to salvage her hairdo and disentangle herself from the bushes.

When she'd finally backed out, she gave me the ultimate threat of Daddy. "You just wait till your father gets home, Mr. Smart Pants, and let's see if you tell *him* to hush." With that, she brushed off her knees and stomped back into the house, letting the screen door slam behind her, which was another standard no-no in our household.

I'd never seen her so angry before.

Fortunately, God gave me a break later that day as I sat and waited in my little Alamo. Daddy called the house to say he had to work late and would not be home until around midnight. Apparently, Mama got lonely, as she was apt to do when Daddy wasn't home, and took pity on me. She let me back inside with nary a swat, and I even got some strawberry shortcake that night. We didn't talk about that episode for years, and that was when she was far enough across the room so, if needed, I could sprint out the door and run into some bushes.

Now another memorable episode happened a few years later, but in this case the rod was not spared from the child.

Mama and I had made our first trip down to see Aunt Hazel and her new husband at their vacation home in Tarpon Springs, Florida. The drive to the Gulf Coast took us over six hours, and as soon as we arrived, I was antsy to get outside. After I had given a big hug to my aunt, and a handshake to Bert, I begged off to go exploring the neighborhood. Mama told me to be back in an hour so we could get ready to go out for dinner. As

I walked out the door, Bert warned me in front of Mama to not go down by the lake; it wasn't safe because of the alligators and snakes.

Now Uncle Bert was a Yankee from New York, and an engineer to boot. What did he know about dangerous reptiles? I grew up on the edge of a swamp and had caught baby alligators while bass fishing; I was adept at shooting water moccasins off willow trees in Aunt Polly's ponds with my 410 double barrel while drifting by in a johnboat.

I just answered ,"Yes, sir," and hightailed it out the door.

I inherited a love of fishing from both my parents, and there is just something that attracts me to even just a little trickling stream. Before you could say, "Don't go there," I was down by the water's edge, gazing into the shallows, watching the minnows dart in and out of the lily pad roots. I wandered over by the dam to check out the runoff water that spilled out into the woods, walked onto the dock and tried to get up close to some pelicans, found an old fishing pole, and looked for some crickets or grasshoppers to use as bait to fish with—and the sun was sinking low. Reality set in when I heard my name being called in the distance, and I looked up to see my uncle Bert yelling for me from across the lake. I was overcome with that deep sense of pure dread that only a young kid can get when he is caught, red-handed, in the act of misbehaving.

"Get in the back of the truck, fellow. Your Mama is worried sick; we've been looking for you for over an hour." I did not know Bert that well, and as he was six-and-a-half feet tall, I did not want to cross him. I got into the truck without a word. When we arrived home, Mama was in a state; nervous by nature, it didn't take much to get her worried, or, as Daddy described, "worked up."

"Where have you been? Are you alright? Look at you—you are covered in mud! Have you been down to that lake?" Her voice kept rising, and Aunt Hazel put her hand on Mama's arm and said, "Now, Joyce, calm down, he's fine," which, of course, did not help one bit. When I didn't answer Mama, she snatched me up by the back of my shirt and hauled me into the guest bedroom.

With no access to a switch, and I guess too embarrassed to ask my aunt for her flyswatter, she pulled off one of her new sandals that she'd bought for the trip, ones with plastic daisies on the straps, and told me to bend over. Mama had a strong arm. She had been an ace baseball player when a kid, and could cast a rod and reel with a great deal of speed and accuracy. My eleven-year-old rear-end was an easy target, and she hit it with all her might and a dead-on aim. Whap! Whap! Whap! The leather on those Sears & Roebuck sandals was getting a real workout, and I was howling. On about the fifth or sixth strike, though, the cowhide had been put through the test, and that shoe broke almost in two.

Mama looked at her broken sandal, then at me, started crying, and grabbed me up in her arms and sat on the bed, telling me to never, ever scare her like that again. I think that was the last whipping I ever got from her, and one that we'd never forget. We laughed a lot about it after I grew up, and I would tease Mama that she was the only woman I'd ever heard of who could wear out a pair of shoes without even putting them on her feet.

The rest of the trip was a real treat, and visiting my Aunt and Uncle became a favorite thing for me to do as I entered my teen years. They were great hosts and went out of their way to make us feel at home and comfortable. Bert enjoyed taking us out to dinner, and he and Aunt Hazel treated us to some wonderful times at a number of tremendous restaurants.

One such spot that we would visit on each trip down would be Pappa's. In the late 1800s, Greek sponge divers flocked to Tarpon Springs, which is known as "The Sponge Capital of the US," and their descendants still comprise a large contingency of citizens in the area. One was Louis Pappas from Sparta, who came over in 1925 and opened what would become one of Florida's most famous restaurants. He located it right on the water by the sponge docks. I was fascinated by the life-size statue of a sponge diver that Mr. Pappas had on display, and the original artwork that graced the walls. He was known for many dishes, one being his Greek salad, which was unusual because it was made with a dollop of potato salad resting in the middle of the traditional greens, olives, and feta. My favorite item to order was the locally caught red snapper stuffed with crabmeat. It would be served piping hot and swimming with butter; I can taste it as I write this line.

We'd also drive over to the historic and Old-World inspired Columbia Restaurant in Tampa's Ybor City. The smell of the fresh-baked Cuban bread would get my stomach growling as soon as we would walk in the door, and it was a grand experience to be served by the immaculate waiters in their black suits and bow ties. I remember having my first taste of gazpacho there; we never had cold tomato soup back home, and I was amazed by how much I enjoyed the explosive taste of the tomatoes and spices along with the course texture of the ground vegetables.

My favorite spot that my aunt and uncle would take us, though, was Clearwater's Kapok Tree Inn, which was the most extravagantly decorated restaurant I'd ever seen. Named for an exotic kapok tree that was just outside its doors, this huge establishment could seat four hundred guests, and it was filled with potted palms, statues, Venetian mirrors, enormous crystal chandeliers, and boasted sets of formal gardens where you could stroll and relax while you waited on your table. The food was highly rated, but in an unusual juxtaposition, not formal or continental. While the interior looked like a palace, the menu was filled with items such as your basic fried Gulf shrimp—which I loved—steaks, seafood, and other fare you might find in a nice, upscale American restaurant. I'll always remember those nights. Surrounded by loving family and in such a rich setting, they were magical to a young fellow from the country.

Mama and Aunt Hazel both were caring and loving ladies, with hearty laughs and good humor, but at the same time no-nonsense and strong willed. Their food was as straightforward as they were; the big meal of the day, supper—or dinner to those in parts of the country outside the South— was always a meat or fish, a starch, and a couple of fresh vegetables. A typical supper might be a platter of pork chops roasted with Vidalia onions, baked sweet potatoes, string beans, and some stewed squash along with a biscuit or piece of cornbread. A relish tray with sliced tomatoes, cucumbers, radishes, and green onions was a standard at each evening meal. We generally didn't have desserts during the week; sweets were a weekend treat. Sunday dinners provided additional dishes, with usually two meats, such as a beef roast and fried chicken, and a couple of extra vegetables or casseroles, along with a cake or pie. Christmas and Thanksgiving were extensive buffets that showcased roasted fowl, a baked ham, ambrosia, pickled peaches, five or six vegetables and casseroles, and a table covered with desserts.

I wanted to share a handful of recipes that were Mom's and Aunt Hazel's standards for the holidays that you might not readily have on hand. I've narrowed it down to three main dishes that were always served, regardless of what else was on the table, as well as one of my childhood favorites. I did not include here how to prepare a ham or bird; those two items are pretty basic in preparation. Mama chose to marinate her smoked ham or pork shoulder with a bottle of Coca Cola, wrap it in foil, and bake it in a slow oven; when it was done, she'd paste it with a brown sugar and mustard glaze. The bird, whether a turkey or capon, was rubbed with butter, seasoned with salt and pepper, placed in a roasting pan with some onions and celery, and baked until golden. A rich gravy would be made from the pan drippings.

The first staple always found on our holiday menu was, and still is, cornbread dressing. This dish is what I'd call "arch Southern" because it is a true food icon of this region. Neither Mama nor Aunt Hazel ever used sage in their dressing; instead, they filled it full of onions and celery. And while I say in several of my recipes it is alright to use good commercial stock, it's not an option with dressing. You must use homemade chicken or pork stock; it is necessary to incorporate some of the fat into the dish to give the depth and flavor needed. Also, please use homemade cornbread and make certain it is not one of those boxed kinds that contain sugar. One final key is to add in real biscuits; some people say breadcrumbs or loaf bread is alright to use, but I disagree. If you don't want to take the time to make your own biscuits, go to the drive-through at Kentucky Fried Chicken and buy some already made. The dressing can easily be put together ahead of time, refrigerated, and then cooked at the last minute.

Cornbread Dressing

Ingredients
3 tablespoons unsalted butter, at room temperature
1 9-inch pan of cornbread (about 6 cups crumbled) made with a good
    brand such as White Lily Cornmeal
3 biscuits (about 2 cups crumbled)
1 quart or so homemade chicken or pork stock, at room temperature
2 cups chopped onion
2 cups chopped celery
3 large hard-boiled eggs, shredded with a fork
2 eggs, slightly beaten
½ teaspoon black pepper

Instructions
1. Preheat oven to 350 degrees F.
2. Butter a 9-x-13 baking pan or large iron skillet with deep sides; it
    should be deep enough to hold 2½ quarts of dressing. Set aside.
3. Crumble your cornbread and biscuits into a large mixing bowl.

4. Pour in half of the stock and mix together with a spatula, mashing until there are no lumps. Add additional stock until you get the consistency of a slightly soupy batter.
5. Add the remaining ingredients and stir well to mix.
6. Pour batter into the buttered dish; bake until the top turns a golden brown, about 50 to 55 minutes (the length of time will vary depending on the depth of the baking dish). The dressing is best served at once but can be covered with foil and reheated in a 300-degree oven.

Servings
Serves 8 to 10

* * *

Mama only used two cookbooks that I can remember growing up. One was *Better Homes and Gardens*, with the red and white checkerboard cover, along with *The Art of Southern Cooking*, which was written by one of our neighbors. Mildred Evans Warren, known to me as "Miss Mildred," lived across the street from us in Perry and wrote a weekly column, *The Cook's Nook*, for the local paper. Over the years she collected a number of popular Southern recipes, and in 1967 compiled them into a wonderful book published by Doubleday & Company that garnered national attention. I still have Mama's copy of *The Art of Southern Cooking*, and it is inscribed: "Happy Cooking, Joyce. It's nice to autograph a book for my neighbor. Ever, Mildred Dec 1969." I remember Miss Mildred well; she was a sweet lady with a lilting voice who let me visit and play with her two English bulldogs, Winston and his aptly named companion, Clementine.

The following recipe is one adapted from Miss Mildred's book, and was one of Mama's favorites. The result is a shiny, delicious confection. We ate sweet potatoes throughout the year. They were baked and served in their jackets with a little butter, sliced and roasted in the oven, or maybe mashed into a casserole. The candied ones here were special and usually reserved for the holidays.

Unless you have a very large pot and can double the recipe, you may need to make two batches if feeding a large crowd. It is important not to overcrowd the pan; if you break the potatoes while cooking, the glaze will not be as clear.

Candied Sweet Potatoes

Ingredients
½ cup water
1½ cups sugar
Dash of salt
4 medium-sized sweet potatoes of about the same circumference, peeled and sliced crosswise into 1- to 1½-inch-thick circles
2 tablespoons unsalted butter, melted
¼ scant teaspoon vanilla

Instructions
1. Mix the water, sugar, and salt in a large stockpot or Dutch oven; heat over medium-high, stirring, until sugar is dissolved.
2. Add the potatoes one slice at a time, trying, if possible, to get them into a single layer. If you cannot, it is fine, but you'll need to pay more attention to the cooking process.
3. Cook uncovered on a steady simmer over medium heat for about 10 minutes; the potatoes will start to shrink as they cook. If the potatoes are in layers, gently move the ones on top down into the pan, careful not to break them.
4. Turn the potatoes over, again gently, so that the cooked bottoms are now facing upwards.
5. Continue cooking for another 15 minutes or so until the potatoes are tender.
6. Mix the butter and vanilla and pour over potatoes. Mix very gently.
7. The potatoes should be a rich, dark, reddish orange color and the syrup a thick, clear glaze.
8. Serve immediately. If not serving when finished, cover and reheat in a warm oven until hot.

Servings
Serves 4

* * *

Another truly Southern dish, and one that was *de rigueur* for both Thanksgiving and Christmas in our household, was collard greens. The FNOB's (food snobs) out there may experience a curling of the upper lip when this vegetable is mentioned, but if cooked properly, they can be wonderful and flavorful. Collards are maligned by many but are an excellent food source, low in calories, high in fiber, and loaded with both vitamins A and K. We ate them throughout the year; Mama would cook huge batches when in season and freeze them in quart containers. The following is my recipe. It is simple and easy to make ahead of time and then reheated. Note that collards, like spinach, reduce in size by probably seventy-five percent of their raw volume when cooked. If preparing for a crowd, you'll need about two pounds, as I have in my recipe. If you don't like the smell of these greens while cooking (an aroma similar to cabbage) you can always cook them outside on your gas grill.

JB's CGs (Collard Greens)

Ingredients
2 tablespoons olive oil
1 cup chopped onion
1 quart good-quality, low-sodium chicken stock
1 ham bone—I prefer Honey Baked—or 2 cups ham, cut into 2-inch chunks
¼ teaspoon red pepper flakes
2 pounds (about 2 gallons) of fresh collard green tops*, torn into 3- to 4-inch square pieces
*Make certain you remove all the large (½-inch or more) stems from the leaves

Instructions
1. In a very large stockpot, heat the oil over medium high and sauté the onion for about 3 minutes, stirring occasionally.
2. Add the stock, ham bone, and red pepper. Bring to a boil, cover, reduce heat to a steady simmer, and allow to cook for about 15 minutes, allowing the flavor of the ham to enhance the broth.

3. Add the collards and bring back to a boil; reduce heat to a steady simmer and cover.

4. After about 3 minutes, stir the collards up from the bottom of the pan. Continue to simmer, covered, stirring occasionally, until the leaves are tender, about 25 to 30 minutes.

5. Remove from heat. Allow to sit for 30 minutes; refrigerate until ready to serve.

6. To serve the collards, remove the ham bone, strain out the collected juices, and reheat.

Servings
Serves 8

* * *

The last recipe I have here invokes a flood of memories for me. It is my aunt Hazel's German chocolate cake, which she made for me each year at Christmas and on my birthday.

The loss of my aunt in 1985 was extremely hard on my mom. I remember to this day when she took the call that her sister had been diagnosed with a terminal illness. I'd never seen my mother, who was so strong and stoic, sob. She lay across her bed and cried and cried, while my father and I stood by and tried to comfort her as best we could. Mama and Aunt Hazel had been very close to one another all their lives; they shared a bedroom growing up and slept in the same bed together until Aunt Hazel married. They raised their children side by side, and I know that Mama looked up to her older sister in many ways, particularly after Ninnie died in the late '50s. As she told me later, it was like losing not only a loving sister, but also a very dear friend.

Whenever I see one of these cakes in the baker's window or on a menu, I recall my aunt's smiling face and how she and Mama would laugh and joke together. I see palm trees and sponge docks, Christmas trees and birthday candles. Hers is the best I've ever tasted.

Aunt Hazel's German Chocolate Cake

Ingredients
Cake
1 cup unsalted butter, at room temperature
2 cups sugar
4 large eggs, separated
1 teaspoon baking soda
1 cup whole-milk buttermilk
2½ cups cake flour
1 4-ounce package German Chocolate, dissolved in ½ cup of hot water
¼ teaspoon salt
1 teaspoon vanilla
German Chocolate Frosting (recipe follows)

German Chocolate Frosting
2 cups sugar
1 cup unsalted butter, melted
2 cups evaporated milk
6 large egg yolks, well beaten
2 teaspoons vanilla
2 cups shredded coconut
2 cups chopped pecans

Instructions
Cake
1. Preheat oven to 350 degrees F.
2. Grease and flour three 9-inch cake pans. Line bottoms of the pans with lightly greased parchment paper.
3. In a large bowl, cream butter and sugar.
4. Add 1 egg yolk at a time into the creamed butter and sugar mixture, beating well.
5. Stir the baking soda into the buttermilk; add to the mixture and stir until just mixed.
6. Add flour, chocolate, salt, and vanilla; mix well.
7. In a separate bowl, beat egg whites until stiff; gently fold them into the cake batter.

8. Pour batter into the cake pans.
9. Bake for 30 minutes and check for doneness. If needed, continue cooking, being cautious with your timing so as to not overcook. Allow to cool completely before carefully removing cakes from the pans.
10. Spread the German chocolate frosting between the cake layers, on the sides, and top of the cake. Handle with care due to the delicacy of the cakes.

German Chocolate Frosting

1. Cream sugar and butter in a mixing bowl; add in the milk and yolks and stir until thoroughly incorporated.
2. Pour the mixture into a medium-sized saucepan. Cook, over medium-low heat, stirring constantly until thick, 6 to 8 minutes.
3. Add vanilla, coconut, and pecans and stir to mix well. Remove from heat and allow to cool to room temperature before using.

Servings
Serves 12

1967 in Perry. Daddy with his tow-headed son.
Same white shirt, same khaki's, same pose

4

My Father

Expert Angler and Ice Cream Connoisseur

Recently, I was in Columbus, Georgia, on business and had been in a succession of meetings for two days. Tired of talking, emails, and office buildings, I decided to take a late-afternoon excursion south to Florence Marina State Park. I was in need of some quiet time outside, and to be by myself.

Located in a very rural area of the state, the park is nestled alongside Lake Eufaula and filled with towering longleaf pines, majestic live oaks draped in Spanish moss, and an abundance of wildlife. I parked and walked down to the marina to take a stroll along the water. The mockingbirds, red-winged blackbirds, brown thrashers, and barn swallows were singing a lively chorus, and it was a soothing balm to be in such a peaceful place away from the hot asphalt of the city.

Because I spent so much time fishing with my folks growing up, I feel closer to them when I'm outdoors. While I don't mean this to sound like a Hallmark Channel advertisement, I can take a walk along a creek or on the banks of a lake and feel the two of them on either side of me, keeping me company just like when I was a child. I had made many trips to Lake Eufaula with them over the years, Daddy pulling his bass boat behind us as we drove the back roads of southwest Georgia on our way for a weekend of fishing. I was thinking a good bit about my parents that afternoon as I looked out over the lake.

I was taking my time along the shore, peering into the shallows, seeing all sorts of fish in the cover of the water lilies, rocks, and tree stumps that were close to shore. The "No Fishing" signs along the marina wall gave the bream and bass protection from anglers, providing them a safe place to congregate. Just a few minutes into my stroll, I noticed a large, spotted gar drifting along just off the bank's edge. The color of dark burnt orange with splotches of white, he'd raise his long, thin snout to the surface about every five or six feet, and then meander on, an ancient, strong creature in no hurry at all to get to wherever he was going.

I chuckled and said out loud, "Lord. That fish reminds me of Daddy."

My father had the reddish coloring of a Scot and sported a head of white hair he kept cut in a short, one-inch buzz. He was not a big man, but he stood a very sturdy 5-feet 8, solidly built and muscled. My cousin, Linda Michelle, always said Daddy reminded her of Popeye the Sailor Man due to his large forearms, one which displayed the tattoo he received while in the Army. He went at his own pace and would not be hurried along for anyone, including Mama, much to her consternation sometimes. He was also one tough fellow. I recall one afternoon walking through the woods to fish on Limestone Creek. Daddy was in front leading the way, and we came across a copperhead directly in our path, sunning itself on the flat surface of an outcropping of rock. Daddy picked up his right foot, slammed it down on the head of the snake with his work boot, and just kept on walking.

Unlike the gar, though, my father did have a soft heart, particularly when it came to animals. My first dog, Hobo, was a little black-and-white mutt Daddy found alongside a country road one morning on his way to a dove shoot. I had that lovable dog for seventeen years. Daddy also rescued a German shepherd someone had abandoned close to our house. It was malnourished and very skittish, staying just on the edge of the woods, away from people. Daddy started setting out food for the dog, first in the woods, then just outside the tree line, then closer in still, until the shepherd finally would let him touch her. "Lady," as she would later be named, never left my father's side after she came to trust him. You'd see the two of them driving around town together in his red-and-white Ford F150 fishing truck; tough old man, tough old dog, and a tough old truck, it was a common site around Perry.

My father was known to everyone in the area as one of the best fishermen in Middle Georgia. He and my mother both excelled at the sport, and they spent many happy days together through the years in one another's company on the creeks and lakes across our state.

To this day, I can still run into one of Daddy's old fishing buddies from Perry or Hawkinsville, and they'll always bring up my father's luck at bringing home a "mess" of fish anytime he set his hook in the water.

One fellow, the son of one of Daddy's best friends, told me once that "if you saw your father getting out of the boat with no fish in his cooler,

Spring 1972, with a string of bluegill caught on Mossy Creek

On Lake Sinclair, still fishing at age seventy-eight

Photo in the *Houston Home Journal,* summer 1967, at the annual
Penn-Dixie Barbeque. I am on the front row, left, with Daddy in the white
shirt beside me. Notice the magnificent stand of longleaf pines. The spray
pond, where I caught the eel, is to the right of the picture.

you'd best turn around and head back home. If they weren't biting for him, they wouldn't be biting for *anybody*."

Mama started her hobby of fishing at an early age back in Clinchfield. My grandfather loved to spend time on the water and took Mama along with him whenever he went, even on night-fishing trips to the banks of Big Indian Creek. Later in life, after Ninnie had passed away, Mama made it a practice to go to Papa's house once or twice a week and fry a pan of fish, make a plate of biscuits, and cook a pot of grits so that he could enjoy his favorite supper.

To her credit, people also often spoke of how good Mama was at filling a basket with an assortment of pan fish. At one Sunday service, her minister joked with the congregation about Mama's passion for the sport: "I was having a glass of tea visiting with Joyce Barrett the other day at her house, and we all know how much that lady loves to fish. She told me at one point, 'Reverend, when I die, I want you all to bury me with my favorite rod and reel, so when I pass over the River Jordan I can see how many fish I can catch.'"

Now while we did not bury Mama with her rod and reel, she did have Daddy sent on to his reward with his favorite Zebco 33 tucked by his side and wearing one of his prized fishing caps.

Interestingly, my mother and father had a competitive streak with one another that was downright comical in terms of fishing. Both were determined to outdo one another, and the victor dearly loved ribbing the one who came up short. After I grew up, I'd always get a phone call on a fishing day from whichever one caught the most on that particular outing. If Daddy had outdone Mama, he would get on the line, and laughing to the point of snorting—which he had the tendency to do, and I unfortunately inherited that trait from him—and say, "Let me get your mama in here and she can tell you how bad I skunked her this morning. She's mad as a wet settin' hen." You could hear him in the background still snorting as he would put the receiver down and go holler for Mama, who would be in another part of the house. "Joyce, come to the phone and tell your son how bad I whipped you today at Mossy Lake!"

If Mama, on the other hand, had out-caught Daddy, you could hear the sweet sense of satisfaction coming across in her voice as she would almost purr telling of her conquest. "Well, we just got back from Big Indian, and all your daddy could do was play with his bait and feed the minnows.

Here, I'll hand him the phone and he can let you know just who skunked who on this fine day."

I started fishing with Mama and Daddy from the time I was old enough to walk and continued to do so right up until each of them passed away. One of my first memories with them on the water was from a summer afternoon on the dock of the spray pond at Penn-Dixie. I was around four years old and fishing with a cane pole. I got a bite, the cork went under the water, and I pulled in the line. Instead of a fish being on the hook, though, I saw this long, slithering black rope of a creature that was curling around itself into knots. Thinking it was a snake, I slammed my pole down on the dock, screaming for Daddy to help me. I was scared to death and next to tears as I watched in horror as the snake crawled, hooked to my line, across the dock. I couldn't understand why Mama and Daddy started laughing and looking at each other like there was some joke; they had always taught me to be afraid of water moccasins and to steer clear of them. Come to find out, of course, what I had caught was an eel. I've hated those damn nasty things ever since then.

Daddy and Mama taught me well, and through the years I've grown to become almost as good at the sport as they were. When I know I'll be traveling through some of the more rural parts of the state for work, I'll take along one of my rod and reels and a small tackle box filled with gear and lures. I like to pull over by the side of a bridge that crosses a fresh-running Georgia creek, do a little casting, rest my mind, and think about growing up with the two best anglers in Middle Georgia. I was a lucky boy.

Back home in those days, it was not uncommon to eat fish more than twice a week, especially during the spring and summer when the sport was at its peak. And just like the vegetables that were harvested and stored, my parent's freezers always held a dozen or so containers of a variety of fish, such as channel cats, bream, bluegill, largemouth bass, white perch, and shellcrackers.

Alongside those vegetables and jugs of fish, you'd also find quart containers of homemade ice cream. My father dearly loved that dessert and enjoyed eating a big bowlful as much as he did standing in his bass boat, pulling in a five-pound largemouth. He perfected a recipe over the years, and it became his specialty in terms of cooking.

The family favorite was peach. He would make the occasional vanilla, strawberry, pineapple, or banana ice cream, and they were all excellent, but the very best were the churnfuls made with world-famous Georgia peaches.

There is nothing like a fresh, ripe peach, one so juicy you have to wear an apron when eating it to keep from staining your shirt. Melissa Faye Green gave a perfect description of the fruit in her book *Praying for Sheetrock*: "A Georgia peach, a real Georgia peach, a backyard great-grandmother's orchard peach, is as thickly furred as a sweater, and so fluent and sweet that once you bite through the flannel, it brings tears to your eyes." Those were just the types of peaches Daddy would use in making his recipe.

He would set out in his truck with Lady, or in later years, his dog Missy, in tow, and drive to his favorite peach stand. The owners knew Daddy would be by a few times a week during June, at the height of the season, and saved the ripest of the fruits for him to pick over. He was extremely choosy in what he selected; he wanted them to be so soft that you could easily press them with a potato masher, but not to the point where they were mushy or bruised.

Daddy would bring the peaches home late afternoon so that he could prepare the churn and allow enough time for it to "sit and cure" in the bucket for an hour or so after supper was served. Daddy so loved his ice cream that he would actually sing to himself while he went about his ritual of making it. You could hear him in the kitchen belting out a verse from "She'll Be Comin' Round the Mountain" or "Pretty Little Girl with a Red Dress On" as he whisked the eggs, peaches, sugar, and milk in an oversized yellow glass bowl.

My job as a youngster was to sit on the hand-cranked churn, atop a layer of old towels, to help keep the ice and rock salt from spilling off the sides. I remember telling Daddy time and again, "Hurry up, my tail is gettin' too cold!" as he'd sit there patiently and methodically turning the crank. As I said, he did not get in a hurry, and you could not rush his ice cream.

So when I think of my father and food, the first things that pop into my mind are big platters of steaming hot, fresh fish and bowls of sweet peach ice cream.

The fish we had were either fried or baked, depending on the time of year and type of fish that had been caught. The smaller varieties of pan fish or small catfish were always seasoned with a little salt and black pepper, dusted with a fine coating of white cornmeal, and fried in a deep iron skillet that had been Ninnie's and that Mama cooked in for decades afterwards. I now use that pan, which must be more than one hundred years old, and the bottom is so well seasoned it shines like polished obsidian.

The larger fish, such as the big channel cats and largemouth bass, would be filleted and cooked in the oven with salt, pepper, lemon juice, butter, and a dash of paprika. I remember a few years ago Mama was watching the Food Network, where a chef was preparing fish *en papillote*. She called me into the room and said, "Would you look at that: they're cooking some French fish dish in, of all things, a paper bag. I cooked the same thing, I just used tin foil instead." Then she thought for a moment and added "But I didn't ruin mine by putting in all those black olives and bell peppers."

Touché, Maman. Keep it simple.

So, of course, after all this reminiscing over my days of fishing and eating ice cream with my father, I'd like to share with you the menu of a typical fish dinner at our house growing up, as well as how to prepare an excellent churn of peach ice cream.

For the baked fish, the process was simple as I mentioned with a minimal amount of seasonings that complemented the delicate white fillets. On the side would be coleslaw, maybe some green beans or stewed squash, and cornbread sticks.

The fried fish dinners were done two ways. One was a very simple supper of just fish, grits, and a pan of biscuits served late at night after we'd had a full day on the water. The other was the one we had the most often, where the fish would be accompanied with homemade tartar sauce, hush puppies, coleslaw, sliced roasted potatoes, and hot buttered biscuits with cane syrup.

A fish fry is one of my all-time favorite dinners, but I have to admit that I don't like to cook them too often. There are so many places that can prepare a wonderful platter of piping-hot, fresh catfish and bring it right to you at the table, saving you the time over a stove tending to bubbling oil. Love's Restaurant on the banks of the Ogeechee River in Savannah comes to mind, as well as Coleman's Lake on the same river, upstate near Louisville, or maybe at Jim Shaw's on Pio Nono Avenue in Macon. Family-owned seafood and fish restaurants are still very prevalent in the South, and if you live in our region there is probably one near you within driving distance.

But once in a while, when I get in the mood for cooking in Ninnie's pan and don't mind getting a little warm over the stove, I'll fix the following menu we had back in Perry:

Menu
~Mama's Fried Fish with Homemade Tartar Sauce
~Sweet Southern Coleslaw
~Hush Puppies
~Home Fries
~Hot Buttered Biscuits with Cane Syrup

Having grown up on fresh, wild-caught fish, I am extremely particular about the kind I serve. If I do not catch them myself, or get them from a friend, I make sure I buy from a respectable purveyor who does not mix in out-of-country, farm-raised varieties on their ice displays. While I am not pretentious about my food, I absolutely refuse to serve anything that came from a pond in Malaysia and was shipped halfway across the world.

My mother was a pro at cooking fried fish and a trooper doing it. She did not care for the way the fish turned out when done in a large outdoor fish fryer; she claimed that those cooked en masse were always "dried out." Instead, she preferred using her oversized iron skillet. Even if we were having ten or twelve folks over for supper, she'd patiently stand over the stove, frying fish after fish in that deep, black pan until there would be plenty for everyone to eat.

Her concept was simple, with no type of marinade or sitting in milk or buttermilk. All she used on her fish was salt, pepper, cornmeal, and good-quality cooking oil. With the thin batter and minimal seasonings, you could really experience the fresh taste of the outdoors.

Mama's Fried Fish

Ingredients
2½ cups white cornmeal, either plain or self-rising
2 teaspoons salt, divided
1 teaspoon black pepper, divided
6 large or 12 small (about 8 ounces each) fresh catfish or other fish,
    such as bream or white perch

Peanut or a good-quality vegetable oil for frying (about 3 cups)

Instructions
1. Mix the cornmeal along with 1 teaspoon salt and ½ teaspoon black pepper in a shallow bowl.
2. Thoroughly rinse the fish under cold running water. Allow to drain but do not dry.
3. Sprinkle the remaining salt and pepper on both sides of the fish.
4. Dredge each fish in the cornmeal mixture, shaking off the excess back into the bowl. Set fish aside on a tray or cooking sheet.
5. Pour two inches of oil into a deep cast-iron skillet (9-inch circumference or so); heat over medium-high until hot, but not smoking.
6. Cook the fish in the hot oil, placing two or three in a batch at a time, being careful not to overcrowd the pan. Depending on the thickness, fry for about 3 to 4 minutes on each side, until a golden brown and the fish firm.
7. Drain the cooked fish on a paper towel or brown paper bag; serve immediately.
Note: save the leftover grease in your pan to fry the hush puppies.

Servings
Serves 6

* * *

My aunt Hazel always made the most flavorful tartar sauce; she filled it with diced sweet pickles and onions. I've added some capers here and a little hot sauce and get very good reviews on the outcome. It is excellent with fried fish, shrimp, or oysters.

Tartar Sauce

Ingredients
1 cup real mayonnaise
2 tablespoons finely minced onion
1 tablespoon finely minced sweet pickles

1 tablespoon capers, drained and finely minced
1 teaspoon juice from the sweet pickle jar
¼ teaspoon hot sauce
1/8 teaspoon ground black pepper

Instructions
Mix all the ingredients together and chill at least 4 hours, or overnight.

Servings
Serves 6

* * *

Coleslaw brings a lot of debate in terms of preparation, with questions on whether or not to use vinegar, celery seeds, pickles, sugar, or sometimes dill, and this consideration also goes for how the cabbage is cut. Should you slice it thickly, thinly, or have it finely ground?

With fried fish and seafood, I like a mayonnaise-based slaw that is sweetened with a little sugar and spiced with some black pepper and onion. The consistency of the ground preparation is also my choice when serving these dishes.

Sweet Southern Coleslaw

Ingredients
1 head cabbage, about 2 pounds (8 gently packed cups when ground;
    see steps 3–4 below)
1½ tablespoons very finely minced green onion, white and light-green
    portions
About ¾ cup real mayonnaise
3 tablespoons sugar
½ teaspoon salt
¼ teaspoon finely ground black pepper

Instructions
1. Cut and remove the core from the cabbage.
2. Slice the cabbage into small, three- to four-inch chunks.

3. Place two chunks of the cabbage into a food processor and pulse until the cabbage is finely ground.
4. Grind the cabbages in batches, placing the ground portion into a large mixing bowl.
5. When you finish the cabbage, add the remaining ingredients and mix well.
6. Place the slaw in an airtight container and refrigerate for 4–6 hours before serving. Stir the slaw once or twice while refrigerated.

Note: the amount of mayonnaise needed will vary depending on the size of the head of cabbage you prepare, as well as your personal tastes. I recommend here adding in ½ cup to start and mix well, and then gradually spoon in more as needed, until it suits you. Remember, you can always add more, but you can't take it out once it's in.

Servings
Serves 6

* * *

Hush Puppies are an absolute "must" for a fish fry; to not have them on your menu would be like serving warm apple pie without the scoop of ice cream. The recipe below produces large, light, and very flavorful fried nuggets that have just a bit of bite from onion, black pepper, and hot sauce. Make sure to follow the instructions with regard to not overmixing the batter; as with pancakes or biscuits, if you stir too much or for too long, the end product will be dense and heavy.

Hush Puppies

Ingredients
1½ cups self-rising white cornmeal
½ cup self-rising flour
1 tablespoon sugar
½ teaspoon baking soda
¼ teaspoon finely ground black pepper
1 cup finely chopped onion

1 large egg, beaten
1 cup whole-milk buttermilk
Couple dashes hot sauce or to taste
3 to 4 cups peanut or good-quality vegetable oil (I use the oil left from
frying my fish)

Instructions
1. With a fork, lightly mix the dry ingredients, including the onion, in a
   large bowl.
2. Add the egg, buttermilk, and hot sauce; gently stir with the fork
   until incorporated, but do not overstir.
3. Lightly flour your hands, dip out the batter a tablespoon at a time,
   and gently shape into a small ball or patty. Place the patties on a
   nonstick cookie sheet and refrigerate for 30 minutes.
4. Using the pan in which the fish were cooked, reheat 2 to 3 inches of
   the oil, adding extra if needed, over medium-high.
5. When the oil is hot and just about to bubble, place 6 to 8
   hushpuppies into the pan, being careful not to overcrowd. Just like
   deep frying any other item, such as fish or chicken, if the pan has too
   many pieces in at one time, the food will not brown or crisp properly.
   Turn occasionally until browned on all sides and done, about 3 to 4
   minutes per batch.
6. Best served immediately. If needed, the hushpuppies can be kept
   warm in a hot oven until ready to serve.

Servings
Makes 16 hush puppies

* * *

The potatoes were another staple for the fish-fry dinner growing up. I'm not
sure why we called them home fries, since they were baked, but that is the
name they were given. A ketchup fanatic, I have a ramekin of it next to my
plate to dip the 'taters in.

Home Fries

Ingredients

2 large (about 2 pounds) Russet or other baking potatoes, washed and
  scrubbed

½ teaspoon garlic powder

½ teaspoon salt

¼ teaspoon ground black pepper

3 tablespoons good-quality vegetable oil

Instructions

1. Preheat oven to 425 degrees F.
2. Slice potatoes crosswise into ½-inch rings. Pat the slices dry with a paper towel and place in a large bowl.
3. Add the remaining ingredients to the potatoes and toss gently to coat the slices.
4. Arrange the potatoes in a single layer on a lightly greased nonstick cookie or baking sheet.
5. Roast for 35 minutes, or until golden brown, turning once during the process.
6. Serve immediately.

Servings

Serves 6

* * *

Another family tradition passed down from Mama's side of the family was having a hot buttered biscuit with cane syrup for dessert whenever you had fried fish. Papa and Ninnie loved this dish, as did Mama, and so do I. The aromatic, distinctive taste of the syrup, which mixes with the silkiness of the butter as it melts atop a light, flaky, piping-hot biscuit, is pure Southern manna.

My mother was a stickler for things cooked and served to her way of liking. She never could understand why seafood restaurants and catfish houses didn't have syrup and biscuit on their menus. But that did not stop her, no, ma'am. Before we'd leave the house to go out for some fried fish, she'd cook herself a couple of biscuits, pour a little cane syrup in a Tupperware container, and zip those babies up in a bag and bring her own. She had no problem at all looking up at the waitress and saying, "Sugar, do you mind taking these biscuits back to the kitchen and warming them up for me? And don't forget to bring me an extra little saucer to pour my syrup in." The lady knew what she liked.

Mama and Daddy kept cane syrup at the house year-round; it was on hand just like many people use honey or maple syrup. Each fall, when the sugar cane had been harvested, we'd make a trip out to the Klondike community to the home of Anna and Sonny Johnson, an elderly African-American couple known for their homemade syrup. The process took most of the day, with a mule walking in circles around a large vat crushing the cane to extract the juice, which was then cooked in a tremendous iron pot, bubbling and simmering for hours. After much skimming, filtering, and gradually reducing the temperature of the massive fire under the pot, the result would be bottles of perfectly clear cane syrup, colored a shade ranging between the darkest of amber to that of strong espresso.

It is hard to find real cane syrup in stores. Read the labels carefully since you'll find that some manufacturers will have slipped corn syrup into their bottles. You can fortunately find some wonderful offerings online, such as Steen's of Louisiana, which has been producing excellent syrup for decades. For a real treat, attend a cane-grinding festival that showcases this old, Southern way of cooking. A few include events held on Oatland Island in Savannah, Dudley Farm Historic Park in Newberry, Florida, where you can pet the sweet mule, Fred, after he finishes his grinding, and at the Wiregrass event in Dothan, Alabama.

Hot Buttered Biscuits with Cane Syrup

Ingredients
1 Buttermilk Biscuit recipe (pages 109-110.)
4 tablespoons unsalted butter at room temperature
½ cup or more real cane syrup

Instructions
1. Make the biscuits following the recipe on pages 109-110.

2. As soon as you take the biscuits from the oven, liberally top them with the softened butter.
3. Place biscuits on individual plates, drizzle with syrup, and serve immediately.

Servings
Serves 6-8

* * *

My father's ice cream recipe is one that the FDA would stamp a large warning sign upon, as it contains five raw eggs. Our family and friends certainly ate hundreds of churns over the years, and according to the experts, we should have died a thousand deaths from salmonella. To save any readers of this book from such a condition, I figured I should come up with a good substitute for Daddy's delicious, but egg-infused, concoction. I pored over a number of recipes from Southern cooks and finally came up with one I feel is very similar to my father's. Full of peaches, it has the same rich consistency and fresh taste that Daddy's had without the density of a custard-based ice cream. I will admit, humbly, that it is the best I've sampled, ever, outside my father's. I think you'll very much enjoy this rich treat.

JB's Just-Like-Daddy's-but-without-the-Eggs
Peach Ice Cream

Ingredients
2 14-ounce cans sweetened condensed milk
1 cup heavy whipping cream
1 cup whole milk
Scant ½ cup sugar
1 teaspoon vanilla extract
About 3 pounds (6 large) very ripe peaches (3 cups mashed; see steps 2–3 below)

Instructions
1. Whisk together the first five ingredients in a large bowl until well mixed. Place in refrigerator until ready to use.
2. Peel and cube the peaches, reserving the juice if possible.

3. Place the cubed peaches in a large bowl, and with a potato masher, crush until very soft, leaving some lumps. You'll need 3 cups of mashed peach pulp.
4. Stir the peaches and juice into the chilled liquid, mix well, and prepare according to your ice cream-maker instructions.

Servings
Serves 8

5

Beaches, Barbecue, and My Aunt Bea

Mama's baby sister, my aunt Shirley Beatrice, was one of the most colorful and interesting people I've ever encountered. She was like a second mother to me, and I was her favorite nephew. She taught me how to drive a stick shift, loved to dance, could swear like a sailor when she got mad, and had a heart the size of Atlanta. She would whisk me off on some adventure, even if it was down a dirt road for a late afternoon Sunday drive, showed me that it was okay to be yourself, and gave me some of the best times of my life.

Aunt Bea was indeed one of kind and marched to the beat of her own, not a different, drummer; her pace and attitude was "all Bea." The three sisters were very close, but Shirley B was somewhat different from Joyce and Hazel. Mama and Aunt Hazel, while no shrinking violets or anyone's patsy, were just more conventional. They each married a local fellow, settled down, and raised a family, but not the youngest Nipper girl. When Papa died, Aunt Bea took her inheritance, bought a new Chevy Bel Air along with a set of Samsonite, and moved to Savannah, where she went to work as a hostess at the Pirates' House and kicked up her heels dancing to country music on River Street.

Now saying this, I'll relay that Aunt Bea did not have any real vices except eating too many potatoes and constantly and clearly speaking her mind. As Mama would say about her, "That Bea just flat doesn't care. She'd as soon tell you to go to hell as give you a kiss at Christmas." I loved her for many reasons, one in particular that streak of independence, and we developed a very close relationship that lasted until she passed away. I can hear her voice as clear as a bell today—I'd walk through the door of her house, with a sack full of Louis L'Amour books and a box of her favorite chocolates, and she'd sing out, "Hey, honey! Come give Aunt Bea a hug!"

My aunt left for Savannah shortly after I was born and soon met and fell in love with a man from Florida. They married and moved to Polk City, where he worked as a manager on a citrus farm. During that time, they had a daughter, my first cousin, Linda Michelle. Aunt Bea named her for my sister and after the Beatle's song "Michelle, My Belle."

The family back in Perry had not seen Aunt Bea since just after her marriage, so one summer in the early '70s, Mama and Aunt Hazel planned a trip to Polk City to see their baby sister and niece. I was about seven years old, and Michelle would have been around three. We made the drive down in the cool comfort of my aunt's wonderful chocolate-colored Cutlass Supreme, which sported a tan vinyl top; I loved that car.

I remember riding by miles and miles of orange groves and eventually turning onto an old county road, the kind paved with hard, packed gravel, and finally then into my aunt's front yard. The house was tucked down a dirt driveway in the middle of one of the stands of orange trees. After we made our way onto the property, I looked out the window and saw this little girl in a pink, two-piece bathing suit, running alongside the car, grinning like there was no tomorrow. She was brown as a nut and covered in streaks from her little pixie haircut and blue eyes down to her toes with rivulets of caked-on sand and dirt.

Mama and Aunt Hazel got out of the car as Aunt Bea came through the screen door, all smiles and her arms open wide, with Michelle now clinging to her leg.

After their hugs and greetings and a few tears, Mama couldn't stand it and had to bear down on her younger sister. Looking at her with narrowed eyes and a furrowed brow, which we call "The Nipper Look," she said in a totally exasperated and not-so-nice voice, "Shirley Beatrice, that little girl is downright filthy! How can you let her get so dirty? You ought to be ashamed letting her run around like that!" Aunt Hazel stood by and shook her head in agreement, and you could hear her "mmm, mmm, mmm" clucking of shared disapproval as the two older sisters tried to set the youngest straight. The sisterly tirade, as always, fell on deaf ears.

"Oh, hell, Joyce, she's been playing outside, what do you expect? Kids will be kids," she said and didn't give it another thought.

I had not been thrilled to learn that I'd be spending a week with a little girl, even if we were kin. But now looking at her, I realized we'd get along just fine. I spent most all of my time outdoors, barefooted and shirtless whenever possible, and got just as dirty as my cousin standing in front of me. At the end of the day, I'd have dirt rings around my neck, in the creases of my elbows and behind my knees, and down into my belly button. Back home, Carrie oftentimes would make me rinse off outdoors with the water hose before letting me back into the house.

My very own Southern Auntie Mame, Shirley Beatrice Nipper Butler,
1960, age twenty-two

Michelle, all cleaned up, age four, 1973

On a trip to Tennessee with a stop at Rock City, 1974

That week, Michelle and I became thick as thieves and have been like brother and sister ever since. However, not long after that trip to Florida, Aunt Bea's marriage ended, and she moved back home to Middle Georgia to be with her family. After their arrival in Perry, the four of us were in one another's company constantly: Mama and Aunt Bea would take us fishing or to the drive-in movies, my aunt and cousin would come watch me play Little League ball, and sometimes we'd do absolutely nothing but sit around the house, read books, and think up something good to eat.

It was during that time that I learned the lyrics to most every country-music hit that was recorded in the late 1960s and '70s. Aunt Bea had a habit of keeping her radio on all night tuned to WDEN, the country station out of Macon. She said it helped her sleep, and you could hear it twanging out the songs until dawn. I supposed through hypnopedia all those words and tunes stuck inside my head, and to this day I can sing along with Tammy Wynette when she tells of her daughter's lamentation "I Don't Want to Play House," or as good old Charlie Pride plaintively asks his wife, "Does My Ring Hurt Your Finger?" My friends, who are mostly Michael Bublé and Diana Krall fans, think it a strictly hillbilly genius, but it may help me win on Jeopardy one day, and besides, I am a Georgia cracker. You can put me in Ralph Lauren finery behind the sleek wheel of a German car, but there is still a lot of red clay in my blood.

The best time of all times with Aunt Bea and Michelle were when the four of us would pack up our things and head out on the road for a vacation. It would not be odd for us to go on two or three a summer, and we covered a lot of asphalt, mostly trekking to the beaches of Florida, with an occasional venture to the mountains thrown in.

Of course, food played an important part of these trips. We'd always leave early in the morning, and Mama would pack a huge cooler filled with sausage and egg biscuits along with milk and juice for breakfast, as well as homemade potato salad, part of a ham, pimento cheese sandwiches, and a fried chicken she had cooked before sunrise for lunch. We'd spread our meals out on the concrete tables of roadside parks found along the old state highways or at rest stops that dotted I-75. Michelle and I didn't know what a Happy Meal was.

The hotels or motels where we would stay always had a kitchen or kitchenette, and Mama would cook most of our dinners there. We'd dine out a couple of times for supper while on our trips and enjoy some fresh seafood, but most of the time our food was still home-style prepared by Joyce Lou. Aunt Bea did not like to cook, so she had beach or pool babysitting duty while Mama was in the kitchen.

And on almost every night, unless it was raining, we'd have something barbecued and cooked on the grill. If there weren't any grills at the motel, we'd ride out to a nearby state park and use one of those wonderful old iron ones that sit up high on a metal pole. St. Augustine was one of our most frequented spots, and we'd usually end up at Anastasia State Park late in the afternoon, heating up the charcoal.

Of course, we'd have the obligatory hamburgers and hotdogs one night, while the other evenings would feature such favorites as barbecued ribs, pork chops, or chicken. To go along with these items, there was some type of salad or coleslaw, and Mama always made sure that vegetables were included as well. Part of our trip when we first arrived would be to scope out the local farmers' market and also find where the nearest vegetable stands were located. I know that all of this work may not sound like much of a vacation, but it was what we were accustomed to doing and it fit our budget.

After I was grown and enjoying a successful career, I would take my mom and Aunt on a vacation each summer, in part as a way of saying thanks for all the times they carted me to Disney World or to the beach, but also because I enjoyed their company. Both Mama and Aunt Bea were voracious readers and could easily keep their noses in a book into the wee hours, finishing a novel in a day's time. I inherited that love of books, and the three of us would lounge around, paperbacks in hand, and spend a week or so reading, eating, and just resting.

Even on these contemporary trips, when I was willing to take them out to eat each night and treat them to wherever they'd like to dine, Mama still preferred supervising the cooking of most of our meals. Reading back over my travel journal from several years ago, I came across the following entry. It shows how we continued our tradition through the years of barbecue and veggies while enjoying the Florida beaches and sunshine.

September 23 to October 1, 2000
Took Mama and Aunt Bea to St. George Island for a weeklong vacation by
the sea. I rented a house there with sweeping views overlooking the beach and
dunes. It was a large home with 3 bedrooms, 3 baths, and a huge living area and
kitchen; a big covered porch was on the east side of the house.
We cooked in 4 nights:
1. Hamburgers, slaw, and baked beans
2. Fried pork chops, green beans, squash, and creamed corn
3. BBQ chicken, potato salad, and butter beans
4. Shrimp perlou, sweet potatoes, and salad.
We ate out at seafood restaurants the other three nights.

After a day romping in the water and maybe having a good nap under the gentle rumbling of a window-unit A/C, a typical meal would include some of the following items, which are often found in Southern picnic fare. I can't eat a rib to this day and not think about those carefree times together, lounging around a picnic table, laughing at something silly one of us said, with barbecue sauce sticking to sunburned smiles.

Menu

~Barbecued Pork Ribs
~Barbequed Chicken
~Mama's Southern Potato Salad
~Baked Beans
~Layered Salad
~Coleslaw
~Cuke-a-dalia Salad
~Southern-Style Butter Beans, Snap Beans, or Peas
~Stewed Squash
~Baked Sweet Potatoes
~Joyce's "Don't Mess with Success" Pimento Cheese
~Banana Pudding

The barbecued or grilled chicken was one of our favorites, and the easiest to cook. Mama simply seasoned it with salt, black pepper, and garlic powder and cooked it over charcoal, with or without barbecue sauce.

The ribs were our first choice on any trip, and Mom liked them more than any of us. For those purists, our method of cooking them will not set well with your standards; however, they come out incredibly moist and full of that wonderful smoked flavor. If you are skeptical about the effectiveness of getting the mesquite or hickory flavor in by the following steps, stand over a charcoal fire with wood chips for a moment or two. It will take two washings of your hair to get the smell out. So trust me.

Barbecued Pork Ribs

Ingredients
6 pounds baby-back ribs (preferred) or spareribs, cut into 1-pound
  portions
½ teaspoon unseasoned meat tenderizer
1 teaspoon ground black pepper
1 teaspoon garlic powder
1 cup or more of your favorite barbecue sauce

Instructions
1. Preheat oven to 350 degrees F.
2. Lightly sprinkle both sides of the ribs with the tenderizer and puncture with a fork at intervals, making sure that the tines go through the membrane on the underside of the ribs.
3. Season with the black pepper and garlic.
4. Completely wrap each rib portion in aluminum foil and tightly seal.
5. Place rib packets on a large cookie sheet and bake in the preheated oven for 1½ hours, or until fork-tender (if you are using thicker ribs than the baby-backs, your cooking time will be longer).
6. During the last half hour of cooking, prepare your grill and soak the wood chips of choice.
7. When the coals are ready, and the ribs done, remove the ribs from the foil and cover each piece with barbecue sauce.
8. Arrange the coals and chips on one side of the grill and place the ribs on the other. If the grill is not large enough to accommodate this

arrangement, just be careful when cooking; you'll need to turn them more often so they don't char too much.

9. Allow the ribs to smoke 20 to 25 minutes, turning occasionally, until well browned and seasoned; they are ready to serve. (Now go wash your hair...)

Servings
Serves 6

I also make my chopped barbecue for sandwiches in a similar way. I season a Boston butt with salt, pepper, and garlic powder and place it and a cup or so of chicken stock in a Dutch oven with a tight lid and bake it slowly for about three hours, until the meat is fork-tender. I then shred the meat when cooled, mix it with barbecue sauce, and put it in a large uncovered baking dish on the grill over the charcoal and wood chips, letting it sit for a half hour or so to absorb the smoked flavor, stirring occasionally.

* * *

My mother's potato salad was so good that you'd go to the refrigerator, stand there with the door open, and eat it out of the bowl with a spoon. Aunt Bea, who never met a potato she didn't like, was especially fond of this dish. Food is a constant reminder to me about family and friends, as it is to any Southerner, and one story can make me laugh out loud with regard to my aunt and her potato-craving taste buds.

On that particular trip to St. George, I got up one morning and walked out on the porch with my morning cup of caffeine, iced tea. Aunt Bea was already up and outside, sitting with a very uncomfortable look on her face.

"Morning, Shirley B. You don't look like you feel good. You alright?" I inquired, plopping myself in a chair across from her.

"No, honey, I don't feel good. I think I might have caught some sort of bug; I'm having the most awful stomach pains. And I know it can't be from what I ate."

"Well, what did you have this morning for breakfast?" I asked, leaning in towards her, concerned.

"A potato salad sandwich. That's all."

That's all. I cocked my head to the side and just looked at her with what must have been an expression of disbelief.

"What?" she asked, in clear puzzlement. "I only had *one.*"

I couldn't believe I heard her right, and asked slowly: "Aunt Bea, you mean you took a couple of pieces of gummy white bread, loaded them up with Mama's thick potato salad, and *that* was your breakfast?"

"Yeah, honey, that's *all* I had. Must be a stomach bug."

Mama and Aunt Bea were bright women, but their logic sometimes took curvy loops and was apt to go around many bends in the road. It would have been a waste of breath to tell her that her condition was more than likely dietary. I just got up, laughing to myself and shaking my head, and went inside to get her a glass of water and an Alka Seltzer.

Here is Mama's potato salad, made in true Southern style. It is delicious, but I don't recommend it as filler for a sandwich.

Mama's Southern Potato Salad

Ingredients

3 pounds Russet or baking potatoes*, peeled, rinsed, and cut into 1- to
    1½-inch cubes

3 quarts water

1½ tablespoons salt

3 tablespoons chopped green onion, white and light green portions

2½ tablespoons chopped sweet pickle

1 tablespoon each finely chopped celery and pimento (optional)

1½ cup real mayonnaise (more or less, according to your tastes)

1 heaping tablespoon yellow mustard

1 teaspoon sweet pickle juice from the jar

½ teaspoon finely ground black pepper

2 boiled eggs, finely chopped

1 teaspoon sweet smoked paprika

Lettuce leaves for the garnish

*The consistency of these potatoes is the key to the texture of this dish;
    you will not get the same effect using harder varieties, such as small
    red potatoes.

Instructions

1. In a large pot, add potatoes, water, and salt. Place on high until just boiling; reduce the temperature to keep the pot at a gentle boil. Stir occasionally and cook for 8 to 10 minutes until just done.
2. Drain the potatoes in a colander; do not rinse.
3. Mix the green onion, pickles, mayonnaise, mustard, pickle juice, and black pepper in a bowl. If using the optional celery and/or pimento, add here as well.
4. Place the drained potatoes in a large mixing bowl. Scatter the eggs on top.
5. Pour mayonnaise mixture over the potatoes and eggs, and with a spatula, gently fold in the dressing, being careful not to break the potatoes.
6. Before serving, place the salad in an airtight container and chill 4 hours or overnight.
7. To serve, place the salad in a bowl lined with lettuce leaves and sprinkle with paprika.

Servings
Serves 6

* * *

Baked beans ranked high on the summertime listing of foods to be served when barbecuing, and my mother filled hers with lots of onions, dark brown sugar or cane syrup, and bacon. Mom made her own sort of barbecue sauce that went into the beans, mixing ketchup, mustard, and Worcestershire sauce together; I cheat and just use whatever good commercial brand I'm going to coat my ribs or chicken in. I sometimes will also try to cut down on the fat content by using precooked real bacon pieces you find at the grocery store. But for the real deal, lay those strips of smoked pork on top and bake away.

Baked Beans

Ingredients
1 28-ounce can Bush's Original baked beans, slightly drained
1½ cups chopped onion
3 tablespoons finely chopped green bell pepper
¾ cup sweet, smoke-flavored barbecue sauce
6 slices bacon or 1 package precooked real bacon bits
1 tablespoon black pepper (only if using sliced bacon)

Instructions
1. Preheat oven to 350 degrees F.
2. Mix all ingredients except for the bacon in a large bowl; if using the bacon bits, add them at this time.
3. Spray a 9-x-13 baking dish with cooking spray. Add the bean mixture.
4. Cut the bacon into 3-inch strips and coat with the black pepper.
5. Lay the seasoned bacon on top of the beans uniformly across the beans.
6. Bake for 45 minutes to an hour, until the bacon is crisping and browning on top.
7. Remove from the oven and allow to cool for 5 minutes before serving.

Servings
Serves 6

* * *

Layered Salad

This layered salad is another favorite and one that was always part of a beach getaway. I like to make it when I have folks over for a summer picnic supper. Besides being a great side for barbecue, it is wonderful, too, with fried chicken. A key to the taste of the dish is to let it sit, covered tightly, overnight in the refrigerator.

Ingredients
1 head iceberg lettuce, torn into bite-size pieces
1 cup diced bell pepper
1 cup diced green onion, white and green portions
1 cup diced celery
1 cup frozen English peas, defrosted and fully drained and wiped dry
    with a paper towel
1 cup real mayonnaise
¼ cup Ranch dressing
½ teaspoon Worcestershire sauce
½ teaspoon sugar
1 cup shredded sharp cheddar cheese
1 12-ounce package of bacon, cooked very crisp and crumbled

Instructions
1. Starting the day before you plan to serve the dish, place the lettuce in a large, deep glass or plastic bowl.
2. Add the other vegetables in individual layers, ending with the peas.
3. In a bowl, whisk together the mayonnaise, dressing, Worcestershire, and sugar. Drizzle this mixture over the top of the vegetables and gently spread out evenly with a spatula.
4. Cover tightly and refrigerate overnight.
5. Uncover and sprinkle the top with the cheese and bacon just before serving.

Servings
Serves 6

* * *

Coleslaw was another summer and picnic standby; the basic recipe is included on pages 53-54 with the fish-fry menu. That dish is one that can be prepared many ways besides the one I provided; do it simple by buying the cabbage pre-sliced in a package, either thick cut or angel hair. Add some sweet pickles, green onions, and shredded carrots if you'd like. It is an easy dish that complements a variety of summer menus.

This next side salad is great on a hot, summer day; the crispness of the cucumbers, along with the sweet taste of the tomatoes and the tang of the Vidalia onions is a cool and refreshing part of a meal. I called it my Cuke-a-dalia Salad.

Cuke-a-dalia Salad

Ingredients
4 large cucumbers, peeled
2 large Vidalia onions, sliced into quarter-inch thin rings
5 tablespoons good-quality vegetable oil
2½ tablespoons white vinegar
1 tablespoon chopped fresh dill
1 teaspoon sugar
¼ teaspoon salt
1/8 teaspoon finely ground black pepper
2 large ripe tomatoes

Instructions
1. Cut the cucumbers in half lengthwise; with a spoon, scrape out the seeds; discard seeds.
2. Slice the cucumbers crosswise into ½-inch pieces.
3. In a large container that can be tightly sealed, place the cucumbers and onions.
4. In a separate bowl, whisk together the oil, vinegar, dill, sugar, salt, and pepper. Pour over the cucumbers and onions. Cover tightly and refrigerate for 4 hours or so.
5. Just before serving, slice off the top ½-inch portion of each tomato and scoop out the seeds and discard seeds.
6. Cut the seeded tomatoes into 1-inch chunks, add to the cucumbers and onions, toss, and serve.

Servings
Serves 6

* * *

Beans and peas were an integral part of our diet, and if they weren't fresh, they came out of our freezer. My sister still buys a variety each summer by the bushel and keeps her freezer filled with them. Because I travel a great deal with work, it is harder for me to keep them in stock, but I have fortunately found that some stores carry a number of good-quality commercial brands, such as McKenzie and Pic-Sweet. For the butter beans, look for the baby sweet or the petite deluxe. The taste is much better than the larger varieties.

The way we prepare our beans and peas is pretty basic and has changed little over the years. As a child, the seasoning for the dishes was a piece of pork side meat, which was similar to a very fatty piece of bacon. Today, I have slimmed it down by substituting either a piece of lean ham or a few slices of bacon with most of the fat cut away. A pod of green cayenne pepper always goes into my pot of peas (I keep a bag or two of these in the freezer during the winter when out of season), and I often like to add some whole okra to the cooking peas about 10 minutes before they are done.

This recipe will work for butter beans, snap beans, crowder peas, or any other Southern pea. The cooking time varies, though. Your butter beans cook quicker than peas and snap beans.

Southern-Style Butter Beans, Snap Beans, or Peas

Ingredients
4 cups good-quality, low-sodium chicken stock
1/3 cup ham, cut into 3-inch chunks, or 4 to 5 slices bacon, some of the fat removed
½ cup chopped onion
1 green cayenne pepper
1/8 teaspoon finely ground black pepper
4 cups fresh butter beans, peas, or snap beans (frozen butter beans and peas may be substituted, but frozen snap beans will not appeal to the Southern palate)
12 small pods of fresh or frozen okra (optional)
3 tablespoons butter

Instructions

1. In a large pot, bring the stock, ham or bacon, onion, cayenne, and black pepper to a boil; reduce and simmer for about 10 minutes, letting the flavors develop.
2. Add your vegetable of choice and return to a boil. Reduce heat to a steady simmer and cook uncovered, 20 minutes for butter beans, 25 to 30 for the peas or snap beans, stirring occasionally. Skim off any foam that may arise and discard.
3. If you are using okra, place the pods in the pot about 10 minutes before the vegetables are done.
4. Remove from heat and drain off most of the water. Take out the pod of cayenne pepper and discard; add the butter, stir until melted, and serve. These reheat easily and can be cooked ahead of time before serving.

Servings

Serves 6

* * *

A bowl of stewed squash was another house specialty, and Mama liked it paired with barbecued chicken and ribs. Daddy, on the other hand, would eat it with whatever was on the table. Of all the vegetables we had served, and there were dozens of them, this was hands-down my father's favorite. He liked his prepared so that the onions in the dish caramelized some, or as we say in the South, "cooked down," giving a sweet taste to dish.

I try to be health conscious, and nine times out of ten, I grill my squash or zucchini these days. But sometimes, when I get a taste for back home, I stew mine and add a little sugar to the pan to help speed along the browning and enjoy a taste of childhood. The following recipe is one that I use today when replicating that favorite of Daddy's.

Stewed Squash

Ingredients

2 slices of bacon

2 tablespoons butter

3 pounds small yellow-neck squash, sliced crosswise into thin circles

2 heaping cups chopped onion*

¼ cup chicken stock

¼ teaspoon salt

¼ teaspoon fresh ground black pepper

¼ teaspoon sugar

*I recommend using regular white or yellow onions with this recipe, and not Vidalia or other sweet brands. The sweeter varieties lose their onion taste when fully cooked.

Instructions

1. In a large skillet with deep sides, cook the bacon over medium heat until crisp; drain off all but a teaspoon or so of the fat. Set bacon aside on paper towels and drain.

2. Add the butter to the skillet, stir and melt, being careful not to let the butter burn.

3. Add the squash and cook for 2 to 3 minutes, stirring occasionally.

4. Add the onions, stock, salt, pepper, and sugar. Stir to mix well. Cover and continue cooking, stirring occasionally, for about 5 minutes, allowing the vegetables to steam.

5. Uncover, and continue cooking over medium-high heat, stirring occasionally, until the liquid has evaporated and the vegetables are slightly caramelized, about 20 minutes.

6. Crumble the 2 slices of cooked bacon and stir into the cooked squash.

7. Remove from heat and serve

Servings

Serves 6

* * *

Baked sweet potatoes were prevalent in the Barrett household, and I still have them at least once or maybe twice a week. A friend of mine recently told me that if I kept eating them so often I was going to "look like a darn sweet potato." Incredibly nutritious and absolutely delicious, their sweet taste pairs particularly well with the richness of barbecued meats.

To prepare, simply place them, unpeeled, on a foil-lined roasting pan and cook in a 400-degree oven for about an hour and a half or two hours, depending on the thickness. They are done when soft to the touch, all the way through the potato. A hint that they are ready is when you see thick, sweet juice being released onto the foil. These can be cooked ahead of time and easily reheated. I like mine bare, but if you'd like to gild the lily, add some soft butter, maybe a little cinnamon, or drizzle a touch of cane syrup on top.

Pimento cheese is another one of those absolute must-have foods throughout the year in Southern households, but especially on picnics or a jaunt to the beach. Everyone seems to have an opinion about how to prepare it, but when I make it, mine is the only one that counts. Like my mama, there are some things that just have to be the way they're supposed to be. Mine is a simple concoction, but there are a few rules that must be strictly adhered to: first, under no circumstances can you use packaged pre-shredded cheese. While convenient to use, these packaged cheeses contain anticlumping additives. Besides keeping the shreds from sticking to themselves, it also prevents the mayonnaise from properly coating the cheese, and you'll end up with a grainy, instead of smooth, consistency. Also, it is written in stone in my mind's recipe slate that there has to be some sugar to go along with the bite of the sharp cheddar cheese.

I will share a secret that is not so big any longer: there is a commercial brand out there that comes mighty, mighty close to being as good as what Mama used to make. If I don't have the time to grate my own cheese and create a homemade dish, Palmetto Cheese is an excellent choice. Known as "The Pimento Cheese with Soul," this spread is one of South Carolina's most sought-after exports. My friends and I use it often in place of our own efforts; we just run over to Publix and buy a batch. And Lord help, they've gilded their Palmetto lily with an additional version that is made with bacon. Talk about good!

So here is my mom's standard for pimento cheese, and the one I use today (unless I have a tub of Palmetto Cheese sitting in my fridge):

Joyce's "Don't Mess with Success" Pimento Cheese

Ingredients
1 pound good-quality sharp cheddar cheese, freshly grated by hand
1 cup real mayonnaise
1 7.5 ounce jar diced pimentos, drained
2 tablespoons sugar
¼ teaspoon finely ground black pepper

Instructions
Mix all ingredients together well and chill 4 hours or overnight in an airtight container. Typically served on soft white bread as a sandwich, it is also delicious as a spread on crackers, stuffed into celery stalks, topped on a burger, or in a breakfast omelet.

Servings
Makes approximately 4 cups, or enough for 12 sandwiches

* * *

Banana Pudding is a dessert of stalwart proportions in terms of popularity here in the South, and still one of my favorite comfort foods. While it is not difficult to make, there are a couple of rules in making this dish that I'm adamant about. If a recipe for this delicacy describes it as "simple," "easy," or especially "no cooking required," you will end up with a halfhearted or even worse attempt at this dessert. While no food snob, I really dislike artificially flavored banana pudding that comes out of a box; bright yellow with a waxy texture and indescribable aftertaste, it is an offense to the senses.

Real, flavorful, and delicious banana pudding requires a homemade touch. The process may take a little more time, but the result is something people will rave about instead of politely pushing it around on their plate. Actually, the very best recipe I have found comes right off the Nilla Wafer box. It calls for cooking your pudding and then pouring the hot liquid over your bananas and cookies, allowing the heat to help bring out the full flavor of the bananas. It is finished off with a sweet meringue and is a fail-proof way to impress the cousins at your next family gathering.

Banana Pudding

Ingredients

¾ cup sugar, divided
1/3 cup all-purpose flour
1/16 teaspoon salt
3 large eggs, separated
2 cups whole milk
½ teaspoon vanilla extract
45 or so vanilla wafers
3½ cups sliced, ripe bananas (about 5 or 6 medium-sized bananas)

Instructions

1. Preheat oven to 425 degrees F.
2. Fill the bottom pot of a double boiler with one inch of water and bring to a boil over high heat.
3. Combine ½ cup sugar, the flour, and salt in the top of the double boiler.
4. Whisk in the egg yolks and milk with the sugar and flour and blend well.
5. Cook, uncovered, over boiling water, whisking until thick, about 10 to 12 minutes.
6. Remove from heat, and stir in the vanilla extract.
7. Spread a small amount of the custard and coat the bottom of a 1½- to 2-quart casserole dish.
8. Cover the custard with a layer of vanilla wafers and then one of bananas.
9. Pour about 1/3 of the remaining custard over the bananas, and continue layering the wafers, bananas, and custard, ending with custard on top.
10. To make the meringue, beat the egg whites until stiff in a bowl; gradually add the remaining ¼ cup of sugar and continue beating until stiff peaks form.
11. Spoon the meringue over the top of the pudding, spreading to cover the entire surface and onto the edges of the dish. Make sure to seal the edges with the meringue so that it does not shrink onto the pudding, leaving a gap of custard.

12. Bake in the preheated oven for about 5 minutes, or until the meringue is slightly browned.
13. Cool slightly before serving, or chill.

Servings
Serves 6

The Cordele Recreation Parlor, still in business today.
Photo courtesy of Shirley Wood and Intelligent Domestication blog.

6

Uncle Telford's Famous Pool Hall Chili Dogs

Cordele, Georgia, the Watermelon Capital of the World, is frequently visited because of its proximity to beautiful Lake Blackshear. However, it is also on the map because of my late Uncle Telford's outstandingly good, raved-about, and highly touted chili dogs. Produced in his downtown business, the Cordele Recreational Parlor, or "the pool hall," as it was commonly called, these hot, steamy delicacies attracted folks from far and wide to the city. You would find people from all walks of life dining together each day, from bankers and barristers to bricklayers and barbers. However, back in those days, you would not find any women sitting at one of the tables enjoying their lunch. Not that my uncle barred women from dining there, it was just that a lady would not be seen in a pool hall, regardless of how good the chili dogs were. For the fairer sex, and for those folks in a hurry, Uncle Telford had a walk-up window installed so that you didn't have to come inside. In an article about the popularity of his business in the January 11, 1972, edition of the *Cordele Dispatch*, it was estimated that between three and four million hotdogs had been sold underneath the neon sign of the pool hall since my uncle moved into the location on historic 11th Avenue in 1948.

Uncle Telford also featured another way to dress up a wiener, the "scrambled dog." Yep, besides a ladle of homemade chili, a touch of chopped onions, and creamy cheese, this baby included some fresh, soft-scrambled eggs for your culinary enjoyment.

Telford Harlston Barrett was Daddy's only living brother by the time I came along, and he was a very big part of my life growing up in the late '60s and early '70s. I dearly loved him and his wife, Martha, and some of the happiest days I spent in my youth were in the company of these two wonderful people. While Uncle Telford was soft-spoken and reserved, at least when I was around him, Aunt Martha was vivacious and bigger than life. Just over 5-feet tall, she was thin as a rail, always had "big hair," big diamonds, a big Cadillac, and a big laugh which was distinctly hers and that she shared constantly. She called me "Scott," my middle name, because she said that there were too darn many "Johns" in our family.

Weekend trips to my aunt and uncle's were something I anxiously looked forward to. Visiting them was paradise for a boy who loved the outdoors and fishing, as their spacious home and property was set on a high bluff overlooking bass-rich Lake Blackshear. The dock house was in itself a wonder to me. It was reached by a wooden, whitewashed walkway and featured a huge fish basket that we retrieved via a rope pulley. Lanterns lit up the water at night for attracting white perch; comfortable benches and chairs along with marine-grade rod and reel holders made it easy to cast out multiple lines, and...there was the phone! Now by today's standards, a phone on a dock is not anything of interest, but in 1969, it was a big deal, at least to me. Heck, we only had one telephone in our whole house at the time in Perry, and that was a party line with my aunt Lil across the street along with another set of neighbors. (For you young folks, a party line was not something cool you said at a get-together; you'll need to consult someone at least fifty years old to find out what it means.)

Also on the property were my cousin Bucky's 15-foot Crest Craft docked in a two-story boathouse as well as Uncle Telford's English setters and pointers that he raised and hunted quail with. Those dogs were his pride and joy and followed him everywhere he went; they were his shadows. Set this scene on the cypress-lined waters of Lake Blackshear, and it provided a dream of a backdrop for me year-round.

The best fishing days, though, were in the spring when the bream and bass spawned and the mayflies emerged. These insects hatch from the water, and as adults are about 2 inches long, with a slim body resembling a dragon-fly, and large, distinctive forewings. One of their unique characteristics is a limited lifespan, which is anywhere from a few hours to a day. Mayflies belong to the order Ephemeroptera, derived from the Greek *ephemora*, meaning "short-lived," and *ptera* for "wings." While they don't bite or sting, mayflies swarm in numbers thick enough to cause automobile accidents because of visibility. And the fish, especially the white perch, love them. There was no reason to buy minnows or other bait during a mayfly hatch; you simply plucked them off the dock, the limbs of a willow, or the screens on your back porch. Thread one on a hook, plop it into the water, and boom: supper would be on the line. There was nothing in the world like sitting out on that dock on a cool summer's night, breathing in the fresh scent of tannin-stained water, looking up at the Milky Way and the bright

Aunt Martha and Uncle Telford at Lake Blackshear
shortly after they were married.

Uncle Telford, front, with his dogs. Daddy is just behind him.

night sky, and pulling in magnificent, hand-sized white perch by the dozen. I was in my own little heaven.

Food certainly played a big role in those visits, as it did in everyday life back home. Of course, fish was a specialty, fresh-caught and prepared on the same day and so good that you could easily overindulge. Fried or smothered quail was also frequently served at the dinner table, thanks to Uncle Telford's love of the hunt and his incredible bird dogs. Aunt Martha was a terrific cook and loved making dinner for us each night, though she did insist Mama prepare the biscuits. She dearly loved Mama's large buttermilk specialties that were the size of the palm of her hand and requested them anytime we were at the lake or whenever she happened to be visiting us in Perry. Surrounded by family, whether on the lake fishing or in the dining room sampling our bounty of the waters and fields, I cherished those times dearly.

Unfortunately, we lost my Uncle Telford way too early in life; he died unexpectedly at the age of fifty-eight in 1973. His death left a big, empty spot in our family. He was such a force in all that we did together on our Barrett side, and I don't know that the balance was every put exactly back in place. This loss shook my father badly. Not only was his loving older brother gone, it also made my dad extremely anxious about his own mortality. His father and each of his brothers had all passed away before reaching the age of sixty, and Daddy was fast approaching that landmark. Mama would half-jokingly tell him he needn't be bothered, since he was the "runt" of the litter, he'd be the one to be around the longest. That didn't stop Daddy from worrying, and if he got a headache that lasted for more than a few hours, he was sitting in the doctor's office to get himself checked out. He let up a bit after he passed sixty-five, and the "runt" of our Barrett clan lived to be one month shy of eighty.

We never stopped missing Uncle Telford; he was the loving patriarch that every family hopes for and we were so fortunate to have. He did leave a great legacy, though, including his love of family as well as his reputation as the most famous hotdog merchant in South Georgia.

While the steamed buns and the use of only the best beef wieners helped create the sensation, it was the chili that made his 'dogs so well loved. And he guarded the recipe very closely. His only child, my cousin Telford Harlston, Jr., or "Bucky," as he is affectionately known, has the recipe in his possession, but it is listed in such large, general proportions that it really can't be replicated exactly. He relates that his father insisted on using very good-quality ground chuck and some specialty chili powder and paprika that was shipped in from New Mexico. But it is in the instructions for quantity where the problems come in: "20 pounds of ground chuck, a large bowl of chili powder, a saucer full of paprika, a handful of onions, another handful of salt, a good amount of tomato soup, and some garlic powder." And, of course, the recipe would have slight modifications; as Bucky said, "Everyone's hand size was different, so there could be extra salt or onions. It didn't seem to matter who cooked it, though; it was always good."

I remember the chili being rather mild, the meat very finely ground, and the consistency thick enough that it easily straddled the top of a hotdog and bun. I took it upon myself to try and come up with recipe similar to what my uncle offered, and through a few trials believe I have a final product that you'll love to slather your own 'dogs with at home.

One of the tricky parts was finding regular chili powder, one that didn't include other seasonings that most chili powder products on the grocer's shelves have inside their bottles. So many of the commercial blends are either bland or too salty. Luckily, I happened upon a jar of New Mexico Chili Powder, with the only ingredient dried chili peppers, at Williams Sonoma. To that I was able to come up with my own blend to include cumin, oregano, and garlic.

Another thing that rather threw me, or at least gave me great pause, was my uncle's use of tomato soup as a liquid base for the chili. While my mom and sister loved a bowl of tomato soup from Campbell's, I was never a fan. At all. But I wanted to follow his formula as closely as possible, so to the store I went and bought myself a couple of cans. To my surprise, it works and works well.

So here is my take, as best as I could reproduce, of my uncle's specialty. It freezes well, so save any leftovers. By the way, the Cordele Recreation Parlor is still in business to this day with the neon sign aglow outside. Stop by sometime and treat yourself to an original "pool hall" chili dog and a cold Co-cola. And give the folks behind the counter a big "Hello" from me.

JB's Chili Dog Chili

Ingredients
3 pounds finely ground beef chuck

2 teaspoons kosher salt
¾ cup very finely chopped onion
3 cups canned condensed tomato soup (do NOT dilute with water)
3 cups low-sodium beef stock
6 tablespoons pure chili powder (no additional ingredients)
6 tablespoons tomato paste
3 tablespoons smoked paprika
1½ teaspoon dried oregano
1½ teaspoon garlic powder
1½ teaspoon cumin
1½ teaspoon hot sauce

Instructions

1. Sprinkle the salt on the beef and mix.
2. Heat a large stockpot or large, deep skillet over medium-high until hot. Add the meat, and allow to brown and thoroughly cook through. As the meat cooks, stir occasionally, and using the back side of a wooden spoon or spatula, break up any large pieces. You'll want the consistency to be like fine gravel.
3. Drain the meat in a colander and discard all but a teaspoon or two of the grease.
4. Place the pan back on the stove and reheat. Add the onions. Stir and cook until soft, about 5 minutes. Do not allow them to brown.
5. Put the beef back into the pan and add the remaining ingredients. Stir to mix well, and bring to a steady simmer. Reduce heat to low, and cook for an hour, stirring occasionally along the way. If the chili gets too thick and starts to stick to the pan, add a few tablespoons of water or beef stock.
6. Server over grilled or roasted hot dogs. Reheats easily.
Note: while some folks would enjoy eating a bowl of this chili by itself, it really is meant more as a dressing for hotdogs and hamburgers. If I were to serve chili as a course, I would include in the recipe a great deal more onions, some chopped tomatoes and bell peppers, and a variety of beans.

Servings
Serves 8

Mama, with my sister, Linda Faye (Sissie), by the front porch
of Aunt Polly's house in Hawkinsville, 1952

Mama and Sissie, Christmas 2000

7

Mama, Sissie, and Their Blue Ribbons

As a toddler, I could not pronounce the word "Linda." Apparently, I enjoyed watching the TV program "Family Affair," and it got in my little head that my sister looked just like the character of "Cissy" who was featured on the show. Able to say "S's" easier than "L's," I began calling her Cissy, and that affectionate name has been how I've addressed her all my life, (though we used the Southern spelling of the name "Sissie").

My sister doted on me when I was a baby and growing up. There are photos of her pulling me around in a cardboard box in the front yard, oftentimes with Brownie, our dog at the time, following along. She was my second love, right there with Mama. I'm still crazy about her and she is as pretty as she was when we were kids.

And while Linda Faye and I both "took after" our father in many ways, we are both a great deal like our mama, getting some of her good genes and also inheriting some of those character "tics" that can be a little irritating.

We are so much alike, we were nicknamed because of these traits by my best friend, Chris. He called my sister "LJ," meaning Little Joyce. He practically lived at our house, and when Sissie was in a snit, would ask, "Hey LJ, what's got you goin' so bad?"

Mama was known to him as "RJ," for Regular Joyce. "I came by the house yesterday when you were at the store, and ol' RJ was givin' your Daddy the devil about somethin'."

Since I was the largest of the three, he called me "XLJ." He still refers to us with these monikers. It wasn't a few months back he used it on me. I can obsess like nobody's business about the least little thing, something I picked up from my dear sweet mama. Chris and I were together, and I was ranting and raving about a family issue that had me more than a little agitated. After several minutes of listening to me beat that dead horse, he finally looked over and said, "Let it go, XLJ. You're about to wear me out!"

One of the ways that Mama and Sissie are alike certainly comes across in food and dining. My sister prepares many of the same types of dishes Mama made when we were kids. She and her husband, Ronnie (or Runnie, as Daddy called him), always have a table full of fresh vegetables and are both great fishermen. If you look in my sister's freezer, you'll find the same varieties of Georgia produce you'd find in Mama's, such as squash, okra, and butter beans, as well as fish and homemade ice cream.

A number of years ago, when the National Fair began in Perry, Sissie became interested in entering some of the food preparation contests. She urged our mother to join her in the competition and submit some of her jars of jams and preserves.

I remember Mama asking if she'd get her jars back, saying, "They cost money, Linda." When she was told no, the judges would eat the preserves and the fair would keep the jars, it took a great deal of convincing for her to let any go out of her pantry.

Mama grudgingly submitted only two items that fall, with the disclaimer that she was not going to "waste any more of my jars, sugar, and all that time over a hot stove." A jar of her stellar fig preserves was sent to the fair, along with another of her special pear preserves, entered under my sister's name since she had helped can them that prior summer. Mama came home a champ with a First Place blue ribbon for the figs, and the pears took the red for second. I understand it was a toss-up of which was the better of the two jars.

The next year, Sissie started talking about what they'd enter that particular autumn. Mama had a variety to choose from: peach, pear, fig, plum, and scuppernong. When my sister came over to the house to help choose which entries, Mama said she wasn't interested in "messing with it."

My sister asked her, "Mama, why in the world not? This is all so much fun."

Shaking her head and slightly rolling her eyes, Mama answered, "Well Linda, you *know* I'd just win again. There's no sport in that. Let those other ladies have a chance." And she was dead serious. Mama's reasoning on situations could be a little skewed at times, but made perfect sense to her, which was all that mattered.

Mama was known to family and friends in Perry for her excellent skills at canning, and winning those ribbons confirmed her talents. She would make dozens and dozens of jars each summer, many of which she gave away at Christmas or for birthdays. When she moved to Savannah after Daddy died, she continued the tradition, with me assisting and learning her techniques and processes. Jars of her confections began being gifted to my friends and major donors, and Mama's reputation for her jams was soon well regarded in her new hometown. An example of this distinction happened at a reception a few years back. I was receiving an award for my work with children's issues, and during the program the speaker introducing me looked out in the audience and saw my mother. She ended my bio with, "And Johnathon's mother, here tonight, makes the best plum jelly I've ever tasted!" I think the jelly got more applause than I did as I walked up to the stage.

Making the preserves was a joint effort, which, of course, was only right, since so many of the jars went to my friends and colleagues. We'd spend a number of weekends going back to Middle Georgia, either to my Aunt Polly's house for pears, or my cousin Joyce's, Aunt Lil's daughter, for figs. We'd drive over to Lane's or Pearson's in Peach County and buy the peaches, and down to the farmers' market in Cordele for scuppernongs and blackberries.

I'd gather the plums we used from the side of the road growing wild. You can't find these tart, flavorful, undomesticated varieties in stores and seldom at produce markets. But they do grow in profusion along the barbed-wire fences bordering the roadsides of Middle and South Georgia. There is a big patch of them along a stretch of highway 96 in West Georgia, but I'm not going to give my sweet spot away; you'll just have to slow down and look for yourself. I've also found them on a couple of country roads up in Bulloch County, and on a long, deserted stretch of US Hwy 321 between Savannah and Columbia. Picking plums is not fun, and I don't enjoy doing it, not one bit, no more than when I was growing up. The bushes are full of thorns and it is easy to get stuck. However, the taste of homemade, wild plum jelly is worth getting the occasional poke and suffering under the oppressive summer sun; it is my all-time favorite on a hot, buttered biscuit.

Mama learned her jelly-, preserve-, and jam-making skills from Ninnie as well as Aunt Lil and Aunt Polly. One of my best memories of Aunt Polly was watching her gather her pears. She would don a big, wide-brimmed straw hat, put on her gardening gloves, and using a very long, wooden pole, knock the pears out of the trees in her backyard. My job as a little boy would be to pick them up and place them in the basket, being careful not to get hit in the head by one of those rock-like fruits.

My sister has not taken to making the jams and similar items as I have, but has become quite the pro at candies and cookies. Aunt Polly taught Mama how to make peanut brittle, and Mama showed my sister. Sissie has taken it to a new level in terms of perfection, winning dozens of prizes and ribbons for her confection. I ran into an old friend here in Savannah the other day, and he told me, "When you see your sister, ask her to please send me some of that wonderful peanut brittle. Tell her I'll pay her for it, just let me know how much and I'll give you the money." She gets these requests constantly; the candy is just that incredibly good.

At Christmas, Sissie always makes each of us in the family our own individual container of peanut brittle, which we covet and hide from each other. If you make the mistake of leaving the candy in a public area of the house, it is considered fair game and will be consumed quickly and completely and without remorse. You will be left with an empty bag, while the moocher's stays safely hidden in some remote corner of a sideboard, closet, or suitcase.

Another gift my sister gives each year is a plate of her homemade candies, many of which come from the recipes of Aunt Lil and Aunt Polly, such as the icebox cookies and my favorite, chocolate macaroons. This past year, however, she came up short and I noticed it immediately. She gave me my horde, and after I peeled back the holiday-colored cellophane, it took me about two seconds to say, "Where are my chocolate macaroons?" Not, "Thanks, this is lovely." No, I wanted macaroons just like every other year, and they were not on the plate.

"I couldn't find the recipe; I don't know where I put it, so I didn't get around to making any this year," was her lame reply.

That off-the-wall reasoning was pure LJ. She knew I had a copy of that recipe; all she had to do was pick up the phone and call me for it.

Never mind that I could make them for myself, that's not the point— she *always* made the macaroons, so why weren't they on that plate? It put a damper on the rest of my Christmas Day. I embrace tradition, which during the holidays is supposed to include a dozen or so of those chocolate, coconut, and peanut butter candies. What's next, no dressing? Why don't we just go out and eat Chinese like they did in *A Christmas Story*? My palate and I were not amused.

(It is not lost on me that I was using a virulent strain of RJ logic in this situation, but I wanted my macaroons, it was Christmas! I suppose it's a good sign I can realize when I'm going down the curvy path of inherited Joyce reasoning. I may one day learn to head it off. Wish me luck.)

Skewed reasoning aside, I do want to share some of Mama's classic Southern jams, jellies, and preserves, as well as the wonderful peanut brittle recipe that has been used in our family for generations.

I'm starting with Mama's pear preserves, which are very simple to make, but take time and patience. The result of your labors will be jars of beautiful amber-colored preserves housed in a rich, thick syrup. It is imperative that you use Southern hard pears, such as the Keiffer. These are not easy to come by, and most are grown on private farms or old homesteads. The softer varieties, such as the Bartlett or Anjou, will crumble during the cooking process, and you would end up with pear sauce or pear butter.

Pear Preserves

Ingredients
6 quarts Southern hard pears
2½ pounds sugar

Instructions
1. Rinse the pears, peel and core. Cut them into large slices, about three inches long and an inch thick. You should have a full 6 quarts when finished.
2. In a 3-gallon stockpot or pan, layer the pears and sugar, starting at the bottom with the pears. Make each pear layer 3- to 4-inches thick, and top with sugar. End with sugar as the top layer.
3. Cover and store in a refrigerator overnight. The pears will release a great deal of juice during this time, which will melt the sugar.
4. Over medium-high heat, bring the pot to a slight boil and reduce to a medium simmer.
5. Cook for 2½ to 3 hours, stirring occasionally, being careful not to break the pears and at the same time not allowing the syrup or pears to stick to the bottom of the pan. When finished, the syrup should coat a spoon.
6. Remove from heat and immediately ladle into hot, sterilized jars and seal with hot, sterilized bands and lids.

Note on jar sterilization: Mama never did a boiling process to sterilize her jars. Instead, she washed them well in hot, soapy water and then placed them in a 250-degree oven for 30 minutes. She'd remove the heated jars from the oven with tongs and immediately ladle in the hot preserves. The jars would then be sealed with lids and bands that came just out of a simmering pot of water on the stove. She must have canned thousands of jars this way in her lifetime, and there was never an instance of spoilage. However, I bow to the suggestions of the USDA and advise you to use the conventional boiling method per manufacturer directions. (Although mine still come out of an oven as written in the following recipes.)

Servings
Makes 4 pints or 8 half-pint jars.

* * *

Mama prepared her figs as actual preserves, and not into jam. She left the fruit whole, keeping a short part of the stem attached to each individual fig. She said this helped the figs stay intact as they cooked, which resulted in perfectly clear syrup.

You'll note that neither her fig nor pear recipe calls for adding lemon slices, which is popularly done by many cooks. Mama found, as do I, that the rind can lend a bitter taste, and since both pears and figs are subtle, you don't want to distract from their gentle flavor.

With figs, you have to be careful that they are ripe, but not overly so. When picking or choosing some from your purveyor, throw out any that are bruised or soft. Also, make certain that the fruit is dry and not allowed to sit in a hot, covered container. If so, you will end up with a mushy, or even spoiled, cooking of preserves.

Mama's recipe card for her figs is rather short; actually it only lists the ingredients. She never wrote down the actual process. Here is how I remember her making them, without aid of written instruction.

Mama's Whole Fig Preserves

Ingredients

6 quarts firm brown figs
3 quarts sugar
2 quarts water

Instructions

1. In a 3-gallon stockpot or other pan, place all ingredients.
2. Over medium-high heat, bring to a gentle boil. Reduce heat to a simmer.
3. Continue cooking for 2½ to 3 hours, stirring very gently during the process, being careful not to break the figs.
4. The preserves are ready when the syrup is thick, the color of iced tea, and coats a spoon.
5. Remove from heat and immediately ladle into hot, sterilized jars and seal with hot, sterilized bands and lids.

Servings

Makes 12 half-pints or 6 pint jars.

* * *

My favorite of all the jellies and toppings that Mama made was the wild plum; they were also referred to as hog plums. The varieties found in Middle Georgia are either a dark, banana yellow or a bright, opaque red. They grow on large, thorny bushes and were at one time very popular on family farms in the South. Most you find now, though, grow in the wild. These fruits are a world apart from the domestic plums sold in stores; the taste of those grown on the roadside, with just Mother Nature as the attendant, is vastly more intense and distinct.

Mom prepared her scuppernong and muscadine jelly exactly the same as the wild plum. These two very Southern fruits are indigenous to the Southeast and were harvested in the wild by Native Americans for a number of uses. While they still grow in the wild and can be found throughout the woods of the South, usually down some rural dirt road with their vines trailing up and along the branches of trees, there are a number of farms that cultivate these fruits for sale. Wine made from the grapes is popular as well.

Both scuppernongs and muscadines, also known as bullises, bullet grapes, or fox grapes, have very distinctive tastes and feature almost leathery skins, a multitude of small seeds, and a soft, jelly-like pulp. You don't actually eat a bullis; you bite into it, suck out the sweet, slightly musky juice, and then spit out the skin, pulp, and seeds. Both of these native wild grapes are from the same family. Scuppernongs are pale green, while the muscadines come in a color range from light purple to aubergine.

Mama's handwritten recipe, which is folded and stained and somewhat general, is listed below with instructions that I've clarified. At the top right of the page she has written and underlined, <u>One Cooking</u>. Mama always stressed to make only one batch at a time; the rule of thumb is that jelly recipes should not be doubled or increased.

Wild Plum or Scuppernong/Muscadine Jelly

Ingredients
6 quarts plums or scuppernongs/muscadines (5½ cups juice)
2 cups water
1 1.75-ounce box fruit pectin
7 cups sugar, measured in a separate bowl

Instructions
1. In a large bowl, crush the fruit in quart batches with a potato masher until the skins are bruised; after each quart is mashed, transfer fruit and juice into a large stockpot.
2. When all the fruit is mashed, pour in the water and place the stockpot over high heat and bring to a boil; stir and reduce heat to a simmer. Allow to cook for 30 minutes, stirring occasionally.
3. Remove from heat and strain the juice through a sieve into another large bowl, gently pressing on the skins and pulp to get all the juice from the cooked fruit. Discard the skins and pulp.
4. Clean your sieve and line it with cheesecloth. Strain the juice through the cloth, being careful not to allow the sediment to flow through. Repeat this step another time or two, or until the juice is clear.*

5. Measure out exactly 5½ cups of juice. If you have more, save it for another cooking. If you don't have quite enough, add a little apple or grape juic.

6. Place the juice and pectin in a stockpot, and bring to a full boil, whisking constantly.

7. Quickly whisk in sugar, bring back to a boil, and allow to boil for *exactly* 1 minute, stirring constantly.

8. Remove from heat and skim off any foam.

9. Immediately ladle into hot, sterilized jars and seal with hot, sterilized bands and lids.

*If you want to make jam instead of jelly, eliminate this step of straining through the cheesecloth. You'll end up with an opaque, thicker spread; while not as pretty in the jar as the clear jelly, it actually has more fruit taste.

Servings
Makes 6 pints or 12 half-pints

* * *

Peach is another favorite, and Mama's tasted like you were biting into a fresh, ripe summer day when you ate a teaspoon of her jam. A number of recipes call for lemon juice to help keep the fruit from browning; however, if you don't allow your peaches to sit before cooking them, the color should be fine, and you don't have that hint of lemon interrupting your peach flavor.

Note: for jams, I have started using the less-sugar or no-sugar pectin. With less sugar, you taste more of the fruit and it turns out beautifully with a jam recipe. However, I have stuck to using full sugar for jellies; the sugar does help gel the juice, and I like a firmer, rather than soft, end product.

Peach Jam

Ingredients
3 cups sugar, divided
1 1.75-ounce box low-sugar or no-sugar-needed pectin
4 pounds ripe, soft peaches (4½ full cups mashed)

Instructions

1. In a small bowl, mix ¼ cup sugar and pectin together with a fork; set aside.
2. Peel peaches and puree in a food processor; leave some lumps.
3. Place the peaches in a large stockpot along with the sugar/pectin mixture and stir well to mix. Bring to a full boil over medium-high to high heat, stirring often.
4. Quickly whisk in sugar, bring back to a boil, and allow to boil for *exactly* 1 minute, stirring constantly.
5. Remove from heat and immediately ladle into hot, sterilized jars and seal with hot, sterilized bands and lids.

Servings
Makes 4 pints or 8 half-pints

* * *

Mama also made crabapple jelly, which she learned from Ninnie as a child; the fruit was picked from Papa's yard or from wild trees growing in the Georgia woods. The yield was a very tart, flavorful spread colored a pale shade of pink. Aunt Lil also made a beautiful and delicious jelly from apples, again relying on her North Georgia heritage for the inspiration. It is not easy to find crabapples these days, so when I recreate this jelly, I seek out apples known for their tartness, such as Braeburn, Northern Spy, or Jonagold.

Tart Apple Jelly

Ingredients
5 pounds of tart apples
5 cups water
1 1.75-ounce box fruit pectin
9 cups sugar

Instructions

1. Stem and core the apples; cut into 3-inch cubes. Do not peel.
2. Add apples and water to a large stock pot and bring to a boil.

3. Reduce heat to a steady simmer and cook for 25 minutes, stirring occasionally.
4. In a large bowl, mash the apples until almost smooth with a potato masher. Place the mashed apples and the juice back into the pot, and cook another 10 minutes, stirring occasionally.
5. Remove from heat and strain the juice through a sieve into another large bowl.
6. Clean your sieve and line it with cheesecloth. Strain the juice through the cloth, being careful not to allow the sediment to flow through. Repeat this step another time or two, or until the juice is clear.*
7. Measure out exactly 7 cups of juice. If you have more, save it for another batch.
8. Place the juice and pectin in a stockpot and bring to a full boil, whisking constantly.
9. Quickly stir in the remaining sugar, bring back to a full boil, and boil for *exactly* 1 minute, stirring constantly.
10. Remove from heat and skim off any foam.
11. Immediately ladle into hot, sterilized jars and seal with hot, sterilized bands and lids.

*If you would like to make jam instead, eliminate the step of straining through cheesecloth.

Servings
Makes 6 pints or 12 half-pints

* * *

Blackberry is another family choice, and one that was coveted by most anyone who came across it. Again, the wild varieties yield more of an intense flavor than the store-bought ones you see, which are induced with fertilizers to make them large and showy, but lack in full berry taste. However, if you can find ones that are truly farm-raised organic, they are an excellent choice.

While I picked many blackberries at Aunt Polly's farm in Pulaski County, located amidst beautiful, green pastures, we'd also make our way into the countryside to gather from other locations. One Saturday afternoon, when I was about two and a half years old, my father, mother, Carrie, and I were down near the little community of Klondike, where a large patch grew along the side of a grove of pines. Now I gather all this from what Mama and Daddy would tell later on, as I can't recall the incident, but it involved meeting up with a rattlesnake.

To get to this patch on my cousin's property, it was easier to crawl through a barbed-wire fence than go through the gate a mile or so down the road. The four of us made our way through, and a small blanket was spread on the ground for me to play on while the adults worked. Just a moment or two after they had started picking and putting the berries in their buckets, a loud rattling sound could be heard coming from the ground. Just near me, under the thick blackberry brambles, was a big, fat, very poisonous rattlesnake.

Carrie, who was in her late sixties at the time, somehow grabbed me up in my blanket, threw me across her shoulders, and did not bother to crawl through the fence with me but in some sprint of agility was able to clear across the top in one large hop and stride. It has been a family story now for almost fifty years of my parents watching in wonder as this elderly, plump lady as much as cleared a track hurdle with a thirty-pound package on her back. Sure wish we had a picture of that scene.

Daddy always carried a gun with him in those days when we'd be in the woods; he shot the snake, and it measured almost 6 feet in length, with a large rattle attached to the end. He took it to the local newspaper, the *Houston Home Journal*, where they took a photo and featured it in the paper, Daddy holding the dead snake with his right arm high in the air, and the snake's tail barely touching the ground.

Snakes are known to stay close to plum bushes, blackberry brambles, and other places where fruit grows to lie in wait as the birds, chipmunks, and other small animals come to feed. So a word to the wise: if you pick fruit in the South, look around and be cautious of "no-shoulders," especially if you don't have an athletic champion to cart you out of there.

Blackberry Jam

Ingredients
6 pints blackberries
1 cup water
1 1.75-ounce box low-sugar or no-sugar-needed fruit pectin
3 cups sugar, divided

Watch Out for Snakes

Fay Barrett is shown with a 5½-foot rattlesnake he shot to death last Sunday afternoon while picking blackberries in the Klondike area. Mr. Barrett said he jumped at least 5½ feet when he spotted the snake. He shot the rattler with a .22 rifle (Home Journal Photo).

Daddy in front of the Houston Home Journal's office

Instructions

1. In a medium-sized pot, crush the berries with a potato masher; add water. Bring to a boil, stir, and simmer for 15 minutes, stirring occasionally.
2. Remove the pot from the stove. Strain the juice from the berries through a sieve, pressing down with the back of a large spoon to get all the juice from the pulp and seeds. Measure out exactly 4½ cups juice.
3. In a separate bowl, mix the box of pectin with ¼ cup of the sugar.
4. Return the 4½ cups juice to the pot and stir in the pectin/sugar mixture. Bring to a full, rolling boil.
5. Quickly stir in the remaining sugar, bring back to a full boil, and boil for *exactly* 1 minute, stirring constantly.
6. Remove from heat and skim off any foam.
7. Immediately ladle into hot, sterilized jars and seal with hot, sterilized bands and lids.

Servings

Make 3 pints or 6 half-pints

* * *

Mama also made a very good pear jam that was a great spread for toast or on a biscuit. It has a nice hint of cinnamon that is a complement to the subtle but distinctive taste of the pears. It is easy to make and a family favorite. Note that while Mama used the hard Southern pears when making her pear preserves, softer varieties, such as a ripe and juicy Bartlett, work better in this recipe.

Spiced Pear Jam

Ingredients

3 pounds peeled, cored, and chopped soft, ripe pears (5 cups)
1 1.75-ounce box low-sugar or no-sugar-needed fruit pectin
3 cups sugar, divided
½ teaspoon cinnamon

Instructions

1. Finely chop the fruit in a food processor; leave some small lumps.
2. In a small bowl, mix the fruit pectin with ¼ cup sugar.
3. In a large stockpot, add the 5 cups of chopped pears and the pectin/sugar mixture. Stir to mix well and bring to a boil over medium-high to high heat.
4. Quickly add in the sugar and bring back to a boil for *exactly* 1 minute, stirring constantly.
5. Remove from heat and add the cinnamon; stir.
6. Immediately ladle into hot, sterilized jars and seal with hot, sterilized bands and lids.

Servings
Makes 3 pints or 6 half-pints

* * *

Before I feature the peanut brittle recipe, I wanted to include two of my specialties that I've made over the years that fit into this chapter and which people very much seem to enjoy: apple butter and spiced pickled okra.

I have always been very fond of apple butter. To me it is a perfect blend of tart, spice, and sweet. Ninnie loved the spread as well, and Mama would tell me of how hers would be used as filling for very tall but thinly layered stack cakes.

In the Appalachian Mountains, where apples grow so abundantly, apple butter has been a staple since the settling of those lands by the Europeans. Preparing this dish was, for generations, an all-day affair, similar to syrup making. Family and friends would gather, and the apples would cook all day under a steady, low fire in large iron pots. Another way to make the butter is to first bake the apples overnight in a very slow oven and then puree the fruit with the spices and sugar.

I use a more modern version that I perfected, which turns out to be the color of burnt umber and has a very smooth consistency. While it contains some spices, you can very much taste the deliciousness of the apples.

JB's Apple Butter

Ingredients
12 cups peeled and cored tart apples, cut into 1-inch chunks
3 cups unfiltered, organic apple cider (not apple cider vinegar)
2 cups dark brown sugar, or more to taste
1 teaspoon good-quality ground cinnamon
½ teaspoon freshly ground nutmeg
½ teaspoon ground allspice

Instructions
1. In a 3-gallon large stockpot, add the apples and the cider. Bring to a boil.
2. Reduce heat to a steady simmer, cooking uncovered for an about 45 minutes, until the apples are very tender, stirring occasionally.
3. With a handheld blender, puree the apples in the pot. (If you do not have a handheld blender, you can puree the apples in your food processor, but be cautious of the hot mixture when handling).
4. Add the sugar; stir and mix well.
5. Continue cooking another 30 minutes or so, stirring frequently so that the mixture does not stick to the bottom of the pan.
6. The butter is ready when you can place a dollop of it on a glass plate and no circle of moisture forms around the butter (it stands dry).
7. Add spices and stir to mix.
8. Remove from heat, and immediately ladle into hot, sterilized jars and seal with hot, sterilized bands and lids.

Servings
Make 4 pint jars or 8 half-pints

* * *

Pickled okra is another Southern food staple, and I think is an excellent companion for a Bloody Mary when watching the Georgia Bulldogs in action, or at any other occasion calling for the libation. These spears are a nice addition to a relish plate or served alongside some deviled eggs for a down-home hors d'oeuvres. I use a hot cayenne pepper in each of my jars, or a jalapeno. Just be careful when reaching into the jar so you don't come up with a pepper instead of the okra; you'll know it first bite, as Justin Wilson would say, "I garw-on-tee."

JB's Spiced Pickled Okra

Ingredients
2 quarts white vinegar
1 quart water
½ cup kosher salt
12 fresh cayenne or jalapeno peppers, whole
12 large sprigs fresh dill
12 garlic cloves, peeled
1 tablespoon black peppercorns
1 tablespoon mustard seeds
120 fresh pods of okra (about 6 pounds), rinsed and drained

Instructions
1. Bring the vinegar, water, and salt to a steady simmer in a large pot.
2. Place the peppers, dill, and garlic in 12 sterilized pint jars.
3. Measure out and add to each jar ¼ teaspoon peppercorns and mustard seeds.
4. Place the okra in the jars, pointed-end down, about 10 per jar, or until packed.
5. Pour the hot vinegar solution over the okra and seal.

Servings
Make 12 pints

* * *

The finale for this chapter is the recipe for the best peanut brittle you'll ever have the pleasure of tasting. It has an almost malted taste, with the flavor of the cooked peanuts mixed in with the boiled sugar. The baking soda at the end sets the caramel color; I'm not sure why, but if I ever get the chance to meet Alton Brown, I will ask him.

This recipe does not contain butter, as many do. My mom said that adding butter not only made the brittle less crunchy, but that it also changed the texture and aftertaste of the candy.

The recipe I have here is the one that Mama made my entire life. It is written out on a notecard that is in my Aunt Polly's handwriting, but on the very back in small lettering it reads, "This is Joyce Giles' recipe." Joyce is my first cousin, Aunt Lil's daughter. I sent an email and asked her if this was her recipe, and she responded, "It sounds like mine, but I haven't made it in so long that I forget." So I don't know exactly who to credit with it, but apparently it was one of the Barrett's.

Note on the steps below: they are exactly how Mama followed them. She did not use a candy thermometer; she relied entirely on hearing the peanuts pop, and if sometimes they did not give off a sound, she would have to go by her olfactory senses. I have it written out exactly as the old, stained, well-used card reads.

The peanuts used for this dish should be raw (not roasted) and, of course, shelled. *Do not use Spanish redskin peanuts in this recipe.*

Peanut Brittle

Ingredients
1 cup sugar
½ cup white corn syrup
¼ cup water
2 cups peanuts, shelled, skins removed
1 teaspoon baking soda

Instructions
1. Cook sugar, syrup, and water until it comes to a boil.
2. Add nuts and cook until the nuts pop, about 3 minutes (or until it smells done).
3. Take off stove and add the teaspoon of baking soda and stir well and pour out thin on a large sheet of aluminum foil.
4. When cold, crack up and place in an airtight container.

Servings
Makes 1 quart container of candy

8

Ringing in the New Year

"In the childhood memories of every good cook there's a large kitchen, a warm stove, and a simmering pot, and a Mom."
—Barbara Costikyan

One of my favorite meals growing up would be breakfast dishes at suppertime. On many weekends, when my father would be off playing poker with the boys or out on a hunting trip, my mom would prepare a delicious meal of eggs, bacon, homemade biscuits, gravy, and grits. Add a glass of cold milk and heap a few tablespoons of Mama's homemade preserves on the biscuits, and it was just heavenly. These mouth-watering memories were the inspiration for my plans for New Year's Eve 2012.

That particular holiday season was a very reflective and downright sad time for me, as we lost several of our older generation, including my mother, through the course of the year.

First, my aunt Martha passed away, which sent a jolt through our whole family. Everyone loved Aunt Martha and her wonderful sense of humor, beautiful smile, and sense of vitality. Even though she was in her mid-eighties, she was the picture of health and so incredibly full of life we all just thought she'd be with us forever. It was a huge loss for many, many people.

Then we lost my Mame. Aunt Bea, who had never smoked a cigarette in her life, passed away from complications due to COPD. I fed her last dinner to her by hand the night she passed away. It about broke my heart. She had always provided such unequivocal love to me and would have, I know, held my hand and told me that "she loved her John-John" if our situations were reversed and she had been sitting by my bedside instead.

Aunt Bea was Mama's best friend, as well as her sister, and she took her death very hard. It was not too long afterwards, in August, that Mama was in ICU herself, where she stayed for two months until she passed away in early October. Losing Mama was the hardest thing I've ever encountered. She was not only my wonderful mother, but our relationship had grown to where we were close friends. And as she depended more and more on me for her well-being, she became almost like my child in many ways. I miss her terribly and think of her constantly, both with smiles and many, many tears. She was the last of that generation, of those who raised me. Fortunately, I have an enormous treasure trove of great memories and recollections, and I am lucky to have had parents and relatives that I loved so much and who were such a big part of my life.

So 2012 was a year of considerable pain for my family and me. It was the first year in all my life—forty-eight years—that I just could not decorate a Christmas tree. And folks, I dearly love Christmas.

As December 31st approached, I was not in the mood to entertain or to be around a large group of folks. Many of my friends kept inquiring about my New Year's Eve plans, but I did my best not to make any commitments or promises. After finally getting a call from Linda Michelle asking for us to get together for the holiday, I figured Mama and Aunt Bea would have wanted us to try and put the past year out of our minds and enjoy a new year's celebration. I *reluctantly* agreed to have a few people over for the night—and it actually turned out to be a really nice way to greet the New Year.

I wanted something simple but good, and for some reason the thought of biscuits and gravy floated over my head one night—I guess a small, sweet biscuit is a good substitute for a sugar plum—and I decided to do a casual breakfast buffet to say goodbye to 2012. The whole concept just felt right, and I knew that I'd be thinking of Mama and Saturday nights back home as I put the dinner together.

Like most of the menus found in this book, you can cook this meal ahead of time—even the biscuits can be made the day before and reheated. I firmly believe a host should spend as much time with his guests as possible, and not be tied to the stove fussing over a last-minute soufflé.

The evening turned out to be therapeutic. It reminded me how lucky I was to have such caring and loving friends and family, and it lifted my spirits with an appreciation for the many gifts I've had in life. There were a few tears in the biscuit batter, though.

My menu gives two choices for dessert. One is provided for those who really are serious about trying to cut back on sweets, and the other is for those die-hard Southern food fans who dearly love their Krispy Kremes. I

With Mama in our front yard, November 1964

Mama and Aunt Bea, 1995

Mama's eightieth birthday party, February 2012, at the Savannah Yacht Club.
The poster shows a picture of my mother, age seventeen, when she became
engaged to my father. She inscribed it to him "My love forever, Joyce."

Mama making a large pan of her "catheads"

say go ahead and splurge—you don't get a glazed KK just any day of the week. Those babies are "special occasions in a box."

Menu

~Egg and Mushroom Casserole
~Roasted Red New Potatoes
~Sliced Honey Baked Ham
~Sawmill Gravy
~Buttermilk Biscuits
~Ambrosia *or* an assortment of Krispy Kreme Donuts

A number of breakfast casserole recipes you find contain ham or sausage, but because this menu already contains meat, I've prepared a dish that features mushrooms instead. It has a very nice texture and taste, similar to a crustless quiche. Easy to make, it is also easily reheated.

Egg and Mushroom Casserole

Ingredients
2 tablespoons olive oil
1 pound sliced fresh button or baby portabella mushrooms
6 large eggs
2½ cups whole milk
1 tablespoon Dijon mustard
3 tablespoons unsalted butter, at room temperature
2 cups shredded Swiss cheese

Instructions
1. Preheat oven to 350 degrees F.
2. In a large sauté pan, heat the oil over medium-high; add the mushrooms and cook, stirring, until lightly browned and all moisture evaporated, about 10 minutes. Set aside.
3. In a large mixing bowl, whisk the eggs until well blended; add the milk and mustard, and whisk until fully incorporated.
4. Grease a 9-x-13 casserole baking dish with the butter.

5. Spread the mushrooms in the baking dish. Sprinkle the cheese on top of the mushrooms.
6. Pour the egg mixture over the mushrooms and cheese.
7. Bake for about 40 minutes, or until just set and starting to lightly brown on top.
8. Allow to sit for 10 minutes before serving.

Servings
Serves 6 to 8

* * *

These new potatoes are a flavorful as well as textured complement to the eggs and give a nice little taste of garlic and onion. You can cook them before dinner and reheat when ready to serve.

Roasted Red New Potatoes

Ingredients
3 pounds red potatoes, unpeeled, and cut into 1- to 1½-inch cubes
3 tablespoons olive oil
1 teaspoon garlic powder
1 teaspoon onion powder
½ teaspoon kosher salt
1 teaspoon paprika
¼ cup fresh parsley, chopped

Instructions
1. Preheat oven to 425 F.
2. In a large bowl, toss the potatoes, oil, garlic powder, onion powder, and salt.
3. Spread the potatoes on a nonstick baking sheet in one layer.
4. Place in the oven and roast for 25 minutes or until done. Stir the potatoes a couple of times during the baking to ensure uniform browning.
5. If making the dish in advance, set the potatoes aside and allow to cool to room temperature.

6. When cooled, cover and refrigerate until ready to serve. Uncover and reheat in a 350-degree oven for 10 to 12 minutes until hot.

7. When ready to serve, sprinkle the potatoes with the paprika and parsley.

Servings
Serves 6 to 8

* * *

We grew up eating biscuits; my mom was known for her large, golden-crusted ones she baked on one of Ninnie's cast iron griddles. Mama would pat the dough out to be the size of the palm of her hand and then press three fingers into the top of each biscuit. When the biscuits were all in the skillet, she'd brush buttermilk on top to create the gold-colored upper crust. Mama told me that these were commonly called "cathead biscuits" because the small burrows on top looked like the stripes on the crown of a butterscotch-colored tabby's head. Aunt Martha particularly loved Mama's biscuits, and when she first became ill, Mama made two big pans for her, wrapped them up in a couple of tea towels, along with a jar of her pear preserves, and sent me on a four-hour car trip to deliver them to her beloved sister-in-law down in Valdosta.

That, my friends, is how you say "love" with food.

While I thoroughly enjoyed Mama's big catheads, I personally like smaller biscuits that will easily break in half so you can butter the middle or fill with jelly. To that end, I've added a bit of additional baking powder and baking soda to the self-rising flour to give the biscuits a little more "rise," and the steps I have listed result in a mini-version of Mama's original method.

Buttermilk Biscuits

Ingredients
2 cups White Lily self-rising flour
½ teaspoon baking powder
¼ teaspoon baking soda
¼ cup plus 1 tablespoon Crisco shortening

2/3 cup whole-milk buttermilk (don't use the low-fat buttermilk or the biscuits won't be as moist)

3 tablespoons melted butter (optional)

Instructions

1. Preheat oven to 475 degrees F.
2. Sift flour, baking powder, and baking soda into a large mixing bowl.
3. Add shortening.
4. With your fingers, very gently rub together the flour and shortening until thoroughly incorporated so that there are no lumps of shortening, about 2 minutes.
5. Drizzle the buttermilk over the mixture.
6. With a large fork, gently incorporate the buttermilk and flour/shortening, folding over and over until just bonded together well; do not overmix. This step is crucial for light biscuits: if you are too heavy-handed with the mixing, the biscuits won't rise and will be hard.
7. With a spatula, scrape the mixture out onto a floured surface.
8. Flour your hands and gently knead the dough a few times
9. Gently spread the dough out until it is a disc about 6 inches wide, and fold it over onto itself. This forms a seam, allowing the biscuit, when cooked, to split apart so you can add your butter or jelly.
10. With your hands, push down on the dough until you get a flat surface that is roughly an inch or an inch and a half deep. You can use a rolling pin, just don't press too hard.
11. Using a floured 3-inch cutter, cut the biscuits out and place on a nonstick cookie sheet or a well-seasoned cast-iron skillet.*
12. Place biscuits in oven, reduce heat to 400. Cook 10 minutes or so until they start to turn a slight golden color and cooked through. Brush with melted butter if you'd like and serve.

*At this point, you can choose to either cook the biscuits through to serve immediately, or cook them until just done so that you can use later. If you want to make them in advance, cook the biscuits for about 7 minutes, or until they *just begin to brown* and are cooked through. Remove them from the oven and transfer by spatula to a wire rack. Allow to cool *completely*. Place them in airtight containers and freeze, or refrigerate if using the next day.

When using frozen biscuits, do not defrost; rather, place them frozen on the cookie sheet. Brush with some melted butter and bake in a 350-degree oven for 5 to 6 minutes until heated through. They are then ready to serve.

Servings
Makes 12 small biscuits

* * *

Sawmill Gravy, according to lore, gets its name from logging camps in Appalachia. The specks of black pepper and bits of sausage supposedly looked like the sawdust that resulted from cutting the logs. The gravy was served to the workers as an inexpensive way to give them a filling and hearty meal.

When preparing the dish below, note that you may have to add some butter to the pan to get the full 4 tablespoons of fat needed to make the gravy properly. The sausage you buy today, particularly from really good sources, contains much less fat than what was common in years past.

Interestingly, I found out why from a visit to the renowned M & T Meats in Hawkinsville, Georgia. On a trip over to see family, my mom wanted to drop by the store, which had been one of her favorite places to shop when she lived in Middle Georgia. It has been in business since 1963 and has one of the very best selections of quality meats you can find in the state. As we were making our selections Mama spotted the owner, Phil Mathis, and called him over to say hello. During the conversation, she asked him, jokingly, why in the world he was charging so much for side meat and streak-o-lean, cuts that have traditionally been some of the cheapest. Phil relayed to us that over the course of the last decade, hogs have been bred purposefully to provide more and more lean meat, and in doing so, the fattier choices are now much less plentiful, thus raising the price. That revelation was a surprise to both of us, but makes sense as Americans have become more health conscious, and pork is now popular as the "other white meat."

Sawmill Gravy

Ingredients
¼ pound good-quality breakfast sausage, made into 4 thin patties
4 tablespoons sausage fat renderings, and butter if needed
4 tablespoons all-purpose flour
2 cups whole milk
¼ cup very strong coffee or espresso
¼ teaspoon finely ground black pepper
Dash of salt, or to taste

Instructions
1. Heat an iron skillet or other pan with deep sides over medium-high heat; add sausages.
2. Cook sausages through, browning well on both sides. When done, remove pan from heat.
3. Transfer sausages to a bowl and coarsely chop or crumble into small, gravel-sized pieces.
4. Place your skillet back on stove over medium heat; if you do not have 4 tablespoons of fat in the pan, add some butter to make up the difference.
5. Add flour and make a roux, whisking; cook for 2 to 3 minutes until the flour starts to brown.
6. Add the crumbled sausage to the pan and stir to mix.
7. Whisk in milk, making certain the flour does not stick to the bottom of the pan. Allow to simmer and thicken several minutes, stirring often.
8. Stir in the coffee, add black pepper, and salt to taste.
Note: the gravy can be made a day ahead, if needed—just cover tightly in a container and refrigerate. Reheat over low flame until hot.
9. Serve hot poured over homemade biscuits.

Servings
Serves 8

* * *

Ambrosia

Ingredients

16 clementine oranges, peeled and segmented

3 dozen or more fresh, ripe, tart cherries, pitted (if fresh are not
available, opt for frozen)

2 cups fresh pineapple, cut into 1-inch cubes

1 cup flaked coconut

¼ cup Cointreau or other orange-flavored liqueur

¼ cup sugar

Instructions

Mix all ingredients together; place in airtight container and refrigerate
overnight. Stir contents occasionally while chilling to mix flavors.

Servings

Serves 8

Part II

Later Years

Dancing in the kitchen with my friend Cathy.
Cooking should always be a reason to have fun.

9

The Way I Cook

"Pull up a chair. Take a taste. Come join us.
Life is so endlessly delicious."
—Ruth Reichl

I have always been a social person. Even in high school I would have parties at home when my parents were away. I remember one in particular my junior year, and it was the night of our school's graduation. The whole class was invited over (there were just thirty-three of us) for a pre-celebration of frozen daiquiris and cheese and crackers before heading on to the festivities. That May evening was unusually warm, and the gym's AC not working too well; the whole junior class could be seen in the bleachers, red-faced and flushed from the rum, fanning themselves with their program books.

My love of being around people is probably due to the fact that I spent so much time alone as a child. Many days it was just Carrie and me around the house. I'd read, play with the dogs, walk down to the creek to fish, all things done pretty much by myself. Not that I was unhappy, far from it. I look back on my childhood with the fondest of memories. But I am at my best when surrounded by friends and family. Because of my affinity for companionship and my love of food, I entertain often at our house. My partner, Tom, and I have hosted a score of memorable get-togethers, both large and small, over the course of twenty-six years. Tom is an interior designer of renown, with projects having been featured in such publications as *Architectural Digest*, *The New York Times*, and *Southern Living*, among others, as well as on television shows, including *Homes Across America*. A graduate of the New York School of Interior Design, Tom has lectured at Sotheby's and worked on projects that span the globe. His impeccable taste and style certainly make an impression when we entertain, whether it is for a formal affair or just a handful of friends eating a bowl of chili or some other simple dish on what we jokingly call "maid's night out."

When I was chosen for Leadership Georgia, a program developed for young business leaders by the Georgia Chamber of Commerce, I participated in a personality profile, as did all the new members of our class. Mine showed dominance in two areas: structure and sociability. This combination is not often seen, but in my case it has resulted in success both with work and on a personal side. I am keenly aware of budgets, timing, and schedules, while at the same time cognizant of what it takes to make someone comfortable and happy in a social setting. It is a winning combination for a party planner or enthusiastic host.

I use both these strengths when entertaining, and through the years have developed a few key guidelines to help ensure the success of the party, while at the same time allowing me the opportunity to enjoy myself along the way. I often watch Ina Garten and find her attitude of hosting very similar to my own. She is quoted as saying, and I paraphrase, "I try to greet my guests with a drink in my hand, a warm smile on my face, and great music in the background, because that's what gets a dinner party off to a fun start." I totally agree.

First, the food I serve is always of excellent quality, but not overly complicated. I believe most people, given the choice, would rather have a simple but delicious meal and the company of their hosts, as opposed to a pretentious affair where there are two empty chairs at the dining table throughout most of the party.

To that end, I make certain most of the dishes and courses served are made in advance and need only slight preparation before being plated. In addition, for any last-minute steps required, I consolidate all the items I will be using beforehand. The French have a culinary phrase for this practice, *mise en place*, which translates to mean "set in place." I have everything needed to put the finishing touches on my dishes premeasured and assembled in appropriate bowls or containers, as well as all necessary utensils and accoutrements out and easily accessible. Plates and bowls for each course are also counted and sitting on the sideboard in order of use. I highly recommend this practice as it is an incredible time saver and helps ensure that your dishes are presented correctly and garnished just right.

To demonstrate my best practices, you'll find that the menus and dishes in the following chapters are all ones that can be made ahead of schedule. I've also tried to make sure the menus are balanced, giving a nice variety of tastes and options so that they would be something you'd like to replicate for your own occasions.

Another standard rule I follow is to never try out new recipes on anyone before I've tasted them myself; your guests don't need to be the guinea pigs with something you saw that looks delicious on the Food Network only to find out just before serving that *it didn't turn out like they made it on TV.* I learned that lesson well. A number of years ago I was having a large dinner party and planned on several courses. I found a recipe in one of my tried-and-true cookbooks for a garlic soup, full of fresh garlic, onions, thyme, and a homemade chicken stock. I followed the instructions to the letter, and it turned out to be SWILL. Down the disposal it went. With no time to cook another course, I had to call around to several restaurants and find a suitable, and now expensive, substitute.

Also, I try not repeating tastes within a course or within a meal. I find that having cheese or any other food served to me four times in four courses is a bit much; variety keeps the menu balanced.

Lastly, and as most of you reading this know, use only the best ingredients, and make sure that they are real. By this I don't always mean the most expensive, but I'd rather have a small amount of really good butter than a whole tub of Promise. Who hasn't bitten into a beautiful looking dish of macaroni and cheese, only to have your taste buds go "what the H?" Low-fat cheese does not a dish make. Use portion control instead of taste control, and the result will be much more satisfying.

Adhering to these best practices has allowed me to have some wonderful times both in the kitchen before the guests arrive and at the dinner table during the course of the evening. The following chapters are examples of those good memories, some elegant, others homey, but all fun and rich featuring family, friends, travel, and wonderful food.

10

Adventures in Dining Out

Whether a restaurant is an upscale, Zagat-notable establishment or a Mom-and-Pop fish camp, if the food is good, I love to eat out. Going back to my childhood, there weren't many restaurants in Perry, although we did boast one of the most well-known dining rooms in Middle Georgia, the New Perry Hotel. The original Perry Hotel dated back to at least 1833. The latest structure, a pale stucco building with a porch reaching three stories high and topped with a classic pediment, was built in 1925. And while the present facility has been in business for many decades, it is still known as the "New" Perry Hotel.

The Green family owned this icon for generations, and their attention to detail made the restaurant and hotel famous and put our little town on the map. The restaurant served food fresh from local farms; I would ride my bicycle around the back of the hotel and see the kitchen staff outside, shucking corn or shelling peas. My favorite dish was Miss Nanette Green's chicken pan pie, along with one of the hotel's hot, buttered yeast rolls. Mama liked to order the cream of celery soup, which was homemade and served with these very small, crusty biscuits rolled out and baked into a crunchy ball. Dessert for me was always their vanilla ice cream that was served with a rich custard-sauce topping. The dining rooms were filled with flowers from Mrs. Green's award-winning garden and placed on tables covered with white linen cloths; on the walls hung colorful framed paintings of camellias and magnolias by local artists.

The occasional Friday or Saturday night supper, or Sunday dinner, at the hotel was considered quite a treat for my family. Besides the very lovely surroundings and wonderful food, you'd also get to meet people from all over the country. Located in the very middle of the state, Perry is known as "The Crossroads of Georgia," with two major highways and an interstate running through my hometown. The New Perry Hotel was an overnight stop for travelers, and the accents in the dining rooms would be a mixture of the four corners of the country. Even after I-75 was built, and there were an influx of chain motels in the area, families still continued to come to this historic inn where the staff always remembered your name.

When I was in my early twenties, I had invited a number of friends to Perry to stay for the weekend as a mini college reunion. My parent's house was too small to hold them all, so the overflow stayed at the hotel.

One of my friends, Amy Swann, from Claxton, was one of the guests at the hotel. Her mother called that first afternoon of her visit and asked the front desk clerk to please connect her with Amy's room. The receptionist told her that she was sorry, but Amy was unavailable to take a call right then. Mrs. Swann, curiosity piqued, inquired as to why her daughter could not come to the phone.

"Oh, Mrs. Swann, Amy's taking a shower right now," was the unexpected answer she received.

"Pardon me, ma'am," returned Mrs. Swann, "but how would you possibly know that she is in the shower?"

"Well, honey, her room is right next to the reception desk, and I can hear the pipes running. She should be out soon, though; she's been in there quite a while. Why don't you call back in about 10 minutes or so?"

You've got to love that exchange. It really evokes what living in a small town can mean.

The New Perry Hotel was my first encounter with fine dining, and over the years, I've had the very good fortune of eating at some incredible establishments. On many occasions it has been due to my being on the road with my job, while at other times it has been traveling for pleasure. My dinners out from barbecue to cassoulet have for the most part been fun and enjoyable. I've loved the lunches with my father over cheeseburgers and fries at the Rexall counter as much as savoring a plate of fresh lump crab at one of Savannah's finest bistros. I firmly believe that besides the food and service itself, a big part of your overall experience results from your own attitude and expectations. It's not to say that I've never had bad service or a totally unpalatable entrée, but fortunately, due to the sheer joy I get from going out, along with some very entertaining and good souls I call family and friends, I can only count on one hand the times that were really frustrating experiences.

One of those few times of irritation comes to mind, and I want to share it with you because it actually was funny after all was said and done. Tom and I were dining at a new spot in town along with another couple, and one

Tom and I, libations in hand, on our way to dinner at The Cloister, 2009

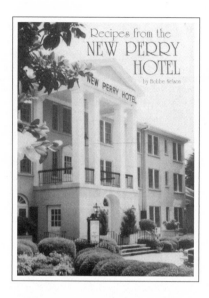

The New Perry Hotel Cookbook

With Bill, Shirley, and Tom at Le Tropicana, Marigot, St. Maarten

of the night's specials was a gumbo featuring grilled andouille sausage. From experience, I tend to find that many places outside the Crescent City and bayous of Louisiana use the term "New Orleans-style" very generally, and I shy away from ordering those items. But I really love these French-inspired sausages and decided to take a chance. When the dish was presented to me, I could look at the meat and tell I might have made a mistake. My first bite confirmed my suspicions. Andouille is typically made of meat that is rather coarsely ground and includes a great deal of spices and garlic; the piece in front of me was as smooth as an Oscar Meyer and the only spice it contained came from a bottle of hickory-smoke flavoring.

I gestured for the waitress and inquired if the sausage was real andouille, which she replied in the affirmative. Now, I worked for many years in college as a waiter and am very conscientious of how difficult a server's job may be, so I go out of my way to be as amenable as possible if there is a problem. I asked her politely to please check with the chef whether or not there might have been some mix-up with the dish.

A few minutes after she made her way back into the kitchen, the swinging doors flew open and the chef, florid of face and looking agitated, came storming over to our table. My father would have described him as looking like he had jets flying up his arse.

"I understand one of you has a problem with the sausage," he huffed, in very poor humor.

"Well, Chef, I wouldn't say I have a problem with it," I said, gesturing to the dish, "it just doesn't taste like andouille. The ones I've always had were much more dense and spicy. Did you run out of the andouille and have to make a substitution?" I asked, and as my friends can attest, asked nicely.

"No, I most certainly did *not* make a substitution. What you have in front of you is genuine andouille." His tone and the look on his face gave a clear indication that he was not happy. "Are you, by chance, a professional chef with formal training from Johnson & Wales?" Without waiting for a response, he pointed a finger to his chest, leaned over the table and breathed, "Because I am."

His nasty and condescending attitude "just flew all over me," as Mama would have said. The Scottish temper I inherited from my parents sprang up like spines on a thistle.

"How nice of them to allow you to graduate when you obviously failed the course on Cajun cuisine, Mr. Professional Chef. You can call this andouille all you want, but what I have here is merely a piece of smoked kielbasa."

One of my friends let out a low whistle. Looking back on this, I should have just let it go, but his attitude was so unpleasant. I know I am not a trained culinary master, but don't serve me a Little Debbie Swiss Roll and tell me it's a "chef-inspired international creation of chocolate and cream confection."

There was a big vein pulsing on his forehead, and if looks could kill, this book would not be in print. Fortunately, without further incident, he turned and marched back off to the kitchen without another word.

He knew that meat came from Hillshire Farms. He just thought his patrons were too far removed from N'awlins to know better. Our waitress, who had been standing a few paces away during the exchange, came back to the table, and with an apologetic grin said, "Chef has issues with folks who disagree with him. Don't worry, I'll take the dish off your bill." Somewhat embarrassed by the whole situation, I assured her that I would gladly finish my dinner and thanked her for her troubles.

My friends and I still refer to this as "The Andouille Incident." On a footnote, the restaurant closed less than a year later. I wonder if they have refresher courses at Johnson & Wales teaching attitude management?

This episode was not the norm for me. The great recollections far outweigh the instances that were difficult. One such occasion was when I was served the most marvelous dish I've ever encountered, and I was able to enjoy it with close friends in a sophisticated and tropical locale. Ironically, despite the beautiful setting and the glory of the food, the dish was extremely modest and simply prepared.

Tom and I were in St. Maarten for the day with our dear friends Shirley and Bill. We've been on more than a dozen cruises with this wonderful couple, who are two of the best traveling companions in the world. Laid back, easy going, and with expert tastes in everything from clothes to food, we have had some incredible times with them over the years. I just enjoy looking at these two together. They met back in the early '60s at the University of Florida—she a tall beauty with cheekbones that would make Lauren Bacall envious, and he a handsome, blue-eyed fellow with an infectious laugh and great sense of humor—it warms my heart to know that two people can have such a full life with one another.

We decided to spend the day on the French side of the island, and for lunch it was recommended we try a place called Tropicana's in the capital city of Marigot. We arrived to find a charming and casually elegant café. Our table underneath the striped awnings overlooked the azure water and onto the elegant yachts and sleek sailboats that were anchored along the bay. The patrons were chatting quietly in small groups; the French accents were soft and fluid and mixed with the sounds of the seabirds and the lapping of the water, it was an idyllic spot for a relaxed and leisurely lunch.

When seated, we quickly ordered a starter course of *pomme frites*, as we were rather hungry and wanted something to nibble on while our main courses were being prepared.

I would never have guessed that "French fries" could taste so good. Cooked to a very delicate, golden texture, they were sprinkled with a small handful of bright green parsley, laced with some very finely minced garlic, and then dusted with just a touch of *fleur de sel. C'est magnifique!* The freshness of all the ingredients, along with the exactness of how the potatoes were prepared—cooked to just the right temperature and without a spot of oil on the platter—made us "ooh" and "ahh" until we ordered a second helping. The entire meal was delicious, but those potatoes were truly an outstanding example of simple food cooked to perfection.

It was a glorious day, and if I live to be a hundred, I'll always remember how I ate the world's best French fries in a chic café on a tiny island in the Caribbean.

As I've mentioned, I do enjoy the company of family and friends, and prefer to have them around most of the time. However, I'll also share that I actually do enjoy dining by myself from time to time; it is, I think, a selfish pleasure. When you are in someone else's company for dinner, you always have to make compromises: you'd rather order a pinot noir, but they'd like a cabernet; you're hungry and would like to select several courses to sample, and they are on a diet and only want a salad. When you dine alone, the choices are entirely up to you.

I am accustomed to eating by myself because I often travel alone overnight with my job. On many trips I am in a town where I really don't know anyone well enough to ask out for supper, and I've learned to entertain myself, very much like the years when I was a child.

For those with food pretentions, you'll probably collectively gasp when I relate that I from time to time find myself eating alone at one of Georgia's most famous family of restaurants, Waffle House. My job does not always take me to the big city, and choices in some places are limited, especially if arriving late in the evening. Even so, I find a fried egg and bowl of grits comforting for supper, and the cooks make the food fresh right in front of your eyes. And I have a lot of very warm memories that took place at these Southern diners.

Growing up, there weren't any establishments that stayed open late in Perry until the Waffle House came to town when the interstate was built. My buddy Chris, my best friend going back to seventh grade, and I would land there as teenagers on many nights and would eat and chat until the wee hours. We built a close relationship with one of the waitresses, "Miss Ruby." Miss Ruby was in her late sixties. She dyed her hair jet black, wore fire-engine red lipstick, smoked Salem 100s, and spoke with an accent that sounded like Tallulah Bankhead if she were from the sticks of South Georgia. We adored her. She'd stand there by our booth and "chew the fat" with us the entire night, gossiping about who had been through the doors of the restaurant that day: good-looking truckers, Yankees who did not know what a "grit" was, and maybe some married man from Unadilla with a woman "who shore wasn't his wife" that came in for a discreet cup of coffee. Even after we'd graduated from high school and left home, whenever we were back in town together, we'd go seek out Miss Ruby. Those simple times may sound boring to some people, but I certainly remember them fondly and would love to be back in her booth today eating some "covered and smothered" hash browns. Miss Ruby left us to her final rest back around 1995; she'd work all her life. Chris and I still talk about her to this day.

The WH also played a part in my Christmas holidays for over a decade. After my nephew's children were born, our family would gather at his home in Milledgeville for Christmas Eve and Christmas Day. I would rent a house on nearby Lake Sinclair for my mom, Tom, and myself for the holidays, and each Christmas morning the three of us would stop by the local Waffle House for breakfast before heading to my nephew's. It was such a festive place those mornings—there would be a decorated, artificial Christmas tree with big tinsel and shiny balls by the door, all the staff wore Santa hats, Rudolph noses, or some other holiday attire, and the place would be packed with diners. When anyone walked through the doors and the bells chimed, customers, cooks, and waitresses all would join in wishing the latest patron a chorus of "Merry Christmas!" Mama would bring one of her Crusty Cream

Cheese Pound Cakes along and give it to the staff and always had a roll of dollar bills so she could hand out extra tips. While Tom, Mama, and I went many places together, I think some of our best times with one another were at Christmas, under the big yellow and black Waffle House sign.

So on any given night, if I'm traveling late and don't want fast food, I find myself back in one of the naugahyde booths, reading a book, sipping on a camouflaged cocktail I've snuck in with me in a Tervis tumbler, and chatting up the staff. I can spend hours in there for the company and memories. I think about Chris and our long thirty-five-plus-year friendship, Miss Ruby and her gossip and sage observations, and, of course, Mama, cake in hand to say "Merry Christmas" to people she didn't even know.

It was on one these solo trips out of town that I had the very best meal ever served to me in a restaurant.

The organization I work for, Junior Achievement, was having a regional meeting in Birmingham, Alabama. I'd never visited there before, but knew of its history and architecture. When I saw the agenda for my meetings and learned that I had at least one night free, I was elated.

I was finally going to eat at Frank Stitt's Highland Bar and Grille.

I had heard of Mr. Stitt over the years, reading numerous accolades with regard to the restaurant and his skills as a chef. I purchased his beautiful book, *Frank Stitt's Southern Table*, and finished all three hundred fifty-plus pages in one evening. You can feel through the wonderful narrative his true love of food and sense his absolute desire to create an exceptional experience for his patrons. I found his recipes to be ingenious creations that combined the very best of the South, and while inventive, they were not in the least bit contrived. I marveled at the book and dining with him had been on my "bucket list" for quite some time.

I talked excitedly to several of my coworkers about going to dinner together; I exalted all the virtues of this top-rated chef and restaurant. To my amazement, no one would go with me. It was during college basketball playoffs, and everyone was all abuzz about the tournament and wanted to watch the games. With no takers, I left them to their wings, beer, and round ball and made a reservation for one. (Not that I would turn down some good hot wings or beer on a normal day, mind you, but we're talking about a world-class restaurant just down the road.)

Wearing my Southern dinner "uniform," consisting of a double-breasted Brooks Brothers blue blazer with monogrammed buttons, a silk rep tie, pressed dress khaki's, and buckled Cole Haan's with no socks, I felt like I fit in nicely with the sophisticated but casually relaxed crowd that filled the restaurant. I wasn't as handsome as some of the fellows, but I was dressed just as well. The hostess showed me to my table, and I was very taken by the interior of the place. Like its patrons, it was elegant without being showy. Colorful and oversized French posters were predominant along with menu displays on large black chalkboards. Art nouveau-inspired lighting fixtures lit the room softly and reflected a nice aura and glow with the warm, chocolate-colored tiled floors. The entire ambiance was captivating. As *Gourmet* aptly described it in a review, "When we dream about an American restaurant, it looks and smells a lot like Highlands Bar and Grill."

My waiter greeted me and I could tell on the spot he was a professional at his craft. Clean-cut and with an immaculately starched white shirt and black vest, he was friendly without being familiar. He did inquire to make sure that there was only one for dinner, and it was I who shared with him why I was dining alone. Relaying I was a great admirer of Mr. Stitt and his cookbook, I told him I was bound and determined to have dinner there that night, regardless if I had company or not, since I did not know when I'd have the chance to be back in Birmingham.

When he returned to the table with my drink order, he said he had taken the liberty of informing the chef of how I came to be dining with them, and Mr. Stitt had apparently asked to meet me. I honestly was beyond thrilled. The waiter led me to the back of the restaurant, and the owner came to greet me just outside the kitchen doors. Shaking his hand, I told him how much I admired his work and how happy I was to finally make my way to his table. He, in turn, was incredibly gracious, thanking me for the compliments as well as for my patronage. He asked what I was going to order; I relayed that I would leave it to him—I wanted a full experience of what he thought his most classic dishes. With that I made my exit, telling him I knew he had a full house of expectant diners and that I was absolutely flattered to have gotten the chance to speak with him. Looking back, I actually would have loved a photo, but I did not have a camera with me, and this was before the age of smartphones.

Again seated, I ordered my second Manhattan—the first one was perfectly concocted with just a touch of bitters and served in an oversized martini glass—and asked the waiter to please pair each course with an appropriate wine. He was a consummate steward, and I thought it would be nice to have the wine courses a surprise to me along with the food.

My dinner was simply excellent with every course. It began with one of the restaurant's signature dishes, stone-ground grits baked in a timbale and infused with freshly grated Parmesan and then covered with a sublime butter sauce laced with country ham and wild mushrooms. The second feature was another Frank Stitt classic: poached fresh asparagus topped with a petite serving of a full-flavored crawfish salad, complemented by a small handful of colored beets, tiny new potatoes, and dressed in a simple fresh herb vinaigrette. Fortunately, my main course was not heavy, as I was already getting to the point, as Carrie would have said, of "having had a gracious plenty." I was served a right-out-of-the-water piece of Gulf flounder that had been lightly sautéed and then gently placed over tender Southern peas and silver queen corn kernels. The chef's sense of balance with his dishes was superb; in every single bite of my meal, the ingredients were orchestrated so that your taste buds could discern even the most subtle of flavors. The man is a genius.

My final course was yet another trademark of Mr. Stitt's, a sweet potato tart that was nestled in a delicate coconut crust and crowned with a savory but sweet pecan streusel. Gilding this sweet lily was a light and extremely well-crafted crème anglaise.

That evening provided the most enjoyable, tasteful and memorable of all my gastronomical experiences. Having dined in so many places on so many occasions, it continues to have the forefront position in my listing of best restaurant meals ever. Unfortunately, Birmingham is a seven-hour drive from my home and not on my direct path at any given time. The bright side, though, is that I do have Mr. Stitt's *Southern Table*, and I use it as one of my most referenced guides. I could use a second copy—the one I have is getting spotted and worn.

It is from that book that I take a recipe and use it in what is my favorite meal to serve, which I call my "All American." It is a menu right out of a classic steak house, such as "Bern's" in Tampa or "Chop's" in Atlanta. Some might say it's more for a man's palate, but most of the ladies in my circle delve into this meal with enthusiasm. As with my other menus, this one can be done ahead of schedule, except cooking the steaks and the green beans. The meat can be preseasoned, so the only thing you have to do is throw it on the grill at the last moment and then steam the beans; within a quarter of an hour you can serve the main course.

Menu

~Hub's Large Roasted Virginia Peanuts

~Jumbo Green Olives with Orange Zest and Oregano

~Classic Shrimp Cocktail

~Grilled Filets of Beef with Beurre Rouge

~Potatoes Au Gratin

~Haricots Verts

~Chocolate Mocha Chess Pie with Bailey's Whipped Cream *or* Strawberry Shortcake with Orange and Brown Sugar Sour Cream

The hors d'oeuvres on this menu help set the stage for the feeling of the rest of the dinner. The peanuts and olives both go well with martinis or some very good single malt, and I like the atmosphere the pairing gives similar to that of taking afternoon cocktails at a gentlemen's club. Hub's is a wonderful variety of large-roasted peanuts: flavorful and cooked until just split, they can become habit-forming. For the olives, I take about two cups and rinse well and then dry on a cloth. I toss them with a couple tablespoons of olive oil and a couple of teaspoons each finely grated orange zest and minced fresh oregano. If you don't have fresh oregano, use parsley. These two dishes look great served in bowls of hand-thrown pottery, polished wood, or a heavy, thick crystal.

I dearly love a chilled shrimp cocktail; I think I might like the sweet but spicy sauce almost as much as I do the shrimp. I've been known to dip a saltine cracker or Captain's Wafer in this horseradish-infused dip while I've waited on my food at any number of seafood houses.

This course can be presented in several ways, with each completely made ahead of time. Sometimes I cut lemons in half and juice them, using the hollowed-out rinds as colorful containers for the sauce. Another presentation is placing the sauce in the bottom of a martini glass and then ringing the glass with shrimp and a wedge of lemon. I also like the shrimp chilled nicely and arranged atop a bed of shredded iceberg lettuce with the sauce drizzled over the dish.

There are several schools of thought to cooking the shrimp: peel them and cook or leave them in their shells and cook; use a court-bouillon for your liquid or poach them in lightly salted water. To me all those ways are fine, but it is important to follow two extremely important rules, regardless of how you choose to cook these delicacies: first, *DO NOT overcook the shrimp.* The meat is so tender, if overdone the texture will be rubbery and there is nothing you can do to repair that mistake. The shrimp are finished cooking when the tail curves inwards and *almost* touches the head-end. You'll also need to remember that, like eggs, shrimp will continue to cook even after removed from their heat source. Second, *always use US-certified wild-caught shrimp.* I will not serve a shrimp that was raised on a farm somewhere across the Pacific. The taste, texture, and freshness between the two choices are incomparable.

Here is my standard recipe for the shrimp and the sauce.

Classic Shrimp Cocktail

Ingredients
½ gallon of water
½ cup Old Bay Seasoning
2 pounds extra-large (21-25 count) fresh, US wild-caught shrimp, peeled and deveined
Cocktail Sauce (recipe follows)
Lemon wedges and parsley for garnish

Instructions
1. In a large stock pot, bring the water and seasoning to a boil.
2. Add shrimp, remove from heat and stir. Cover with a tight fitting lid.
3. Allow the shrimp to poach for 5 minutes; check for doneness. If needed, place lid back on and allow to continue poaching until just done. The shrimp are finished when the tail end almost touches the head end of the body.
4. Pour into a large colander and shake off excess water. Do not rinse.
5. Place in an open container and refrigerate until no longer hot (you don't want to cover the shrimp at this point, which would make

them retain their heat and continue cooking). When cool to the touch, cover tightly and chill 2-4 hours.

6. Serve the shrimp on chilled plates with the cocktail sauce, and garnish with lemon and parsley.

Servings
Serves 6-8

Cocktail Sauce:
Ingredients
1 cup ketchup
1 tablespoon Worcestershire Sauce
1 tablespoon freshly squeezed lemon juice
1 ½ tablespoons prepared horseradish (not the creamed style sandwich spread)
1 tablespoon dry gin (optional—including this ingredient gives an additional "umph" that brightens the sauce even further)

Instructions
Mix all ingredients together, cover and chill 2-4 hours.

Servings
Makes 1+ cups of sauce, enough for 8 shrimp cocktails
* * *

Saturday nights in the summer usually meant steaks at our house in Perry. Daddy liked T-bones, and so that is all we ever had. I didn't realize there was another cut of steak until I was in my mid-teens. Mama would prepare a potato-casserole dish to go with the meat, alternating layers of sliced potatoes, Vidalia onions, butter, and a good bit of black pepper. We'd also have a salad that was full of tomatoes, cucumbers, green onions, and radishes all atop a bowl of lettuce, and on the side some buttery garlic rolls. The standard dessert would be strawberry shortcake that she made with her Crusty Cream Cheese Pound Cake. I think that was my favorite meal as a kid, and decades later I continue the tradition.

For the steaks in this meal, I cook each person a petit, thick-cut filet. I prepare them very simply so not to overwhelm the taste of the very tender meat. The beurre rouge is a lightly seasoned butter sauce that coats the steaks with just the right amount of additional richness. You'll want to make the sauce in advance to allow the flavors to meld, so plan this step several hours before you plan to cook your meal.

Grilled Filets of Beef with Beurre Rouge

Ingredients
Ingredients
8 six-ounce filets, cut 2-plus inches or thicker
1 tablespoon kosher salt
1½ teaspoons freshly ground black pepper
Beurre Rouge (recipe follows)

Instructions
The steps here are simple. Season the filets with the salt and pepper, set aside, and allow to come to room temperature. Meanwhile, prepare your grill. Cook the steaks over an open flame to the temperature of your liking; timing will depend on the thickness of the meat. For medium rare internal temperature should be 135 degrees, and 140 for medium. When finished cooking, set aside and allow to rest for 5 minutes. To serve, place a tablespoon of the beurre rouge on top of each steak. The flavored butter will melt and coat the meat.

Servings
Serves 8

Beurre Rouge
Ingredients
¼ cup dry red wine
1 bay leaf
1 tablespoon finely minced shallots
1 tablespoon minced fresh thyme
½ cup unsalted butter
Dash of kosher salt
1 tablespoon finely minced fresh parsley

Instructions

1. In a saucepan, add the wine, bay leaf, shallots and thyme; cook over medium high heat, stirring, and reduce until 2 tablespoons of the liquid remains.
2. Remove the bay leaf and discard.
3. Add the butter to the pan, allowing it to melt, and stir in the salt and parsley.
4. Pour into a container, stirring to mix well. Cover tightly and refrigerate for 4 hours or overnight. Allow to soften at room temperature before serving.

Servings

Makes ½+ cup, enough for 8 steaks

* * *

My potatoes au gratin recipe is framed from *Frank Stitt's Southern Table*; it is a staple on many of my dinner menus and one of my all-time favorite dishes. I've made a couple of changes on the basis of the ingredients. You may ask, "How can you possibly improve on one of Mr. Stitt's recipes?" The answer is that I cannot, however, I love the taste of garlic and butter together and like the way a touch of nutmeg brings out the flavor of the cheese. This dish can be cooked ahead of time, placed on the back of your stove, and reheated just before serving.

Potatoes Au Gratin

Ingredients

5 to 6 large Russet or other baking potatoes*
4 tablespoons unsalted butter, at room temperature
3 large cloves of garlic, sliced very thin lengthwise
1 cup freshly grated Gruyére or Parmesan cheese
Scant 1/8 teaspoon freshly grated nutmeg
1 tablespoon kosher salt
2 cups heavy cream
*I don't suggest using Yukon Gold, red, or other waxier varieties, as they do not absorb the cream as well.

Instructions

1. Preheat oven to 350 degrees F.

2. Peel potatoes and cut crosswise into ¼-inch slices. Place them in a bowl of cold water and soak for 10 minutes.
3. Meanwhile, rub the bottom and sides of a large casserole dish (9-x-13) with the butter.
4. Scatter the sliced garlic on the bottom of the dish.
5. Remove the potatoes from the water and dry them thoroughly on paper towels or cloths.
6. Place a layer of potatoes in the dish, allowing them to slightly extend over one another. Sprinkle the layer with a couple tablespoons of the cheese, pinch of nutmeg, and dash of salt.
7. Continue to layer until you've used all your potatoes.
8. Carefully pour the cream around the edges of the dish, making certain that you cover the entire circumference of the pan.
9. Cover the potatoes with the remaining cheese and any nutmeg.
10. Bake uncovered on an upper rack until done, about an hour. The top should be a nice golden color, and the cream absorbed fully into the potatoes.
11. Allow to cool slightly before serving.

Servings

Serves 8

* * *

I love the very thin variety of green beans, haricots verts, available now in stores. They are easy to prepare and a nice alternative to asparagus. I often buy them in prepackaged, 8-ounce bags. To serve eight guests, you'll need two of these packages. Steam them in the microwave for about 90 seconds per the bag instructions. When ready (being careful of the steam), remove the beans from the bags and toss with bit of kosher salt, a teaspoon or so of olive oil, and maybe a couple of tablespoons of freshly chopped parsley; they are then ready to serve.

If the beans are purchased loose, make sure to trim any remaining vine pieces off the end and rinse thoroughly. Place them in a microwaveable container, cover, and cook for 90 seconds to 2 minutes, depending on the depth of your dish. Season as suggested in the prior paragraph.

* * *

The chocolate chess pie is simply prepared as well as delicious; the whipped topping with a splash of Bailey's finishes it off very nicely.

Chocolate Mocha Chess Pie with Bailey's Whipped Cream

Ingredients
½ cup unsalted butter
1 1-ounce square unsweetened chocolate
2 large eggs
1 cup sugar
Pinch of salt
3 tablespoons espresso or very strong coffee
1 unbaked deep-dish piecrust
Bailey's Whipped Cream (recipe follows)
Powdered cocoa, shaved chocolate, or a sprig of spearmint for garnish

Instructions
1. Preheat oven to 350 degrees F.
2. Melt butter and chocolate in a saucepan over low heat. Set aside.
3. In a large mixing bowl, beat eggs well; whisk in sugar and salt until thoroughly mixed.
4. Whisk in melted chocolate and butter followed by the espresso.
5. Pour into the unbaked pie crust.
6. Bake for 35 to 40 minutes, or until set. Allow to cool completely before slicing. Top with the Bailey's Whipped Cream and garnish with powdered cocoa, shaved chocolate, and/or fresh spearmint.

Servings
Serves 6-8

Bailey's Whipped Cream

Ingredients
¼ cup cream cheese, softened to room temperature
3 tablespoons confectioner's sugar
1 cup heavy whipping cream
¼ cup Bailey's Irish Cream

Instructions
1. In a large mixing bowl, beat the cream cheese and sugar until no lumps are left. Add the cream and beat on high speed until thick; add the

Bailey's and continue to beat for another minute, or until the consistency of a thick pudding.

2. Serve immediately or cover tightly and refrigerate up to 4 hours.

* * *

One of our family's favorite desserts was Strawberry Shortcake, and Mama often made it with a Crusty Cream Cheese Pound Cake. She dearly loved these cakes and they were one of her signature dishes in terms of sweets. I remember helping her bake the last few she put together, as her arthritis had made it too difficult for her to stand long enough to mix all the ingredients.

This pound cake is the best I've ever tasted; the thick top crust rises up and splits to look like caramel-colored bark, while the interior of the cake is dense and moist. It is a great to eat by itself, or you can pair it with fresh fruit and a cream topping to make a showy dessert, as I have featured here.

I came up with the topping recipe because I was tired of using plain whipped cream. I wanted something providing a rich taste and consistency, but didn't want an actual frosting. Fiddling with some sour cream, I discovered this gilding agent, which incorporates two wonderful tastes, brown sugar and orange. It is an excellent companion to the cake and fruit and does not make the dish too sweet or overly heavy.

Strawberry Shortcake with Orange and Brown Sugar Sour Cream

Ingredients
1 Crusty Cream Cheese Pound Cake (recipe follows)
Orange-and-Brown-Sugar Sour Cream (recipe follows)
4 cups fresh strawberries, halved lengthwise
Mint sprigs, violets, or thin strips of orange zest for garnish

Instructions
Slice the cake and place on individual dessert plates. Spoon ¼ cup of the topping and ¼ cup of the fresh berries on each slice. Garnish with a spring of mint, a violet, or strip of orange zest, and serve immediately.

Servings
Serves 8

Crusty Cream Cheese Pound Cake

Ingredients

1 cup unsalted butter, softened at room temperature
3 cups sugar
½ cup shortening
1 8-ounce package cream cheese, at room temperature
3 cups cake flour, sifted
6 large eggs
1 tablespoon vanilla extract

Instructions

1. Preheat oven to 325 degrees F.
2. Cream the butter, sugar, and shortening in a mixing bowl.
3. Add the cream cheese, beating continuously over medium-high speed until the ingredients are fully incorporated.
4. Continuing to mix, alternate flour with eggs, starting and ending with the flour, mixing until just blended. Do not overmix.
5. Mix in vanilla.
6. Pour into a greased and floured 10-inch tube pan. Bake for 1 hour and 15 minutes, or until a toothpick or wooden skewer comes out clean. Cool to room temperature before removing cake from pan, being careful not to disturb the crusted top.

Servings

Serves 8 to 12

Orange-and-Brown-Sugar Sour Cream Topping

Ingredients

2 cups sour cream
½ cup packed dark brown sugar
1 tablespoon finely grated orange zest

Instructions

Mix ingredients together and refrigerate in an airtight container until thoroughly chilled, about 2 hours.

Servings

Makes 2 cups (enough for 8 slices of Strawberry Shortcake)

11

Dinner with a Cookin' Fool

"Cooking is at once child's play and adult joy. And cooking done
with care is an act of love."
—Craig Claiborne

On many occasions, I've had people over to celebrate a birthday, anniversary, or some other milestone, though sometimes I just get in the mood to throw together a dinner and go into what Tom calls my "cookin' fool" state of mind. I don't need a concrete reason to invite folks over or to entertain; it is all just a part of how I have fun, enjoy life, and express my affection to my loved ones and friends.

The kitchen is my space. If I am awake and at home, nine times out of ten you'll find me here. I have a sizeable Edwardian chair in the room that Tom purchased in London at the Bermondsey Antique Market. With its deep seat and large arms, it fits me to a "t" and is a comfortable spot to rest and watch television as the food is cooking. At Christmas, my favorite time of year, I decorate a small Fraser fir or cedar tree with vintage ornaments, many of which I had as a child, and set it atop the marble countertop. Since I spend most of my time in this room, I want some spirit of the season keeping me company. I have framed photos of family and friends on the deep windowsills that look out over the garden, and culinary-inspired paintings and other pieces of art on the walls; it is my favorite place in the whole house.

As I mentioned, I have over the last several years developed a renewed appreciation for Southern cuisine and often incorporate those dishes into my dinners and parties. The following menu contains some of my favorite recipes, and it can be dressed up for a formal dinner or presented casually at a low-key supper. It includes bowls of delicious sweet potato bisque, a shrimp and grits recipe that I've adapted over the years to my tastes, and a twist on the old favorite standby, key lime pie.

In my kitchen with friends for a holiday dinner

With Shirley and Barbara at my house New Year's Eve;
the toque was a tongue-in-cheek sort of gift from my friends.

Menu

~Plains Cheese Ring
~Tomato Sandwiches
~Johnathon's Sweet Potato Bisque
~Shrimp and Grits
~Grilled Okra or Petite Baby Butter Beans
~Rosemary and Parmesan Biscuits
~Key Lime Pie with a Shortbread Crust

I have always loved Rosalyn Carter's "Plains Cheese Ring"; there is something about the sharpness of the cheese, the nutty taste of the pecans, and bite of the onion covered with the sweet, aromatic taste of strawberry preserves that is truly pleasurable. Men enjoy this dish as much as women, and there is rarely any left over after a party.

I go by a standard recipe I've modeled from the *Savannah Style* Junior League Cookbook and always use Kraft's Cracker Barrel Sharp Cheese (in the gold and black foil wrap); it lends a real creaminess and richness to the texture of the dish that you don't always find in sharp cheddars, which can be crumbly or brittle.

Plains Cheese Ring

Ingredients
1 pound sharp cheddar cheese, hand shredded*
1 cup finely chopped pecans
1 cup real mayonnaise
6 green onions, chopped finely, using white and light green portions
Couple dashes of hot sauce
2 cups strawberry preserves
Crisp crackers or wafers

Please do not be tempted to take a shortcut and buy pre-shredded cheese; with its anticlumping additives, it will not properly absorb the mayonnaise or flavor of the other ingredients.

Instructions
1. Mix all the ingredients together except for the preserves and firmly pack into a springform pan.
2. Cover with plastic wrap and chill overnight.
3. Unmold onto a cake stand or other decorative platter and "frost" the top with the preserves. Serve with crackers.

Servings
Serves 12 to 14

* * *

Tomato sandwiches were a staple in our house during the summer when I was a child. They were simply made with mayonnaise and a little salt and black pepper. If the fruit was especially ripe, you'd choose to eat the sandwich standing over the kitchen sink so the dripping red juice would not spill onto your clothes.

When I moved to Savannah and attended one of my first cocktail parties, I was outright surprised to see this simple food being served in such an elegant setting. The party was held in a stunning nineteenth-century home, and our hostess had an enormous sterling silver tray piled high with small, bite-sized tomato sandwiches sitting atop a magnificent mahogany sideboard. And let me tell you, those canapés were going as fast as the staff could keep the platter filled. I came to learn quickly that it isn't a "real" Savannah party if you don't provide tomato sandwiches; they are a must-have. It is this sort of absolute sense of self that Savannah has that endears me to the city, where the people know that elegance does not need to be showy, but rather in good taste. And to me, tomato sandwiches are definitely good taste.

For mine, I use Sunbeam King Thin for the bread, which is a soft, accommodating blanket for the sweet slices of tomato. And I make them small, using a champagne flute to cut the bread so the sandwiches are around 2 to 3 inches in diameter and easily consumed in one bite. If you can find good, fresh Roma tomatoes, they work perfectly here because of their size. If you cannot locate Romas, choose another flavorful, ripe tomato that you can trim to fit the bite-sized bread rounds.

Tomato Sandwiches

Ingredients

4 ripe Roma tomatoes, preferably, 2 to 3 inches in diameter

¼ cup cream cheese, at room temperature

½ cup real mayonnaise

¼ teaspoon Lawry's Seasoning Salt (or kosher salt)

1/8 teaspoon finely ground black pepper

Optional: 2 teaspoons finely minced basil or dill, or 1 tablespoon real
   bacon bits

1 loaf Sunbeam King thin or other soft white bread

Instructions

1. Slice tomatoes crosswise into ¼-inch thick rounds and place on
   paper towels to drain.
2. In a bowl, beat the cream cheese until very soft. Add the mayonnaise
   and continue beating until fully incorporated.
3. Add the seasoning salt and black pepper; stir to mix. (You may add
   any optional seasonings as well.) Set aside.
4. Cut the bread out in rounds; do not include any of the crust.
5. Spread a bit of the mayo mixture on each round of bread and use 1
   slice of tomato to make each sandwich. Serve immediately. If you are
   preparing these in advance, place them in an airtight container, with
   a very lightly dampened paper towel or two between layers, and chill
   up to 4 hours until ready to serve.

Servings

Makes 16 to 20 sandwiches, depending on size

* * *

The bisque is a recipe I've come up with that gets rave reviews from guests.
It is a velvety smooth soup that can be served in your grandmother's Royal
Doulton for an elegant dinner or a country crock to set the mood for a rustic
autumn get-together. The gilding of the dish with crème fraiche sets it off in
terms of taste and presentation.

The soup can be frozen and then defrosted and served; it does not lose flavor or consistency.

Johnathon's Sweet Potato Bisque

Ingredients
3 medium-sized sweet potatoes, baked (3 cups peeled and mashed)
¼ cup unsalted butter
¾ cup chopped Vidalia onion (or other sweet onion)
2 tablespoons minced fresh thyme
4 large crushed allspice berries
1 quart homemade chicken stock (or other high-quality, low-sodium stock, such as Kitchen Basics)
1/8 teaspoon salt
¼ teaspoon curry powder
½ teaspoon cinnamon
2 tablespoons dark brown sugar
1 8-ounce container crème fraiche, sour cream, or heavy whipping cream

Instructions
1. Preheat oven to 400 degrees F.
2. Place potatoes on a small foil-lined pan; bake for 1½ to 2 hours until done. The potatoes should be soft to the touch throughout. Set aside to cool.
3. Peel cooled potatoes and set aside.
4. In a Dutch oven or large pot, melt the butter and sauté the onions over medium-high heat, stirring; cook until tender, about 5 minutes.
5. Add thyme and crushed allspice, stir and cook another minute or so to mix well. Add stock, bring to a boil, reduce, and simmer for 10 minutes. Remove from heat and allow to cool.
6. In two separate batches, add half the sweet potatoes and half the soup mixture to a blender. Puree on high speed until smooth. Pour both batches into a storage container.
7. Add salt, curry, cinnamon, and sugar to the puree, and stir until blended well. Cover and refrigerate overnight.

8. To serve, reheat soup in a large pot to a steady simmer. Ladle into bowls, and place a dollop of crème fraiche, sour cream, or whipped cream on top.

Note: Don't be tempted to add additional spices until you have allowed the soup to chill and the flavors to marry overnight; they will develop as the soup sits. The point here is to allow the spices to complement the taste of the sweet potato, not overwhelm it, so just a hint of curry and cinnamon is needed—you don't want your guests to taste those spices and go, "Oh, another curried soup." Subtlety here is key.

Servings
Serves 6 to 8

* * *

My shrimp recipe is uncomplicated but takes a little longer to prepare than some; however, the end result is worth the efforts. Total prep and cooking time is about an hour, which is mostly spent peeling and deveining the shrimp. If you allow your seafood purveyor to do the dressing, it will save you a good 20 minutes. This dish is also one that tastes better as it sits for a while, allowing the flavors of the shrimp and gravy to marry. The ingredient I like to use in this dish that is a little different from many similar recipes is coffee. It adds a great depth of taste to the gravy. You'll see that I use coffee or espresso in a few of my dishes in this book. After you prepare them for yourself, you'll understand why.

Shrimp and Grits

Ingredients
3 slices bacons
½ cup chopped onion
2 tablespoons diced green or red bell pepper
1 clove, or 1 teaspoon, diced fresh garlic
½ cup chopped fresh tomato
4 cups low-sodium chicken stock
1 teaspoon sweet smoked paprika
½ teaspoon dried thyme
½ teaspoon dried oregano
¼ teaspoon freshly ground black pepper

1 bay leaf
3 tablespoons butter
3 tablespoons flour
¼ cup very strong coffee or espresso
2½ pounds fresh large, US wild-caught shrimp, about 48, peeled and
deveined
½ teaspoon of Old Bay or your favorite Cajun or Creole seasoning
8 cups cooked stone-ground grits, instructions following
¼ cup fresh chopped parsley for garnish

Instructions
Shrimp
1. In a large stockpot or Dutch oven, cook the bacon until crisp.
   Remove bacon and set aside.
2. Drain off all but two tablespoons of the bacon fat.
3. Over medium-high heat, add the onion to the pot, and cook for 1
   minute, stirring occasionally.
4. Add the bell pepper and garlic, stir, and continue to cook for 2 to 3
   minutes, until the vegetables start to become soft.
5. Add the tomato, and stir.
6. Pour in the stock, stir and mix well. Make sure to scrape up any of
   the bacon bits that might be stuck to the bottom of the pan.
7. Add the paprika, thyme, oregano, black pepper and bay leaf.
   Crumble and add the reserved bacon. Bring the mixture to a gentle
   boil, stir, reduce to a simmer, cover and cook for 20 minutes. Stir
   occasionally.
8. Remove from heat and strain the stock mixture through a sieve into
   a bowl, pushing down on the vegetables with the back of a spoon to
   release all the juices. Set the bowl aside.
9. Return the original Dutch oven or pot back to the stove over
   medium heat; add the butter.
10. Mix in the flour, and whisking, make a roux, stirring constantly.
    Cook until it turns a golden color, about 5 minutes or so.
11. Whisk in the strained stock and bring to a steady simmer. Stir until
    it thickens, about 7 to 8 minutes.
12. Add the coffee or espresso, stir to mix.
13. Toss the shrimp in a separate bowl with the Old Bay or kosher salt.

14. Add the shrimp to the thickened gravy, and stir occasionally, cooking until *just done*, about 5 minutes. The shrimp are done with their tail-end curves up to almost meet the head section.
15. Remove from heat, and either serve immediately, or chill immediately, as the shrimp will continue to cook after being removed from the stove.

If making ahead of time and you need to reheat the shrimp, do so on the stovetop (don't be tempted to use the microwave). Bring to a steady simmer but do not boil; if overheated, the shrimp will become tough. Ladle the shrimp and gravy over your grits and sprinkle with the chopped parsley.

Grits

Prepare the grits according to the instructions on the container, but for 1 part of the water in the recipe use whole milk instead. For example, if you are making 4 servings, and the instructions read 1 cup grits and 4 cups water, use 1 cup milk and 3 cups water. When the grits are done, they should be thick and creamy with the consistency of a rich pudding. If during the cooking process they become too stiff and difficult to stir, add a few tablespoons of milk as needed. Be careful not to add too much liquid, though; you can't remove it once it's poured in, and with slow-cooking stone-ground grits, adding more grits at the last minute is not an option.

Note: Most gourmet grocers carry these grits or you can find a number of places to order online, such as Carolina Plantation, Barker Creek, or Nora Mills. Make sure that you have real, stone-ground grits; their consistency and taste are needed in this dish. If these types of grits are not an option, choose real grits, or quick grits if you have no other choice. However, under no circumstances use instant grits. You can use either yellow or white grits, both are completely acceptable. These can be cooked ahead of time and reheated over a low flame when ready to serve. Make sure you stir them along the way as they heat so as not to stick to the pan, and add any milk or water as needed.

Servings

Serves 6-8

* * *

Fresh okra is an incredible side dish that can be made in a hurry at the last minute, but it does not work well for larger crowds. If you have a party of eight or fewer it can be easily done on an inside or gas grill. It is best to cook these in a grill basket that you can shake or stir; I have found that skewers don't work well. If the okra is large enough not to slip through the grill, they can be cooked individually, turning them with tongs as they roast.

Grilled Okra

Ingredients
36 pods of medium-sized okra (don't be tempted to get really large pods, as they can be tough)
2 teaspoons olive oil
¼ teaspoon kosher salt
1/8 teaspoon freshly ground black pepper

Instructions
1. Preheat your grill.
2. Toss the okra with the oil and salt and pepper.
3. Grill over high heat until the pods start to stripe but are still a bright green, shaking your grill basket or turning the okra over occasionally, about 3 to 5 minutes.

Servings
Serves 6

If you choose to use the beans, I suggest McKenzie's Petit Deluxe Baby Butter Beans if you can't find fresh. These are easily made ahead of time and then reheated; they make a great pairing of tastes and texture with the main course. Follow the recipe found in the Beaches, Barbecue, and My Aunt Bea chapter, found on pages 73-74.

* * *

You need something to help clean the scrumptious gravy off your plate, and these herb-and-cheese-laced biscuits do the trick nicely.

Rosemary and Parmesan Biscuits

Ingredients and Instructions

To the basic biscuit recipe you find in the New Year's Eve menu on pages 109-110, add ¼ cup grated Parmesan cheese and 2 tablespoons minced fresh rosemary to the biscuit dough just after you have finished incorporating the Crisco. Add the buttermilk and continue with the recipe instructions.

* * *

The key lime pie recipe is one that I've used from my friend Janis Owens, the wonderful author and cook from North Florida. Her secret in making this a standout dish, besides cooking it with a significant dose of Southern Cracker love, is the use of fresh lime zest in the filling. I have adapted the recipe somewhat; first, by doubling the filling recipe (one of those few times when I think more is better than less), and I make the crust using shortbread cookies and nuts instead of graham crackers.

Key Lime Pie with a Shortbread Crust

Ingredients

2 cups shortbread cookie crumbs (I use Keebler Sandies shortbread
    cookies and crumble in the food processor)
¼ cup finely ground pecans
¼ cup sugar
¼ cup unsalted butter, melted
1/8 teaspoon cinnamon
1 cup key lime juice (if you can't get fresh, which is difficult, use a
    reliable organic, not-from -concentrate brand, such as Santa Cruz)
6 teaspoons very finely grated lime zest
4 large egg yolks
2 14-ounce cans sweetened condensed milk
Whipped cream and slices of lime for garnish

Instructions

1. Preheat oven to 350 degrees F.

2. In a large bowl, make the crust by mixing together the cookie crumbs, nuts, sugar, butter, and cinnamon. Put the mixture in a nonstick pie dish; using your hands, press evenly over bottom and up the sides, making certain it adheres and sticks.
3. In another bowl, beat the lime juice, zest, egg yolks, and milk until thoroughly incorporated.
4. Add the filling to the crust and bake for 18 to 20 minutes. Remove and refrigerate overnight.
5. To serve, top with whipped cream and slice of lime.

Servings
Serves 6 to 8

The living room of our mountain house with Mr. Murphy
in his favorite chair

12

In the Cool of the Blue Ridge Mountains

As a youngster, my family would make trips each summer to the north Georgia mountains to visit Daddy's family. I fell in love with the beauty of places such as Sautee and the Nacoochee Valley and decided when I was in my early thirties to buy a weekend getaway. I found a spot on Reece Creek, right off of Nottely Lake. It was a small, cute house facing a rolling meadow where the creek meandered through. I had a heyday venturing out to buy rusticated furnishings and vintage fishing gear. When it was finished, it was a little gem of a spot that looked like an old but comfortable fishing cottage.

But as much as I loved the place, the house was too small to have any people join me for the weekend. With only one bathroom, it proved a little awkward on a couple of occasions, if you know what I mean. Because of its location, adding on to the house was not an option, and after a good bit of discussion, Tom and I decided to sell it to buy a larger house in the mountains together.

We searched on a radius that would limit us to five hours travel one way. If you look at a map, you'll see that Savannah is really in the southern region of the state and that Georgia is the largest state east of the Mississippi, which translates into a long distance to any hill country. We eventually ruled out North Georgia simply because of those logistics and the exhaustive necessity of having to drive through Atlanta.

Many of our friends encouraged us to buy in Highlands, North Carolina, where several of them spend parts of the summer. We both love Cashiers and Highlands and visited there often, but we'd be seeing the same people through the summer as we did the rest of the year. The area is very much like a "Little Savannah" during the high season, as the following humorous story shows.

Chris and I had taken a week off up to the mountains and had rented a sporty Mustang convertible to make the drive. We made a stopover in Highlands for a couple of days. Before we checked into the inn the first night, Tom, who was back in Savannah, had already heard that we had arrived. Apparently, as Chris and I made our way down Main Street that first afternoon to buy a few things at Bryson's Food Store, someone from home spotted us in the car. We did have the top down, and, knowing us, we were listening to an '80s song, such as "You Dropped a Bomb on Me" or something by Rick James, so we probably did stand out. When I phoned Tom that night, he relayed that a "friend of a friend" said that they had seen "Johnathon and another young fellow up in Highlands this afternoon carousing down Main Street in a flashy convertible, and they looked like they were having *just the best time.*"

Proving that in the South, you can't go anywhere and get away with anything.

While I'll admit we more than likely had the music turned up, I can assure you we were *not* carousing. I don't dance in public, at least not on a main street. And we weren't drinking either. Chris does not imbibe, and I make it a rule not to have a cocktail until after 6 p.m., just on principle.

In the end, we opted to look in upstate South Carolina and near Hendersonville, North Carolina, drawing a line at Asheville because of the distance. We spent a number of months touring dozens of properties, and after another long day of viewings, had one final house to inspect. It was located in the small community of Gerton, which sits atop the continental divide halfway between Asheville and Lake Lure.

Driving into Gerton fifteen minutes before our appointment, we found a charming hamlet that included a picture-postcard white-clapboard church set on a grass-covered knoll, a small general store, and community center that backed up against a rushing creek. There were dozens of Arts and Crafts-style bungalows and houses, all centered around a huge meadow called "The Commons" by area residents.

The house we were coming to see had been on the market for some time. We knew from having spoken earlier to the realtor that it was in need of extensive renovation, but that was really what we were looking for. Tom loved refurbishing houses and had restored more than thirty over the course of his career. We came up the drive to find a cottage that was similar in style to the locally favored Arts and Crafts movement. The downstairs was all native stone and built into the side of the hill, and the second story was board and batten. You could tell right away, even though the bones of the house were good, a whole lot of major TLC would need to be provided.

As we got out of the car to walk around and were peaking in the windows before the realtor arrived to let us in, we heard this angelic music

My little fishing cottage near Blairsville, Georgia

With friends Lisa and Mason, and Mr. Murphy,
enjoying an afternoon outdoors

floating through the trees. We looked at each other, amazed at the unexpected sound, as chimes played out from the little church's carillon "A Mighty Fortress is our God," a favorite hymn of mine. We spoke at the same time: "This is it!" We later learned from our new neighbors that the church, Bearwallow Baptist, was made famous as the cover photo for one of Charles Kuralt's coffee-table-style travel books.

With this omen of good tidings, we zipped through the house with the realtor and made an offer on the spot. Within a couple of days, we'd reached a price with the owners, and soon the house was ours.

After a few months of work, we were left with an incredible property that was both beautiful and so very, very comfortable. We turned the entire downstairs, which was 60 feet long and 20 feet wide, into one large expanse. We often joked that the cottage was our "single-wide," as the whole house was just one room deep. The entire back wall of the room was original native stone, along with an impressive fireplace topped with a signature keystone of the stonemason—a local gentleman, a Mr. Owensby, who was instrumental in building dozens of homes in the area. The front wall was knotty pine with custom-made windows and French doors that all provided a large view of Bearwallow Mountain. Tom installed a gourmet kitchen that opened into the room so that whoever was cooking would not be separated from the other guests downstairs. The renovation included a wet bar, where we hung a bronze bat chandelier and named it "The Bat Bar" in honor of the closest town, Bat Cave, just down the mountain. The whole public area of the house flowed wonderfully for guests, and we hosted a number of parties and dinners there for our visiting friends and for the new ones we made in the area.

There were three bedrooms upstairs, all done with knotty-pine walls and ceilings. Each boasted its own interior bathroom, which was extremely convenient with overnight guests; you wouldn't run into anyone heading down the hall to use the facilities with curlers in her hair or wearing just his boxers. We prepared one of the rooms especially for Mama. Tom put a colorful Brunschwig & Fils wallpaper picturing cardinals, orioles, and blue jays in the bath and hung on the walls some of my sister's original paintings she had done of camellias. The twin bedroom housed my collection of vintage fishing gear along with a great watercolor painting of a school of bream, and I draped my favorite plaid Ralph Lauren blankets on the beds. The master bedroom showcased an antique North Carolina chest of drawers and carried on the Arts and Crafts motif of the area with wallpaper in the bath featuring block-style images of squirrels, bears, and other wildlife that would fit right in at a Roycroft exhibit.

The outside porch ran the length of the building, and from it you looked right into the 4,000-foot splendor of Bearwallow Mountain, which was a verdant green in the summer, an array of golds and crimsons in the fall, and dusted with snow in the winter. A dozen hundred-plus-year-old boxwoods, standing more than 8-feet tall, dotted the property, planted when the original homestead was built during the last century. Maples and other hardwoods towered over the house, and we had another dozen or so mature dogwoods, all of which stretched down the yard to the road. Under the canopy of the trees was a dark, forest-green carpet of periwinkle.

I also love to garden, so I put in a colorful flowerbed filled with coneflowers, daylilies, zinnias, purple salvia, cleome, and bee balm, with herbs that grew like they were bushes. I planted curly-leaf parsley in massive pots along with red dragon-eared begonias that the hummingbirds loved to visit. The stems would get so large that the parsley just cascaded over onto itself. The chives grew thick as grass and bloomed beautiful lilac-colored balls all summer, and the thyme just exploded. It was heaven for me when cooking.

I hung a bird feeder in the garden, and the variety of birds that were attracted to it was just amazing. One of my favorite things to do when at the house was sit outside and watch all the titmouse, towhees, goldfinches, hummingbirds, cardinals, woodpeckers, and rushes flit in and out of the garden. However, after a while, I had to remove the feeder and just scatter the seeds on some of the flat rocks outlining the garden and along the ground for the birds. After I replaced the feeders for the umpteenth time and spent hundreds of dollars on them, I decided not to fight the bears anymore. Yes, the bears apparently love sunflower seeds. I awoke late one night for a trip into the bathroom, and as I looked out the window I could see very clearly under the bright moonlight a big brown bear on its haunches wrestling open my $100 squirrel-proof bird feeder. Bearwallow Mountain was aptly named.

After the project was completed, we began inviting friends up for long weekends, and some of the best times of my adult life were spent at what we began calling "TommeeJon Lodge." We'd spend our days touring through the Blue Ridge Parkway, exploring Asheville, or just sitting quietly reading a book. Evenings always found us with a little libation, maybe a game of cards, and, of course, good food. Quite a lot of memories were made there.

One episode is a story that still gets told today, even though it happened over a decade ago. One couple, who will go unnamed, was visiting with us for Halloween. Although married for well over thirty years, they still experienced the same feelings for one another that you generally would associate with honeymooners, and it was a well-known fact amongst our set of friends. After dinner that Saturday night, and another round of gin rummy, Tom and I said our goodnights and headed upstairs. The couple decided to stay and continue to enjoy the fire that was still going. Well, apparently the heat of the fire flamed their passions, and they became engaged in some very deep affection. So caught up with their attraction to one another, they failed to notice that somehow the flue on the fireplace had become unhinged and dropped down, and smoke began to fill the room. Suddenly the fire alarm downstairs started to ring and screech. The husband jumped up from the couch where they were *in flagrante delicto* and fell immediately against our very substantial wooden coffee table; it seemed his pants and Fruit of the Looms around the ankles tripped him—he sported two lovely, purple-colored bruises on his shins the next day. Our lady friend was able to help him up, finally, and he opened the doors and shut off the alarms. Tom and I had hurried downstairs in the middle of all this to see him in his underwear on a chair tugging at the fire alarm on the living room ceiling—I laughed so hard my sides hurt.

There are other funny and touching stories I could share, but none as interesting as that one.

So on to food. Western North Carolina is a food-lover's haven, and the concepts of organic produce, farm-to-table food, and healthy eating are all not just a fad, but a real way of life for so many people there. You find hundreds of small farms amidst the countryside around Asheville where you can choose from an enormous variety of fruits and vegetables, some that you can pick in the fields or buy already bagged. Many of these places put their food in little sheds out by the roadside, and it is an honor system to pay. You'll also find numerous farms providing free-range meats. One, Hickory Nut Farms, is located just down the mountain from our house, and they have some of the best sausages, meats, and eggs that I've ever tasted or cooked. Tailgate sales of cheeses, honey, jams, and other items accompany the vegetables and meats and can be found throughout both Asheville and Hendersonville each weekend

With all this wonderful, natural food at my disposal, it was a real treat and adventure to put together meals. Probably nine out of ten times my dinners would include something that I fixed on the grill, too. I love to be outside, and unless it was pouring rain, I'd be using charcoal. Even in the freezing cold of the winter, with my mom fussing at me that I was crazy and was going to catch pneumonia, I had the outdoor fire going.

The menu I have here is an example of what I might prepare for company on a summer's night in Gerton, and features a combination of fresh vegetables and fruits, along with grilled meat. Since our dinners in the mountains were much smaller, and a great deal more relaxed and informal, I did not mind making it a group affair for my guests and have them in the kitchen to lend a hand with the preparations.

Menu

~Smoked River Trout Platter
~Roasted Beet Salad
~Honey and Herb-Marinated Pork Roast
~Tomato Pie
~Fresh Corn with Butter and Chives
~Blackberry Cobbler

Trout are plentiful in the mountains of Georgia, Tennessee, North Carolina and South Carolina. I love angling for these beautiful fish, and have enjoyed many afternoons casting into a bold, rushing stream. Of course you can catch and smoke the fishes for this dish yourself, but there are dozens of purveyors that prepare them commercially and can be purchased online or in any number of grocery stores. This dish is an absolute hit without fail, and one that I create often for parties. You can substitute hardwood-smoked salmon if you cannot find the trout.

Smoked River Trout Platter

Ingredients

2 8-ounce packages cream cheese, softened to room temperature
2 4-ounce packages hardwood-smoked river trout, skin removed, flaked
 into pieces
¼ cup chopped fresh chives
¼ cup chopped fresh dill
¼ cup capers, drained
1 tablespoon finely zested lemon
1 package Bremner Wafers or other thin crackers
Lemon slices, sprigs of parsley, dill, chives for garnish

Instructions

On a large serving platter, spread the cream cheese out smoothly into a
 large, ½-inch deep disc. Sprinkle the trout across the cream cheese,
 and top with the chives, dill, capers and lemon zest. Garnish and
 serve with crackers.

Servings

Serves 8 to 10

A nice variation on this dish is to top Kettle Brand baked potato chips
(use the baked variety because they are flat) with a small portion of crème
fraiche or sour cream, and then add your trout and fresh spices. These
gourmet nibbles are nice to serve as a passed hors d'oeuvres and are simple to
make. I promise that they will bring a great deal of compliments from your
guests.

* * *

The starter course in this menu is full of summer flavor from the mountains;
it can even be a main course for some of your vegetarian guests. I love adding
watercress to this salad; the fresh bite of this green can just set your palate
aloft. It grows wild in the small creeks in North Carolina, where you can
wade out into the shallows and pick it for your table.

Roasted Beet Salad

Ingredients
Salad
6 small red or other-colored fresh beets
1 tablespoon olive oil
½ teaspoon kosher salt
2 tart apples, cored, peeled, and cut into 18 slices, lengthwise
6 1-inch slices soft cheese, such as a chevré or Cambozola
8 cups loosely packed fresh, seasonal baby greens, including watercress
Dash of salt and freshly ground black pepper
1 small red onion, or other sweet variety, sliced into very thin rings
1 cup walnut or pecan halves (roasted or fresh)
Vinaigrette Dressing (recipe follows)

Vinaigrette Dressing
1 tablespoon good-quality red wine vinegar
½ teaspoon Dijon mustard
1 teaspoon of freshly minced herbs, such as tarragon and thyme
1 teaspoon finely minced fresh garlic
1/8 teaspoon sugar
3 tablespoons extra virgin olive oil

Instructions
Salad:
1. Preheat oven to 350 degrees F.
2. Peel the beets and toss with the olive oil and salt. Place in a baking dish, cover, and cook for about 45 minutes until tender but firm. Remove from oven and cool; slice into 18 pieces. This step can be done ahead of preparing the dinner. Cover and chill until ready to use.
3. Arrange 3 slices each of the beets and apples, along with a wedge of the cheese, on six individual plates.
4. In a large bowl, sprinkle the greens with a few dashes of kosher salt and a couple grinds of black pepper; mix lightly.
5. Add the onions, nuts, and dressing to the lettuce; toss and place on top of the other items on the plate. Serve immediately.

Vinaigrette Dressing:
1. Mix vinegar, mustard, herbs, garlic, and sugar in a small bowl and allow to set 10 to 15 minutes or more for the flavors to marry.
2. Slowly drizzle in the oil, whisking the entire time, to incorporate. The dressing may be made ahead and refrigerated; whisk again thoroughly before using.

Servings
Serves 6

* * *

There is something about roasted, smoked meats with a sweet, savory glaze that I just thoroughly enjoy. This recipe can be done with pork, chicken or lamb. The marinade came from my friend Stan Applebaum and his charming and gracious wife, Tanya. Stan and Tanya hosted me for dinner one evening in their lovely Gainesville, Georgia home, and Stan had prepared the absolute best rack of lamb I ever put in my mouth using this recipe. (You can substitute lamb here using two eight-chop racks to serve eight people). Here I'm keeping with a Southern mountain theme and using boneless rib-end pork roast. Note that I brine the pork before cooking to ensure a moist and tender roast. Because of the brining steps, and the marinating, you'll need to make allowance for timing when scheduling your dinner. However, the whole process is simple and can be made in advance to grill at the last moment.

Honey and Herb-Marinated Pork Roast

Ingredients
¼ cup kosher salt
3 cups water
2 2-pound rib-end boneless loin pork roasts
1 cup olive oil
½ cup Wildflower or other honey
1/3 cup Worcestershire sauce
1 tablespoon chopped garlic
½ tablespoon freshly ground black pepper
½ teaspoon dried thyme

1 tablespoon chopped fresh parsley
3 tablespoons chopped fresh rosemary—Stan advises that you cannot
use too much fresh rosemary
2 tablespoons melted butter

Instructions
1. Dissolve the kosher salt in the water. Put the pork in a deep bowl or
zipper-locking storage bag and pour the salted water over it. If using
a bag, put it in a deep-rimmed pan in case it leaks. Refrigerate
overnight.
2. Remove the roasts from the brine, drain, and dry with a paper towel.
Place in a gallon storage bag or a pan that is deep enough to hold the
meat.
3. Place the oil, honey, Worcestershire, garlic, pepper, thyme, parsley,
and rosemary in a tightly sealed container; shake vigorously to mix
well. Pour the marinade over the roasts, coating well. Cover tightly
and refrigerate for 4 hours.
4. Prepare your charcoal or gas grill and have ready to cook.
5. Place pork on the grill; cover and cook for about 5 minutes.
6. Turn meat and continue cooking until the meat is medium—a light
pink on the inside—maybe 15 more minutes depending on the
temperature of your grill and the thickness of the roasts.
7. Allow meat to sit for 10 minutes before slicing it into 1-inch thick
medallions.
8. Pour the collected juices from the rested meat in with the melted
butter; drizzle this sauce over the medallions and serve.

Servings
Serves 6

* * *

Tomatoes are one of the most favorite of all summer foods; growing up
you'd find a whole platter of these sliced on our table for dinner, with just a
touch of salt and pepper. We ate them baked, stewed with okra and Vidalia
onions and a hint of bacon, in soups, and in one dish called escalloped
tomatoes, where you baked the fruits with cheese and bread crumbs. Mama

would can jars of them in the summer so that throughout the year we'd have tomatoes from our gardens.

This dish is one that I take particular pleasure in preparing and serving. The flavor of the tomatoes makes your taste buds sing bite after bite. Besides serving this pie with a dinner like we have here described, it is also excellent for breakfast with some soft scrambled eggs, or for a vegetarian lunch where you can pair it with a tossed salad. In this menu, it's rich, bright acidity is a great balance for the sweetness of the corn and pork.

Tomato Pie

Ingredients
1 unbaked deep-dish pie shell
1½ pound ripe tomatoes
1 teaspoon Dijon mustard
1/8 teaspoon freshly ground black pepper
3 tablespoons plus 1 cup freshly shredded Parmesan cheese
1 teaspoon finely minced fresh thyme
¼ teaspoon kosher salt
3 tablespoons good-quality real mayonnaise
1 tablespoon olive oil

Instructions
1. Preheat oven to 350 degrees F.
2. Line the bottom of your pie shell with aluminum foil and fill with 1 cup dried beans or pie weights; bake for 10 minutes. Remove foil and beans, and set the shell aside.
3. Cut the top quarter off each tomato, carefully remove the seeds, and discard seeds. Slice the seeded tomatoes crosswise ¼-inch thick, and lay the slices on paper towels. Pat dry.
4. Brush the bottom and sides of the pie shell with the mustard.
5. Place one slightly overlapping layer of tomatoes in the bottom of the shell and sprinkle with a bit of the black pepper, Parmesan, thyme, and salt.
6. Continue layering as above until you use all your tomatoes or the pie is full just below the crust's edge—if you have any slices left over, make yourself a tomato sandwich!

7. With a whisk, mix the mayonnaise and olive oil until very smooth, about half a minute. Gently dabble the mixture over the top layer of the tomatoes with a brush.
8. Place a pie ring on the top of the pie to prevent the edges from overbrowning. If you don't have one, cut several 3-inch wide strips of aluminum foil and gently wrap the edges of the pie with the foil.
9. Place the pie on a cookie sheet and bake for 20 minutes.
10. Remove the pie from the oven and sprinkle 1 cup of Parmesan on the top. Place back into the oven and bake another 15 to 20 minutes, or until the cheese is melted into the mayonnaise and the top is browning slightly.
11. Remove from heat and allow the pie to cool completely before serving. The dish can be made ahead of time and refrigerated until ready to use. Serve at room temperature.

Servings
Serves 6

* * *

Corn was another vegetable that we ate growing up prepared several different ways: boiled with a little salt and black pepper, cut off the cob and mixed with some fresh baby butter beans to make a succotash, or my favorite, creamed corn, where you scraped the kernels and "milked" the cob to get all the juice, and cooked it in a deep iron skillet with a little cream and butter and maybe a sprinkle of bacon. All three variations found their way into our freezer, and we'd enjoy corn throughout the year. The fresh corn in the summer, just picked and served that day, is manna to my palate. Here I keep it simple, where you can really taste the flavor of the sun and rain; it can be cooked ahead of time, refrigerated, and then reheated quickly.

Fresh Corn with Butter and Chives

Ingredients
¼ cup kosher salt
2 quarts of water
6 large (or 10 small) ears of fresh corn, shucked and silk removed
¼ cup unsalted butter
¼ cup fresh chives, finely minced
Kosher salt and freshly ground black pepper to taste

Instructions
1. In a large stockpot, bring water and salt to a boil; add corn. Stir occasionally so the ears rotate evenly in the water; cook 5 minutes and remove from heat.
2. Drain corn in a colander and rinse with cold water. Shake off excess water and dry with a towel.
3. Cut the kernels from the cobs into a large mixing bowl; cut down so that you get the whole kernel, but not part of the cob itself.
4. Melt the butter in a skillet, stir in the corn, and heat thoroughly; add chives and season with any kosher salt or black pepper based on your tastes and serve immediately. If you want to make this ahead of time, do not add the chives until you are ready to reheat.

Servings
Serves 6

* * *

Blackberries have to be one of my all-time favorite fruits, and when I learned that they were so good for you—filled with antioxidants and low in carbs— I've added more in my diet and keep a package of the fresh berries in my refrigerator during season to eat as a snack or with my oatmeal. Like many of the foods we ate growing up, these were harvested and Mama either froze them for pies or canned them as jam. One of the last times I spent a whole afternoon with my Aunt Polly, who is now one hundred and nine, was one summer when she was in her late eighties. She asked me to take her to the farm so we could pick some blackberries; she donned her straw sun hat, put on her gloves, collected a few pails, and off we went. Now at the time I was in college; I played tennis, rode my bike to class, jogged every day and was in good shape. I have to tell you that little lady ran my legs off across those pastures and fields and I ended up with sunburn and a sore back, along with more than a few brambles stuck in my hands.

In North Carolina, you'll see cars parked all along the grassy embankments along the Blue Ridge Parkway in the summer, and folks lined up picking these berries up and down that scenic highway. I always think about Carrie and the rattlesnake incident whenever I come across this scene. I believe the wild ones are the best; while they are not as large or showy as the ones you'll find in the markets, which have been cultivated for their size, they impart an enormous amount of fresh berry flavor.

When I was a child, Mama, Carrie and my Aunts would all make their blackberry cobblers with homemade dough that they rolled out by hand. In later years, Mama discovered an easier version that was just a delicious, and I've included that recipe here. I like to cook and serve this cobbler in a cast-iron skillet not just for the presentation, but also because it produces an incredible crust. Note that you can substitute any fruit in this recipe; however, you may need to alter the sugar content depending on the sweetness of your selection.

Blackberry Cobbler

Ingredients
5 to 6 cups fresh blackberries
1½ cups sugar, divided
½ cup unsalted butter
1 cup self-rising flour
¼ teaspoon cinnamon
Dash of kosher salt
1 cup whole milk
Whipped cream or vanilla ice cream along with mint sprigs for
   garnishment

Instructions
1. Preheat oven to 375 degrees F.
2. In a large bowl, toss the berries with ½ cup sugar. Set aside.

3. Add the butter to a large cast-iron skillet or baking dish; place the skillet in the oven and melt the butter and allow the skillet to get hot, about 6 to 7 minutes. Be careful not to let the butter burn.
4. In the meantime, make the batter by mixing together the remaining sugar, flour, cinnamon, salt, and milk. Whisk to incorporate.
5. Pour the batter into the hot skillet and onto the melted butter; do not stir.
6. Spread the fruit on top of the batter; again, do not stir.
7. Bake for 45 minutes or until the batter is set and turning a golden brown.
8. Serve warm with a dollop of whipped cream or scoop of ice cream and garnish with a sprig of mint.

Servings
Serves 6

In Sandy's kitchen on Ossabaw looking after the "Buco"

13

Dining on Ossabaw Buco

Georgia is graced with barrier islands that I believe to be some of the most magical and beautiful places in the world. Our state's coastline is situated in a cusp between the Carolinas and Florida, which results in high tides as the water rushes to collect into this C-shaped area. These islands provide a buffer from the sea and have helped create more than a third of all the salt marshes in the US, giving the coast a fertile area for aquatic sea life.

As well as being some of Mother Nature's finest work in the Southeast, the Golden Isles are also steeped in history. Before there was a Jamestown, Spanish settlers founded a mission on St. Catherine's Island, called Santa Catalina, and the coastal area played an active role during both the Revolutionary and Civil wars.

Today, some of the islands are heavily inhabited, while others are carefully guarded from the intrusion of mankind. I've been fortunate to visit most of them, and, of course, enjoyed some delicious food with each of the trips. The most well-known of all are the tourist destinations, such as Tybee, St. Simons, and Jekyll Island.

I visit Tybee often, as it sits just fifteen miles from Savannah. A number of our friends have cottages on the island, and we've enjoyed some great times there at oyster roasts, shrimp boils, and barbecues. There are also a number of casual restaurants serving fresh seafood and providing a strong dose of local atmosphere, such as The Crab Shack, whose tagline is "Where the Elite Eat in Their Bare Feet." This slogan gives good insight into the island, which is probably one of the more eclectic towns you'll visit on the Eastern Seaboard. Where else can you be a part of a ritual such as the annual "Beach Bum Parade," where people from all walks of life strut down the main street, Butler Avenue, to celebrate their uniqueness? Tybee is known as a drinking village with a fishing problem. If you want to have a good, uninhibited time in a place where folks fully believe that you should "live and let live," make a trip to Tybee.

Down the coast are Jekyll, St. Simons, and Sea Island, outside the port city of Brunswick. Jekyll is a state-owned island with miles and miles of undeveloped beach. Famous for its history with America's most wealthy citizens, families such as the Morgans, Rockefellers, and Carnegies formed what would become the world's most exclusive enclave in the nineteenth century, The Jekyll Island Club. Supposedly one-sixth of the world's wealth would be represented when the club was in session during the wintertime. The extravagant "cottages" they built, as well as the incredibly grand centerpiece to the development, the club's hotel, can be visited and seen today. I'd recommend to anyone that wants a romantic and memorable escape to make a trip here and enjoy the splendor of what was once the Gilded Age.

St. Simons and Sea Island sit side by side and are favorite places to visit; these sisters are the two unrivaled royal princesses on the coast. This area is a golfing paradise, and people flock here from all over the world to stay at the renowned five-star Cloister and the venerable King and Prince. I spent many childhood weekends on St. Simons and still continue to make trips down for a respite at least three or four times a year as an adult.

My favorite spot to dine is at Bennie's Red Barn, an institution that has been around for generations. Housed in—yes, a big red barn—the interior has 20-foot high ceilings, huge exposed beams, an immense fireplace, and serves some of the best steaks and seafood I've ever put in my mouth. If I'm visiting the island with friends, we always have dinner at Bennie's and then make our way to one of the local dance clubs and put some mileage on our soles as we shag to beach music or jam with some old-school rock. One night I was in Ziggy's, where both locals and tourists gather for the great bands and reasonably priced libations, with a group of girlfriends. Tired of dancing together, the girls started venturing out for some male hoofers, and my friend Gaye, from Atlanta, approached one nice-looking gentleman standing by himself and asked if he'd like to join her. With a big, wide Kennedy-like grin, he replied, "Love to. Let me ask my wife." Gaye turned redder than the tulips on her Lily Pulitzer sundress as the man's wife walked up and slipped her arm through her husband's. Fortunately, the lady was good-natured. "Sure, take him off my hands for a while. Just bring him back in one piece." Gaye recovered, and off to the dance floor they trotted to the strains of the Tams singing "Be Young, Be Foolish, Be Happy."

The truly remarkable spots on the coast are the islands protected from overdevelopment, all of which are accessible only by ferry, such as Sapelo, where you can stay in the tiny hamlet of Hog Hammock, a community of

Tom with Sandy West at her home on Ossabaw Island

At Bennie's Red Barn on a night out with the girls
to celebrate my fiftieth birthday

Mama, Tom and I at the Weekender on Sapelo

descendants from the island's slave population. One spring weekend, Tom and I took my mom over to visit and stayed at the Weekender, a rustic set of buildings in the heart of the village. The first day we spent touring the island; we strolled through the ruins of an eighteenth-century plantation, Chocolat, dug through Indian mounds to find pottery, collected shells on the beach, and ended our first afternoon with a good bit of wine and food prepared by the owners of the inn. The dinner was a low-country feast including roasted oysters, shrimp perlou, fried hush puppies, deviled crab, and a peach pie. The story here is one we teased my mom about for all the years that followed. Seems Mama was so tired, and with all the plentiful wine and the magnificent Gullah food, she went to bed and fell into a deep, deep sleep. A few minutes after she had turned in, Tom and I heard a loud, crackling noise. I thought it was the flock of crows I saw roosting in the pine trees outside the cabin, and when I went outside to investigate, I picked up an old conch shell by the screen door and threw it into the pine thicket. You could hear the birds cawing and flapping their wings as they took off. I went back inside, and settled down with my book, but we could still hear the rumbling noise. Come to find out, as I walked down the hallway to my room later that night, the noise was coming from Mama, snoring up a storm, dreaming, I guess, about how delicious deviled crab can be with a glass or two of chardonnay.

Another barrier island that we have had the chance to visit is Cumberland, an extraordinary place filled with rich history. Nathaniel Greene, the Revolutionary War hero, purchased land there in the 1780s, and wood for the construction of the famous warship the USS Constitution, "Old Ironsides," came from the island. In the 1880s, steel magnate Andrew Carnegie's brother, Thomas, purchased most of Cumberland and started construction of a fifty-nine-room Scottish mansion named Dungeness. The island came into modern fame with the marriage of John Kennedy, Jr., and his fiancée, Carolyn, who tied the knot in the tiny First African Baptist church in 1996.

Tom and I spent a wonderful winter weekend there several years ago at The Greyfield Inn, a beautiful island retreat built for Mr. Carnegie's daughter in 1900. It is rated as one of the country's top places to stay, and it well deserves the distinction. One of the prettiest sites I've experienced in all my years was on Cumberland. Tom and I had finished cocktails and dinner with the other guests and carefully walked by flashlight across the meadow in front of the inn to the caretaker's cottage where we were staying. Cumberland is known for its herds of wild horses, and these majestic creatures often graze the meadow, and in doing so, leave behind piles that you don't want to step in. We meandered our way back through the dark, using the lights to sidestep the horses' "presents," and took to our beds. I woke up very early the next day to a chilly morning. There was a heavy frost on the ground, and as I wandered outside on the porch, I was astonished to see that entire meadow was covered with hundreds and hundreds of bright red cardinals. They speckled the ground like someone had thrown out a bushel full of cranberries onto a white marble floor. I stopped counting when I passed fifty, and there were three or four times that many left. I've never seen such a colorful flock of birds before in all of my travels, and I was just amazed at such a glory of nature on this cold, beautiful dawn. It was a magical moment for me, a present from God, and something I'll always remember.

On another jaunt we had the good fortune to visit Little St. Simons. This island is covered with cedar trees, which drew the attention of the owners of the Eagle Pencil Company in New York at the turn of the twentieth century. The company purchased the island to use the trees to manufacture pencils, but found out after the sale that the cedars were too bent and misshapen from the constant coastal winds to be of any use. However, the company's president, Mr. Berolzheimer, fell in love with the beauty of the island and built a small, rustic lodge there for his family. Since his ownership, the environmental stewardship of the land has continued, leaving thousands of acres virtually untouched by man, except for the original lodge and cottages that make up the resort.

A retreat to LSSI is a must for nature lovers and for those who want to experience fresh, organic, and fantastic food. When I spent the weekend, one of the inn's naturalists took me fishing in the saltwater marsh. We found a sweet spot on a tidal creek containing a number of exposed oyster beds, and using a bright-colored soft plastic jig lure, and casting just by the oyster beds, I caught my day's limit that afternoon. The guide took the fish back to the inn, cleaned the trout, and gave them to the chef, who prepared them the next morning for breakfast; he lightly dusted the filets with cornmeal and flour, sautéed them with a little butter and parsley, and served them over soft scrambled eggs with cheese and a side of stone-ground grits. Life does not get much better than that, at least for me.

Now while I have great affinity for all these places on the coast, I believe that the largest gem in the crown of the Golden Isles is Ossabaw. It is one of the most verdantly colored landscapes imaginable—from the foliage of the towering pines and outstretched live oaks to the slender reeds of the spartina grass and the rustling fans of the palmettos, the island is a hundred shades of green. Even the marsh water is tinged the soft color of sage. I cannot describe here in words that will adequately give justice to the tranquil, peaceful, and majestic beauty Mother Nature has imposed on this spot; you need to see it for yourself. While visitation is limited, the island is open to the public and is owned now by the state of Georgia. Before you go, I would suggest reading *Ossabaw—Evocations of an Island*. Photographer Jack Leigh captures hauntingly beautiful shots of the wildlife and forests, as does the incredibly talented artist Alan Campbell with his paintings; James Kilgo, master of prose, narrates the magnificent story.

This historic island was home to American Indians four thousand years ago, and if you paused for a few solitary moments under the forest's canopy, you probably could well imagine seeing a native ancestor quietly walk by, so untouched is the landscape.

This preservation is due to one woman. While the Hindus have Aranyani, the goddess of woods and animals, and the Celts look to Druantia, queen of the Druids, to teach them the sacred ways of the forest, Ossabaw has Eleanor Torrey West. Known as Sandy to her friends, she is 100 pounds of equal parts determination, tenacity, intelligence, and good humor. Sandy's parents, a very prominent and wealthy couple from Michigan, purchased the 26,000-acre island in the 1920s. On the west end of the parcel they built a stunning, pink stucco Mediterranean-style house reminiscent of a Palm Beach manse, where Sandy still lives, alone, at an age past the century mark. Sandy fell in love with this coastal paradise as a child, and when she inherited the property, she was determined to keep it from modern development. She envisioned an island sanctuary for future generations where people could learn about the environment and the natural sciences, and for artists to have a place for reflection and to study and hone their talents. With the help of then-governor Jimmy Carter, Sandy sold the island to the state of Georgia for a fraction of its worth, with restrictive stipulations setting permanent and perpetual limitations on the use of Ossabaw.

Thousands of people enjoy the island's splendor each year, but the mansion is not open to the public, and your only way to see its mystique is by invitation of the island's matriarch. Through a close mutual friend, Lisa White, Tom and I have had the chance to spend several weekends over the years with Mrs. West, each of which was a special treasure. Fewer people stay as her guest than sleep in the Lincoln bedroom in a year's time, and I was just as tickled, if not more so, to be under Sandy's roof.

On one such trip I was the designated chef for a special occasion, our friend Monica's birthday dinner. Lisa and I grew up twelve miles down the road from one another, she in the town of Fort Valley and I in Perry. Our friends in Savannah call us "the cousins," as we hail from the same red-clay part of the state and bring with us our soft, Middle Georgia accents (which can get a little more pronounced after a few nips of bourbon). Monica, our Monique in the Girl's on the Grill Book Club fame, and I met at a cocktail party downtown just after I moved to Savannah and forged a long and wonderful friendship based on our affection for books, good food, and fun times. Monique is known for her love of life and deep-rooted sense of good humor. She livens up any room where she is found and can illuminate even the dullest of party yawners. A few years ago Lisa and I were at a dinner engagement—one Monica had to bow out of because of the flu—in which one of the guests dominated the conversation with boring orations about trips abroad, and detailing the monologues as if the rest of us had never left the confines of Chatham County. Lisa leaned over to me at one point and whispered, "Lordy, honey, Monique sure left a big hole at this table tonight." And she was right.

The trip over to Ossabaw is by boat, space is limited, and not only do you have pack yourself, you have to bring your food as well. Our weekend away was for ten guests, plus Sandy and another friend, so the boat had to make a couple of runs of the thirty-minute crossing. I felt it best, after considering I would need to cook for a dozen people, and Sandy's kitchen—while immense—was totally unfamiliar to me, that I should prepare most of the meal in advance and take it with me.

After thinking over my options for a menu, I decided to do a braise, which is always better prepared in advance. I set out to make a dinner around a dish I called Ossabaw Buco, which was basically my osso buco recipe, but it was an easy play on words that we still talk about today. To round out the rest of the meal, I looked to the house as an inspiration to carry on the theme. The dining room is styled after the Mediterranean design of the manse and features tiled floors and walls, an immense oak dining table and matching oversized chairs, and a massive wrought-iron chandelier, all original to the house from the 1920s. It is, as you can imagine, a wonderful place to sit and dine. Here is my menu, with its southern European continental flavor.

Menu

~Individual Charcuterie Plates
~JB's Awesome Ossabaw Buco
~Dottie's Creamy Saffron Rice
~Tomatoes Provencal
~Blood-Orange Sorbet with Almond Biscotti

The charcuterie is a wonderful and easy way to serve an impressive first course. And while I include a recipe for a chicken pate here, these meat spreads can be purchased at most any gourmet food store across the US. Be sure to use large serving plates, or chargers, for this course so that each item can be showcased.

Individual Charcuterie Plates

Ingredients

Chicken Liver Paté (recipe follows)

Pickled Onions (recipe follows)

Toast points (either homemade or commercially prepared)

24 cornichons

24 very thin slices of prosciutto

24 large green olives

16 slices of a bold, flavorful cheese, such as an aged Gouda

4 cups fresh baby arugula

Pinch of kosher salt and freshly ground black pepper

½ teaspoon red wine vinegar

½ teaspoon olive oil

Instructions

1. Unmold the paté and cut into 1" slices, or spoon the spread into small ceramic pots. Place the paté on each charger or large plate

2. Arrange a tablespoon or so of the pickled onions and a few slices of toast points next to the paté.

3. To each plate add three cornichons, 3 slices of prosciutto, 3 green olives, and 2 slices of cheese.

4. In a separate bowl, lightly sprinkle the arugula with salt and freshly ground black pepper, and toss with the vinegar and oil.

5. Spread the dressed greens on the plate, and serve immediately.

Servings

Serves 8

Chicken Liver Paté

Ingredients

2 tablespoons olive oil

¾ cup chopped onion

½ cup chopped sweet apple (peeled)

2 fresh bay leaves

¼ teaspoon freshly ground nutmeg

1/8 teaspoon cinnamon
¼ teaspoon finely ground white pepper
1 large clove of garlic, minced
¼ teaspoon kosher salt
1½ pounds fresh chicken livers, trimmed of any sinew or fat, washed
   and drained
1½ cups unsalted butter, softened to room temperature

Instructions
1. Heat the oil over medium-high in a large skillet; add the onion,
   apple, bay leaves, nutmeg, cinnamon, white pepper, garlic, and salt.
   Sauté for about 5 minutes until the onion and apple are soft.
2. Add the livers, and continue to sauté over medium-heat, stirring and
   cooking until the livers are just done, about 10 minutes.
3. Remove from heat and discard the bay leaves.
4. Add the liver mixture and butter to your food processor and pulse
   until smooth.
5. Line a small loaf pan with plastic wrap or foil; add the paté, cover,
   and chill overnight.
6. To serve, unmold the paté, and cut into 1-inch thick slices, or spoon
   into small ceramic crocks.

Servings
Serves 8

* * *

The pickled onions are a very popular accompaniment to paté, and I get requests for the recipe often. I was first introduced to this delicious condiment from Emily Belford, whom I consider to be one of the next generations of wonderful cooks here in Savannah. This dish also goes well with roasted meats.

Pickled Onions

Ingredients
1 cup sugar
1 cup red wine vinegar
1 pound red onions, sliced thinly
4 allspice berries
½ teaspoon kosher salt
2 teaspoons minced fresh thyme
1 fresh bay leaf

Instructions
1. In a large saucepan, stir together the sugar and vinegar over medium-high heat until the sugar is melted.
2. Add the remaining ingredients, reduce heat to medium, and allow to simmer for 5 minutes, stirring occasionally.
3. Remove from heat, set aside, and allow the onions to sit in the mixture for an hour.
4. Drain the onions, remove the bay leaf and berries, and refrigerate the onions in an airtight container overnight. The onions can be stored in the refrigerator for 3 to 4 days.

Servings
Serves 8

* * *

The osso buco recipe here is one that I've cooked numerous times, and the key to making it turn out successfully is to thoroughly brown the meat.

JB's Awesome Ossabaw Buco

Ingredients
8 medium-sized lamb shanks, about ¾ pound each
½ teaspoon each kosher salt and freshly ground black pepper
¼ cup olive oil, plus more if needed
1 cup chopped onion
1 cup chopped carrots
1 cup chopped celery
4 large cloves fresh garlic, sliced thin lengthwise
3 cups good-quality, low-sodium beef stock
2 cups hearty dry red wine
3 tablespoons fresh chopped rosemary
2 tablespoons fresh chopped thyme
½ teaspoon each finely grated lemon and orange zest
¼ cup packed fresh parsley, chopped

Instructions
1. Preheat oven to 350 degrees F.
2. Wash lamb and dry thoroughly. Season with salt and pepper.
3. In a large Dutch oven or deep skillet, heat 2 tablespoons of oil over medium-high heat.
4. Brown the shanks on all sides, 2 to 3 at a time; do not overcrowd the pan or the meat will not brown properly. Set browned shanks aside as you finish. You will probably need to add the other 2 tablespoons of oil after your second batch.
5. Add the onion, carrots, celery, and garlic to the pan and cook over medium-high for 3 to 4 minutes, stirring occasionally.
6. Add the stock and wine and deglaze the skillet by stirring to loosen the pieces of browned lamb that will have been left on the bottom of the pan.
7. Add the rosemary and thyme; stir to mix.
8. In a large, deep roasting pan or roasting dish, arrange the shanks in one layer (they may have to overlap depending on the size of your pan).
9. Pour the stock mixture over the lamb.

10. Cover tightly with a lid or foil; bake for 2 hours or until fork-tender.
11. When done, carefully remove the shanks and set aside; strain the gravy from the pan through a sieve into a fat separator, pressing down on the vegetables to get all the juice. Discard the fat.
12. Remove the drained vegetables from the sieve and put into a bowl. Mash the vegetables with the back of a large spoon until a thick consistency; add the defatted pan drippings and stir to mix and create a gravy. If too thick, add in a little more stock and wine.
13. Place the meat back into the roasting pan and pour the vegetable gravy over the shanks.
14. Cover and refrigerate overnight.
15. To serve, reheat uncovered in a 350 degree oven until hot. Place each shank on a serving plate, and garnish with the zest and the parsley.

Servings
Serves 8

* * *

My dear friend Dottie Lynch, a Savannah native who, in her youth studied at the Sorbonne, gave me this rice dish. She is a wonderful cook and hostess. This recipe incorporates the flavors of risotto but is much easier to make, as it doesn't require all the stirring, which is monotonous and time consuming. While it pairs well with other meats and poultry, such as roast pork or grilled chicken, it is the perfect side for the Ossabaw Buco.

Dottie's Creamy Saffron Rice

Ingredients
2 tablespoons unsalted butter
2 tablespoons olive oil
½ cup minced shallots
¼ teaspoon saffron threads
2 bay leaves

2 cups Mahatma's Valencia rice (or another good-quality short-grain rice)

4 cups low-sodium chicken stock

1 cup freshly grated Parmesan cheese (do not use packaged, pre-shredded cheese)

Instructions

1. In a large saucepan, melt the butter with the oil over medium-high heat.
2. Add the shallots and sauté, stirring, for about 2 minutes, until soft.
3. Add the saffron and bay leaves; stir to mix.
4. Add the rice. Stir and coat the rice with the oil and butter.
5. Add the stock, stir, and bring to a boil.
6. Stir again, cover tightly with a lid, and reduce heat to a simmer. Cook for 20 minutes.
7. Remove from heat; allow to stand in the sauce pan for 5 minutes or so.
8. Uncover and add the shredded cheese; stir well to mix and allow the cheese to melt. Serve immediately.

Note: if you would like to make this in advance, cook through step 7 and either set aside until ready to use or refrigerate. When ready to serve, add a couple of tablespoons of water and stir to mix well. Then place the pan over medium heat, allow it to heat through, and follow with step 8.

Servings

Serves 8

*   *   *

The tomatoes Provencal dish proved to be a little more last-minute intense than I wanted, and getting those rosy red babies over on the boat without bruising, bobbing up and down with the waves and wind, was a task in itself. However, I knew that the taste of the dish would complement the meal enough to make the effort. And I just brought another half dozen in case some of them got smashed.

Tomatoes Provencal

Ingredients

8 ripe, fist-sized tomatoes
½ teaspoon kosher salt
1 tablespoon red wine vinegar or other flavorful, full-bodied vinegar
¼ cup olive oil, plus more as needed
1 cup finely chopped onion
3 tablespoons each minced fresh basil and thyme
1½ cup Panko bread crumbs
1 teaspoon sugar

Instructions

1. Preheat oven to 350 degrees F.
2. Slice a very thin section, about 1/8 of an inch, off the bottom of each tomato so that it will sit upright on a cookie sheet when baked. Do not cut through the wall of the tomato.
3. Slice the top ¼ section off of each tomato. Carefully scoop out the seeds and discard the seeds.
4. Sprinkle the inside of each cut tomato with the salt and vinegar.
5. Set the halves, top-side down, on a cookie sheet or rack for 30 minutes to drain.
6. Meanwhile, in a saucepan, heat the ¼ cup of oil over medium-high heat; add the onion, stir, and cook for about 6 to 7 minutes until tender and translucent.
7. Add the herbs to the onion mixture; stir and cook for another minute.
8. Add the breadcrumbs to the onions and spices. Stir to incorporate fully. If the mixture is too stiff (it should be a consistency that is fully moist) add a few drizzles of additional oil.
9. Take the tomatoes and, one by one, gently shake out the moisture collected inside the cavities into the sink.
10. Sprinkle the sugar into the tomatoes.
11. Carefully stuff each tomato with the crumb and herb mixture until just full.

12. Set bottom side up on a nonstick, lightly greased cookie sheet and bake for 30 minutes or so until heated all the way through, but not to the point of being overcooked and mushy. Serve immediately.

Note: you can make these ahead of time to the point of step 11; cover and refrigerate until ready to bake. I would not, however, advise allowing them to sit overnight uncooked.

Servings
Serves 8

* * *

Because the lamb is such a rich dish, I thought we'd need something light to round out our palates and to ward off having to get up at 1 a.m. and reach for an Alka-Seltzer. I chose a blood orange sorbet, which is amazingly full flavored and refreshing, and placed a couple almond-flavored biscotti next to it for added taste and texture.

While reading this book, you know that I love to cook and prepare things by hand. However, some dishes can be purchased already made and delicious from the gourmet grocer. This course is one of those examples. I can't easily replicate a gelato or sorbet, particularly when using a fruit such as a blood orange. I have found the recipes for it, certainly can make it if I put my mind to it, but in the end, Cia Bella's and other gourmet brands are as good as homemade. And if I use them, I usually have time for a nap.

Paris at the Musée d'Orsay

14

Culinary Inspiration from Outside the Borders of Dixie

I have always loved to travel and am ready to take a trip at the drop of a hat. Tom says this about me: "He's like an old hound dog. Mention the word 'Go,' his tail will start to wag and he's ready to jump on the back of a pickup truck and take off." Daddy and Mama would often comment on my affinity for going places, observing, "That boy *straight loves* to stay in the middle of the road." In my mind, it doesn't really matter the destination, it just matters that I'm going somewhere.

Growing up, my trips were those taken with Aunt Bea, Mama, and Michelle during the summers, with just a few that included my father. After he returned home from his service overseas, where he saw action in Italy and North Africa, Daddy did not care to leave the safe, rolling hills and meandering rivers of Middle Georgia. He would take us on a trip each year to North Georgia to see family, or maybe down for a long weekend on St. Simons, but otherwise, the furthest he was interested in traveling would be over to Lake Eufaula or down to Lake Blackshear to fish. He was perfectly content to stay close to home.

As a kid, I would trek up the short hill from our house to the public library, where Mrs. Alice Gilbert, our town's librarian, would help me choose books about foreign lands and countries. I would sit on the library floor in the small travel section and leaf through volumes of selections that had pictures of the crystal-blue waters of the Caribbean, the magnificent snow-covered peaks of the Alps, and the country villages of Provence, promising myself that one day I would see all of those spots.

My first trip abroad was to Cancun with Chris when we graduated from college. He and I were walking in downtown Perry one spring afternoon and took notice of an advertisement at the town's exclusive (meaning only) travel agency. Their portable marquee sign, the kind with removable plastic letters and an arrow made of lights at the top, read "Visit the Beach in Cancun, Mexico! Ten nights, including air, only $279!"

We looked at one another and at the same time said, "Where the hell is Cancun?" This was 1986, mind you, and Cancun had been nothing but a deserted island just twenty years before. Intrigued, Chris and I went in, spoke with the agent, and after a quick phone call to the parents, came out with tickets to see our first glimpse of the Caribbean. We had a tremendous time, but I came away with few food experiences to relate. At twenty-two and just out of college, my taste buds were more in line with *cervezas* and tequila, and we celebrated graduation with more of a liquid diet, so to speak.

A few years later, living in Savannah, I met Tom, who was a well-seasoned traveler, having spent time across Europe and in faraway places such as India, Bali, Japan, Singapore, and Taiwan. He was actually one of the first merchants to travel to China when the country opened for foreign trade in the mid 1970s, buying container loads of furnishings to import back to his business on Hilton Head. Over the last twenty-six years, he and I have taken some wonderful trips together, and our upcoming cruise over Thanksgiving will be our twenty-ninth sailing. We've seen some fabulous places, met a number of extraordinary people, and sampled a wide array of incredible cuisines. Each of those trips, particularly the ones to Europe, have inspired me in terms of cooking and entertaining, and I've always brought home ideas and recipes to use in my own kitchen.

Our trips, regardless of where we go, consist mainly of two things: first, historical and cultural sites, and secondly, food. The sightseeing is a little easier to determine, as you know that if you are in Madrid you need to visit the Prado or if you're off to Paris you will want to climb the steps to Sacré-Coeur. For the serious-minded epicurean, though, finding the right spots for dining takes detailed research.

Word of mouth from fellow travelers is a great way to start, particularly when it comes to sampling smaller, out-of-the-way spots that may not be written about in popular media. My next reliable sources are the professional publications and websites, such as Zagat's, Frommer's, and Fodor's. If we're traveling with friends, we'll each investigate the various reviews, coming up with our top choices; those restaurants that coincide are our first picks. And I always inquire of the locals. I frequently ask not just the concierge or hotel staff, but also the taxi driver or the curator at the art museum. I believe those who live in the area are the ones who know best where to recommend going or, rather, to avoid.

I'd like to share some of my gastro experiences from a couple of trips to Europe, including sample menus from each of those places. I'm also going to throw in information about New England. While not across the pond, it is

Cathy and Carolyn digging into their lobsters.
I had already finished my lobster roll and was hoping,
like one of the seagulls, that they might throw me some scraps.

so different from the Deep South, I feel it is almost a different country, albeit one with some extraordinary and exemplary food.

I have only made two trips to New England and am anxiously awaiting another. Until I was invited there to visit, I have to admit that seeing the upper Northeast had never been on my radar screen of travel sites. Except for the parts I'd been exposed to in school, such as Longfellow's *Midnight Ride of Paul Revere* and Hawthorne's *The Scarlett Letter*, I really did not know much about that area of the country. I was aware of the New Englanders' reputation for being rather reserved, and as far as the food went, I just knew that in Maine they ate a lot of lobsters and apparently clam chowder was a well-known commodity.

I am so very glad that I decided to go. From the time I set foot in the region, I was enthralled by all the aspects of my sojourns. The landscape and countryside is not just picturesque, but stunning, from the Green Mountains of Vermont to the rock and conifer-covered inlets of Maine. I fell in love, too, with the small towns, each which was set around a Common, or Green, along with their beloved whitewashed Unitarian churches, centrally placed town halls, and the prominent public libraries. I'd like to schedule my next trip for Christmastime, and have a Currier & Ives experience to see these quaint villages covered in snow and decorated for the holidays.

The people were, as I had heard, quiet and not exceptionally outgoing, but at the same time extremely kind and welcoming. We Southerners are a decidedly effusive bunch and don't always understand when others don't follow suit. Sometimes we just have to "take it down a notch or two" when it comes to interacting with people who don't share our outward enthusiasm. I came to admire these New Englanders and their Yankee spirit and found it very easy to speak and connect with them. All it took was a smile and an introduction and I was able to make friends in each city and every small hamlet I traveled through.

The cuisine from this area of the States is reflective of the New England people and their attitudes. It is straightforward, uncomplicated, and, as the saying goes, "the real thing." It is also exceedingly gratifying and enjoyable. Their approach incorporates a great deal of organic, farm-to-table offerings, both at home and in the local pubs and restaurants. The seafood from the cold waters of the north Atlantic is also a mainstay for that entire region. One of the best gifts I ever received was from our traveling companions Bill and Shirley, who have a summer home in the coastal town of Damariscotta, Maine. They shipped me a large box of the most exquisite oysters. From the river that bears the same name as the town, the oysters were large, full-bodied, and had a briny flavor that was delicious and distinct. I grilled them in their shells and ate every one, right by myself, with some homemade cocktail sauce. It was a blissful few moments of life.

The first of the two trips we made up North was with our friends Carolyn and Cathy. We stayed in the exquisite little town of New London, New Hampshire, and forayed each day in a different direction, from Vermont to Maine.

Every meal we had was a culinary experience. Our first outing was at the famous Harraseeket Lunch and Lobster Company in South Freeport, Maine. The restaurant is family owned and for decades has served thousands of people on its stunning waterfront location overlooking the boats and pleasure-crafts dotting the harbor. We sat outside and feasted on freshly cooked lobster that had been pulled from the Atlantic that morning, and I sampled what was my first lobster roll. It was, as they say, love at first bite.

The entire trip was filled with incredible food wherever we ventured. Our next excursion took us west to the award-winning Simon Pearce Restaurant, The Mill, which sits adjacent to the waterfalls on the Ottauqechee River. I was enchanted by the spot, and, actually, when the meal was over, did not want to leave. The meal was another consummate New England food experience with the offerings simple but crafted from the very finest of fresh ingredients.

We heard from friends who had eaten there that we absolutely had to sample The Mill's Vermont cheddar soup, and the recommendation was a meritorious one. I have had cheddar soups before and was never impressed with those selections like I was with this dish. Oftentimes these soups can be grainy and overly strong, or in the reverse, unimpressively bland. This recipe was velvety smooth but fully imbued with the distinct taste of cheddar along with a subtle flavoring of fresh herbs and garlic. We all could have eaten a second helping.

My most enjoyable dish on this trip, as it seems to be on many of my dining encounters, was one of the most modest of offerings in terms of construction and ingredients. This appetizer consisted only of a small, delicate johnnycake, which is a cornmeal patty. It was cooked on a hot griddle until crisp and lacy and then lightly drizzled with maple syrup. Mama would have loved it; it was a Northern version of her syrup and biscuit. In this case, I could not help myself and did order a second helping, and pushing even more moderation behind, sent my most effusive and enthusiastic of Southern compliments back to the chef.

Our second and most recent venture to the Northeast was to visit Bill and Shirley to stay with them in their New England saltbox house set back in the woods just outside of Damariscotta. On this trip we explored the famous craggy coast of Maine, visiting such historic and beautiful places as Booth Bay Harbor, Camden, and the Acadia National Forest.

I discovered on this trip two extraordinary things: fried whole-belly clams and the wild Maine blueberry.

According to the Maine Office of Tourism website, "Fried clams are to New England what Barbecue is to the South." I had never been impressed with clams, though, as the ones I had sampled before this trip were those little strips of fried muscle which held little seafood flavor and were of the consistency of rubber bands. Our first outing was for lunch, and we were sitting at a restaurant on the banks of the Damariscotta River, which is famous for its Ipswich clams. Shirley relayed to me that since I so loved eating fried oysters, I would very much enjoy authentically prepared New England fried clams. As it turns out, the distinction "whole belly" means that you are actually being served the entire clam, and not just the chewy part. When the basket arrived, full of crisp, oddly shaped fried nuggets, I dipped one in the tartar sauce and popped it in my mouth. What a food revelation: soft in texture, sweeter than an oyster, and full of the briny essence of the Atlantic, they were to become my food of choice for each meal throughout my stay.

I have the habit of ordering the same thing when I find something I truly love in an area where that dish is popularly made. When I was in Victoria, British Columbia, one of North America's most beautiful cities, I learned that a local specialty was fish and chips. The Georgia boy in me took over my palate and I happily and ardently ate fried halibut and chips each and every one of the five days we stayed on Victoria Harbor. (Interesting to note, people always assume that only the South fries fish, but they certainly put batter and oil to use up in Canada and New England.) Same situation in Key West; kicking health issues to the back of my mind, every single morning my breakfast was a piece of key lime pie. Live each moment while on vacation to the fullest, I say.

So for seven full days, I sampled as many restaurants' preparations of these fried gems as I could and cannot wait to get back to the north coast and go through additional platters of my now-favorite New England dish.

The other wonder of the New England food world that came to my taste buds' appreciative attention were the tiny wild Maine blueberries that burst with an intense and aromatic sweetness. The berries are grown on more than 60,000 acres in the state, either in fields or in the glacially formed rolling plains, called "barrens." These fruits were prized and cultivated by Native Americans for centuries well before the Puritans landed at Plymouth Rock. The variety found in Maine is indigenous to the State and are known as "low bush" blueberries, growing on short shrubs that spread through underground stems. I was only familiar with the cultivated "high bush" type that we have back in Georgia, which rise up to ten feet and produce a much larger, though admittedly here from a loyal Southerner, not quite as flavorful of berry.

I ate these petite, indigo-colored morsels as often as I came across them, heaping ladles of cobblers, pies and crisps, stacks of pancakes, and scoops of ice creams onto my plate. They were also excellent eaten right out of the bowl from the refrigerator. I ate so many I thought I may start to look like Violet Beauregarde from *Willy Wonka*, who turns into a fat blueberry.

Now besides finding out that there was so very much more to clams than just elasticity, and that the Maine wild blueberry packs a helluva taste sensation, I also experienced one of the most scenic and idyllic backdrops for dinner in all our travels while on this trip. Mutual friends of ours with Bill and Shirley, the Pierces, invited us by their house for cocktails, and these four expats from Savannah promised to treat us to a meal in one of the loveliest settings in the state. Our destination turned out to be the acclaimed Anchor Inn Restaurant in the tiny village of Round Pond, located just a short drive out onto the scenic Pemaquid Peninsula. Housed in a completely unimpressive structure of weather-worn shingles and a tin roof, you don't expect to be so awed and completely enchanted by what you'll see on the other side of the building. Situated just off the edge of Round Pond Harbor, we were given a 180-degree view of the water on this circular bay, ringed with large outcroppings of grey, sloping rocks and topped with incredible towering pine trees. The salt air and fresh scent of the conifers wafting through on a cool breeze completed the setting of what was, in my opinion, quintessentially Maine. Mother Nature went even further to impress us that special evening, as we were able to view the moon rise up over the harbor, larger than usual, reflecting and shimmering back on the night water. Tom says to this day it was the most beautiful moonrise he had ever seen in his life. We lingered over dinner until the restaurant was ready to close, enjoying some wonderful food (yes, I had fried clams), warm conversation, and an incomparable setting.

I relished all my time spent in Maine and throughout New England, and I'm hoping I will be able to enjoy some sleigh bells and hot cider up that way some holiday very soon.

My menu here is simple, but a great representation of tastes and dishes of Northeastern cuisine. While my new food love is the fried whole-belly clam, it is extremely hard to find them outside of New England, and so I did not replicate those here; instead, I put forth another Maine staple, the lobster roll, as the entrée. The meal begins with that fantastic offering of Vermont cheddar cheese soup, and is finished off, of course, with blueberries. And staying true to my efforts, all can be made ahead of time with little last-minute work so you can prepare in advance before your company arrives.

I've served this menu for a couple of special landmark birthdays for friends here in Savannah, and the guests have always enjoyed the casual trip to New England taken at my dining table.

Menu

~Vermont Cheddar Cheese Soup
~Maine Lobster Roll with Gourmet Potato Chips or Home Fries
~Wild Maine Blueberry Pie

The Mill Restaurant where I had the cheddar soup is owned by Simon Pearce. This company was started by Mr. Pearce in 1971, and its specialty is the design and creation of handmade blown glass and pottery. You can see the master artisans at their craft while visiting the restaurant.

The company's website shares recipes, and fortunately their delectable soup is on that list. That said, it did take some dissembling in terms of steps and process to make it "user-friendly." The recipe below is adapted from their offering. It can easily be frozen, then defrosted and reheated. Just be careful to not allow it to get too hot—you do not want it to simmer—if it does, the consistency will suffer.

The cheese used in the recipe is from Cabot Creamery, a family dairy cooperative that has been in business in New England since 1919. Their products can be found at grocers throughout the country and are easy to spot with the "Cabot" logo printed in bright red across a green outline of the state Vermont. The nice folks at Cabot actually donated a wonderful selection of cheeses for me to use at a large cocktail reception for the major donors and authors at the Savannah Book Festival a few years back.

Vermont Cheddar Cheese Soup

Ingredients
1½ quarts water
½ cup each carrots and celery, very finely and thinly grated on a hand
  grater
5 tablespoons unsalted butter
¼ cup finely minced onion
1 teaspoon finely minced garlic
6 tablespoons all-purpose flour
1 teaspoon finely minced fresh thyme
1 bay leaf
¼ teaspoon kosher salt
1/8 teaspoon freshly ground black pepper
¼ teaspoon hot sauce
12 ounces grated Cabot sharp cheddar cheese
1½ cups heavy cream

Instructions
1. In a large pot, bring the water to a boil; add the carrots and celery and cook for 2 minutes, until tender. Pour the vegetables into a sieve and drain the water into a large bowl. Set the carrots and celery aside in another small bowl.
2. Return the strained water into the pot and bring it to a steady simmer.
3. In a large stockpot, melt the butter over medium heat. Add the onion, cook for 2 minutes, stirring occasionally.

4. Add the garlic, stirring, and sauté for another 2 minutes, until the onion and garlic are tender.
5. Whisk the flour into the butter mixture and incorporate well. Turn the heat down to low and cook for 10 minutes, stirring occasionally. The roux should become a light tan color.
6. To the roux add the heated water in two batches, whisking after each addition to incorporate well. Continue to whisk slowly after all the water is included and the mixture is smooth and creamy.
7. Add the thyme, bay leaf, salt, pepper, and hot sauce. Stir to mix well. Continue cooking for several minutes, stirring occasionally, until thickened. Remove the bay leaf.
8. Add the grated cheese to the pot, stirring until melted.
9. Puree the reserved carrots and celery in a food processor; add to the cheese mixture and stir in well.
10. Whisk in the cream. Mix well and cook over low heat until the soup is heated through and thick. Be careful not to allow the soup to come to a simmer or boil. Serve immediately.

Servings
Serves 8

* * *

The lobster roll can be found in white-cloth restaurants or on roadside stands, and wherever we sampled these utterly simple but profoundly heavenly creations, there was never even a crumb left from the toasted buns. The choices of preparation for the filling do not vary too widely, usually finding nine parts lobster to one part mayonnaise and a few spices.

Two keys to the successful finish of this dish are buttered and toasted hotdog buns, as well as how you cut the lobster meat. The claw meat of the lobster is extremely tender and should be left in larger pieces. The tail meat is much denser, and I recommend chopping it more finely.

Lobster meat is rich in terms of taste and depth of flavor, as well as in pricing. Outside of New England, it is not uncommon to find these at $20 a pound, and if you need five pounds to make six rolls, well, you do the math. They can also be unsettling to cook for the soft-hearted, as you do it while they are alive. Shelling them can also be a little difficult. I recommend having the professionals at your local seafood market or grocer steam the lobsters for you; usually they will do this at no extra charge. Many places, particularly if you are a good customer, will also shell the lobsters and remove the cooked meat. However, if this is not an option, I've included how to cook the lobsters below.

While there is no substitute for using lobster in making this recipe, I have sometimes in the past made shrimp rolls to serve instead. I use three pounds of fresh, US wild-caught shrimp and cook them in the same way as the shrimp cocktail recipe found on pages 131-32, then proceed as you would with the lobster-roll recipe below. The result is delicious, nestled in those buttered and toasted hotdog buns, and I'm sure you'll enjoy them. But, of course, shrimp just is not in the same strata as lobster. But if you are not ready to shell out $100-plus just for the main course at dinner, use the prawns instead and give the dinner a little Southern twist.

Cooking the Lobsters:

1. Prepare a pan of ice water large enough to hold the lobsters; I put the stopper in and use my sink for this step.
2. Bring a 4-5 gallon pot of water to boil; add ¼ cup salt per gallon of water.
3. With a pair of tongs, place the lobsters one at a time in the pot and cook until bright red and the tail is curling, about 10 minutes. Remove from the boiling water and place them in the ice-water bath. Allow them to cool there for several minutes.
4. Remove the lobsters and twist off the claws and tail. Using a lobster cracker, nutcracker, or large pair of pliers, crack the claws and carefully remove the fragile meat. Next, crack the tail and remove the meat; with a sharp knife, cut a line down the length of the lobster, remove the intestinal trail, and discard.
5. Chop the claw meat into ½-inch chunks and dice the tail into ¼-inch pieces.

Maine Lobster Roll

Ingredients
4 1¼- to 1½-pound lobsters, cooked and prepared per above
1½ teaspoons finely minced celery
2 teaspoons finely minced chives
¼ teaspoon finely minced fresh tarragon
1½ tablespoons fresh lemon juice
2-plus tablespoons good-quality, real mayonnaise (or more to taste)
2 pinches freshly ground black pepper
6 hotdog buns
3 tablespoons unsalted butter, melted
3 cups shredded Boston or other soft green-leaf lettuce

Instructions
1. In a large mixing bowl, gently toss together the lobster meat, celery, chives, tarragon, lemon juice, mayonnaise, and black pepper. Cover tightly, and chill in the refrigerator 2 to 4 hours.
2. Just before serving, heat your nonstick griddle, large sauté pan, or grill over medium-high heat. Brush all sides of each bun with the melted butter. Cook the buns, turning after a moment or two, until lightly browned on each side. If you would rather, you may also toast them in a preheated 400-degree oven.
3. Place ½ cup of the shredded lettuce in each bun and stuff with the lobster salad. Serve immediately.

Servings
Serves 6

* * *

I like to serve a side of gourmet, thick-cut potato chips, such as Kettle Brand, with my lobster rolls. The texture of the crispy chips is a nice complement to the soft lobster meat and toasted bun. Of course, you can make your own, but I don't care to go through those laborious steps with a lot of hot grease when I can buy them already made. Also, the home fries I use with the fish fry menu on page 56 make a very nice accompaniment as well.

* * *

The dessert on this menu is easy to make in advance and then warmed just before serving.

I purchase Wyman's of Maine wild blueberries in the frozen food section at the grocer for this pie. There are also other brands available that will give you that exquisite, intense taste; just ask your grocer. I will stress to you that using cultivated blueberries will not give you the same concentrated berry taste as the ones from the wilds of the Pine State.

Wild Maine Blueberry Pie

Ingredients
1 16-ounce package rolled piecrust (2 crusts)
¼ cup all-purpose flour, divided
2/3 cup sugar
¼ teaspoon cinnamon
Dash of salt
5 cups frozen wild Maine blueberries
1 tablespoon unsalted butter
1 egg
1 tablespoon water
Whipped cream or vanilla ice cream

Instructions
1. Preheat oven to 375 degrees F.
2. On flat surface, unroll one pie crust and dust one side with 1 tablespoon of flour. Place dough, floured side down, into a nonstick pie pan. Cut off excess shell, allowing ¼ inch or so overhang.
3. Mix the 3 remaining tablespoons of flour, sugar, cinnamon, and dash of salt together in a large bowl. Add in the blueberries and toss well.
4. Pour the berries and flour mixture into the pie pan.
5. Cut the butter into small pieces and dot evenly over the berries.
6. Cover the dough with the second crust, folding the ends together and crimping to seal.
7. Cut 6 small slits in the top of the pie with a sharp knife.

8. Whisk the egg and water together until well combined and brush over the crust.
9. Place the pie on a cookie sheet and bake for 45 minutes or so until the crust is browned and the pie cooked through. If the edges of your pie begin to brown too quickly, remove from oven and cover the pie's border with a pie ring or strips of foil.
10. Remove from heat and allow to cool for 20 minutes or more before slicing.
11. Serve each slice with a dollop of whipped cream or a scoop of ice cream.

Servings
Serves 6

* * *

One of Tom's and my best traveling experiences was a ten-day tour of Spain with our friends Carolyn and Brooks. What a magnificent country on so many levels: the people are both stylish and gracious, the architecture as well as the topography remarkable, and the food some of the best in the world.

We started off in Madrid, whose inhabitants are the ultimate in terms of fashion chic. I was fascinated watching the elegantly dressed ladies in their furs and silk scarves and the gentlemen sporting double-breasted camel-hair overcoats promenading, along with their dogs, in front of the Palacio Real. Everywhere you turned, the citizens were bedecked in the most tasteful attire, and I can't help but admit I felt somewhat dowdy, even in my Cole Haans and Brooks Brothers blazer.

From Madrid, we made a wide circle through the country, visiting the Alhambra in Granada, where I learned that the beautiful oranges hanging from the trees in the palace were a bitter fruit, best used for perfumes and not to be eaten. Being a skeptic, I had to try one for myself, and the first bite was spit right back out and into my handkerchief.

Other sites included such ancient cities as Toledo, which is surrounded on three sides by the Tagus River and is known for the immense four-towered Alcazar that dominates the city's skyline. We also visited Málaga on the Costa del Sol, where Picasso was born, and dipped our toes in the waters of the Mediterranean. The next stop was Gibraltar. This enormous rock is known as one of the Pillars of Hercules from ancient myth, and the highlight of our stay was the steep taxi ride to its top, where you looked over what appeared to be an expanse of blue glass to see Africa in the distance. I was not crazy, though, about visiting with the famous Barbary apes, which were scattered all over the site. I do not, under any shape, form, or fashion, like monkeys. These overly friendly creatures wander freely and will even sit atop your head; they found Carolyn's large diamond-stud earrings incredibly fascinating. No one is really sure how these monkeys arrived on Gibraltar; legend has it that there was once an underground tunnel linking Africa to what was then called Mons Calpe, and they crossed through ages ago. To the British people who occupy this land just off the coast of Spain, it is believed that as long as the Barbary monkeys exist on the Rock of Gibraltar, the territory will remain safely under English rule.

Stops were made to other wondrous places, such as Coronado and Seville. My favorite site, though, throughout the entire trip was the awe-inspiring city of Ronda. Founded before the sixth century, the Romans built the city atop two limestone escarpments that overlook a 300-foot deep canyon, the El Tajo. The view looking down into this spectacular ravine is nothing short of breathtaking. The beautiful white, sculpted cliffs form a sheer drop to the Guadalevin River below, and it was one of the loveliest natural scenes I'd ever experienced. I would go back to visit in a heartbeat.

Throughout our trip, we sampled meals and dishes that were almost indescribably good. The French and Italians get more press about their culinary offerings, but I would put Spain on par with either of her romance language-speaking sisters. The origins of Spanish cuisine resulted from the diverse history of the country, very similar to how the dishes of the South developed. Our food has the influences of the Scotch-Irish settlers in Appalachia, the French in the Creole areas of the Gulf, the Native Americans who added so much to our diet, as well as the styles brought from Africa during the eighteenth and nineteenth centuries. In Spain, there have been a variety of cultures that have occupied and lived on the Iberian peninsula, including the Phoenicians, Jews, Romans, and, of course, the Moors, all who shaped the food and customs of modern-day Spain. This history, along with the abundance of fruits and vegetables from the fertile plains and the bounty of seafood from the surrounding waters, ensures that a trip to Spain is a delight for the food lover.

Tom and I in Toledo, with the Tagus River to his left
and the Alcazar between us

While the country is famous for many foods and dishes, such as their olive oils, almonds, wines, cheeses, and, of course, paella, they are best known for their cured meats. This centuries-old process is considered an art form, just as wine making is revered in France. One very sought-after variety is the Jamon Iberico de Bellotta, a ham from that comes from free-range pigs that have a diet made solely of wild acorns; it is very expensive and only recently been allowed as a US import. More commonly known Spanish meats are the spicy chorizo sausage along with the jamon serrano, which is made in the arid mountains of Spain and means, in literal translation, ham of the mountains.

We had exceptional meals, especially at dinner, for those two weeks and had a most jovial time doing so. It was an interesting experience eating in the Spanish restaurants. We are not early diners, tending to make reservations at a restaurant around 8 p.m., giving me time to have a quick nap, and fix myself a "gettin' ready drink" cocktail of a little bourbon before I go out. On our first night in Madrid, the concierge made a reservation for us at our normal time; we arrived to find the bistro completely empty. We knew that the Spaniards took their meals late, but this seemed out of the ordinary. We wondered if the guidebooks had steered us wrong, and the establishment had taken a downturn. However, by the time we finished our meal at 10 p.m., the place was packed with patrons and there was a line out of the door. This lonely beginning happened throughout our stay, and Tom remarked one night, laughingly, that we looked like two old retired couples down in Boca who wanted to make sure they didn't miss the $10 Salisbury steak early-bird dinner special.

My favorite dish on the trip was again one of the most simply prepared that I sampled. It was a platter of fresh anchovies, which had been given a light dusting of flour and cooked quickly in a deep fryer, then served immediately with a garlic mayonnaise. It was more than just *delicioso*, it was phenomenal. The fish were so amazingly delicate yet full of fresh sea flavor, and the creaminess of the spiced mayonnaise was a perfect accompaniment. I'd never had an anchovy before that was not out of a can packed in salt or oil, and this presentation was an amazing revelation.

I've come up with a menu that I serve based on a selection of Spanish dishes, and like the others presented, is one that can be served to guests without a great deal of last-minute work. The prevalent flavors I recall from my trip were those of oranges, saffron, seafood, and olives, and I've incorporated them into the menu. I recently recreated this dinner as a thank you for friends of ours who took care of our pets while we were on a trip out of the country. They all gave rave compliments about each of the courses and asked for second helpings of both the gazpacho and paella; Savannahians do love good food.

I chose paella as the main course, not just because it is probably the most famous of all Spanish entrées, but also because of the ease in constructing in advance. True Spanish chefs would maybe disagree with how I go about making the dish, but I'm not a chef and don't always have the time and resources to replicate exactness. Not many of us do have that expertise, so instead of exactness in some dishes, I make a concerted effort that the essence and root of the dish are a part of the final result.

Remember that many of the dishes we enjoy today, such as the French bouillabaisse and cassoulet, have humble origins, as does paella. While the basis of paella is rice, the cooks of long ago would use rabbit and snails along with whatever vegetables were on hand to make the dish complete.

Speaking to this fact, a number of years ago I was chairing a lecture series for Historic Savannah Foundation focusing on Southern culture, and one of my guest lecturers was a very well-known Southern chef. She planned to make a catfish stew for her presentation, and I took her shopping and assisted in procuring the items she would need for the dish. As we roamed the grocer's aisles, she told me that she was a "purist" and very much liked getting back to the real roots of age-old Southern fare. This statement was said after she filled the cart with bottled water to cook the fish in, which got a slightly raised eyebrow and sideways look from me. Then later, unloading the car, she found that she was missing a vital item needed to cook the dish. "Oh no! (expletive, expletive) I forgot to pack my nonreactive stockpot! I need a nonreactive pot to make the stew! Johnathon, do you have one I could borrow?" She was seriously upset.

I tried not to laugh as the following scene entered my mind:

It is 1895, and the setting is a small camp built on the banks of the Ogeechee River in the thick forests of East Georgia. Husband has just returned from a day of fishing and sits down at the make-shift table, hungry and ready for supper. His spouse puts down a plate in front of him and steps back. Husband looks down, and then in amazement asks, "Wifey, whars the catfish stew you promised t'make? I have a mess of channel cats all cleaned and dressed out in that tub yonder. This ain't no supper here on this table!"

Hands on hips and jaw thrown forward, she answers, "What you see is what you gone git. You wuz in such an all-fired hurry to leave to git shere that you forgot to put my nonreactive stockpot in the buggy. And what's more, you left erry jug of fine mountain sprang water settin' right on the back porch. How you 'spect me to cook a catfish stew without my nonreactive pot? Huh? And what I'm 'sposed to do 'bout water? Git it out of the river where they swam? Hmph! You cain't cook a catfish stew worth eatin' without the right pot and the right water. So there you go."

With that, Wifey turns on her heel and flounces into the tent, and poor ol' Husband is left to eat cold cornpone and leftover fried fatback because of his unfortunate negligence.

Okay, so my imagination can conjure scenes of sarcasm sometimes, but you get the general gist of what I'm trying to relay. It is fine to be serious about your food, but you can also be flexible.

With most of the forms of paella, there is rice and saffron and the food is cooked over an open fire. Seafood is generally included in some shape or form, and a few vegetables. Bearing this in mind, I created the following recipe that is not exactly prepared as a chef in Valencia might serve, but the end product does speak clearly "paella."

The other courses are done with a nod to Spain and in total create a lovely meal that evokes an old-world feeling that can be prepared in a modern American household.

Menu

~Hors d'oeuvres of sliced Serrano Ham, Olive and Almond Tapenade, Manchego (or other Sheep's milk cheese), and Grilled Bread
~Gazpacho Andalusia
~Paella of Shrimp, Chicken and Chorizo
~Crema Catalana with Apricot Compote

For the hors d'oeuvres, a lovely platter can be made to showcase these items, all which mix so well together. Serrano ham is found in most markets; for six people choose 1/3 pound, thinly sliced. Monchego is a classic, strong

Spanish cheese and is usually available in most gourmet markets; if not in stock, find a half pound of another selection that is made with sheep's milk.

With the bread, buy a long, thin baguette and slice into ½-inch rounds; brush with olive oil and some crushed garlic and either grill or bake until toasted. To store, allow to cool completely and place in an airtight container until ready to serve.

The tapenade combines two of Spain's most popular condiments, olives and almonds. Spread it on the toasted baguette to serve. It is an easy and delicious spread.

Olive and Almond Tapenade

Ingredients
½ cup almonds
1½ cups good-quality pitted green olives, rinsed and patted dry (a 6-ounce jar)
1 tablespoon chopped fresh oregano
1 teaspoon finely minced garlic
¼ cup extra virgin olive oil

Instructions
1. Grind the almonds fine in a food processor.
2. Add the remaining ingredients and puree until smooth.
3. Refrigerate stored in an airtight container until ready to use.
4. Serve on toasted baguette slices.
May be stored in the refrigerator for 2 to 3 days.

Servings
Serves 6

* * *

Gazpacho is a very popular dish in Spain as well as the US, but its ancient beginnings are far off from the traditional dish we mostly know on today's menus. The most popular of contemporary versions comes from Andalusia, in southern Spain, and has a tomato base; in some forms, bread is incorporated in this dish. Supposedly, this soup started out simply as bread soaked in vinegar with perhaps some garlic or chopped vegetables; tomatoes were not introduced to Spain until the mid-1500s. The Romans ate this bread-and-vinegar version, and the tradition is even referenced in the Bible. The Book of Ruth, chapter 2, verse 14 reads: "And Boaz said unto her, at mealtime come thou hither, and eat of the bread, and dip thy morsel in vinegar."

In keeping with what we know is popular, I have included a recipe that showcases tomatoes, onions, peppers, celery, and cucumbers. Invigorated with some Spanish sherry vinegar, it is a very flavorful and at the same time nutritious dish.

Finding good, ripe tomatoes is not always easy and so sometimes I cheat when making this dish. The shame, the shame...but I openly admit to using a shortcut on more than one occasion, and it turns out perfectly well. Purchase a container of a very good salsa, one preferably that does not contain cilantro. Salsa already has most of the makings of gazpacho, containing, along with the tomatoes, onions, peppers, and garlic. With just the inclusion of a handful of ingredients, including cucumber, celery, olive oil, and a good-quality sherry vinegar, you can "doctor" the salsa up into a quick and good gazpacho.

A key ingredient here, as in several Spanish recipes, is to use a good-quality sherry vinegar, preferably a Reserva. This aromatic vinegar is a specialty of Spain, provides more flavor than regular red wine vinegar, and is not as strong on the palate as balsamic.

Gazpacho Andalusia

Ingredients

6 cups peeled, seeded, and chopped fully ripe tomatoes, about 8 to 9 medium-sized fruits
1½ cups V-8 juice
1 cup finely chopped cucumber, seeded
½ cup finely chopped red bell pepper
1/3 cup finely chopped celery
1/3 cup finely chopped red onion
1½ teaspoon minced garlic
1 teaspoon finely minced fresh jalapeno
½ cup olive oil
3 tablespoons sherry vinegar, preferably an aged Reserva
1 teaspoon kosher salt
1 teaspoon ground cumin
Chives for garnish

Instructions

1. Place all ingredients except garnish in a large mixing bowl; stir and combine.
2. Take half of the mixture and puree until smooth in either a food processor or blender; add the puree back to the mixing bowl.
3. Place the soup in an airtight container, cover tightly, and refrigerate 4 hours or more.
4. To serve, place in chilled bowls and garnish with a sprinkle of chives.

Servings

Serves 6

* * *

The paella recipe I use below is full of the flavor of saffron, a key ingredient, as well as combining the taste of seafood with the smokiness of grilled chicken and chorizo. It can be made ahead of your dinner, and reheated easily in a hot oven. Serve this with slices of good European-style bread along with small bowls of olive oil for dipping.

Paella of Shrimp, Chicken, and Chorizo

Ingredients
2 cups water
2 teaspoons kosher salt
1½ cups frozen petite baby butter beans
1 pound boneless, skinless chicken thighs
1½ pounds fresh, large US wild-caught shrimp, peeled and deveined, tails left on
½ teaspoon kosher salt
¼ teaspoon freshly ground black pepper
2 teaspoons sweet smoked Spanish paprika
2 teaspoons dried oregano
½ cup olive oil, divided
¾ pound smoked or fresh chorizo sausage (if unavailable, substitute andouille)
2 large onions, peeled and sliced into 1-inch rounds
1 large red and green bell pepper, each sliced into 1-inch rounds
1 cup frozen English peas, thawed and thoroughly drained
1 recipe of Dottie's Creamy Saffron Rice (omitting the Parmesan), pages 178-79
¼ cup dry sherry
¼ cup chopped flat-leaf parsley
2 tablespoons finely zested orange peel

Instructions
1. Preheat your charcoal or gas grill.
2. In a medium-sized pot, bring the water and 2 teaspoons kosher salt to a boil, add the butter beans, and cook al dente, about 18 minutes. Drain in a colander and set aside.
3. While the butter beans are cooking, toss the chicken and shrimp in two separate bowls with half each the salt, black pepper, paprika, and oregano. Drizzle on ¼ cup olive oil and toss again.
4. Grill the chicken until done, about 15 minutes, turning occasionally. Place on a baking or cookie sheet and set aside.

5. Grill the chorizo until done, about 20 minutes for fresh sausage, 10 minutes or so for fully cooked, smoked varieties. Place on the sheet with the chicken.

6. Turn your oven on to 350 degrees F and preheat.

7. Grill shrimp, using skewers if needed, turning a time or two, until just done, about 5 minutes, when their tail-end is almost touching the head portion. Remove from heat and place on a separate sheet and set aside.

8. Toss the onions and peppers with the remaining olive oil; grill, turning occasionally until just charred and tender, about 10 minutes. Remove from heat and set aside.

9. Chop the chicken and chorizo into bite-sized chunks, making certain to reserve the liquid that has collected in the pan while the meats were cooling.

10. In a large mixing bowl, place the saffron rice (omitting the Parmesan); add the meats and shrimp, pouring any collected juices into the rice as well.

11. Add the cooked vegetables and English peas. Toss well to thoroughly mix.

12. Pour paella into a large, lightly oiled baking dish and drizzle with the sherry. Cover tightly and place in the preheated oven. Heat for 20 to 25 minutes, until hot.

13. When ready to serve, sprinkle each plated portion with the chopped parsley and orange zest.

Servings
Serves 6 to 8

* * *

Crema Catalana is one of the most popular dessert dishes in Spain, and a very close sister to France's crème brulée. The major differences between the two dishes is that the Spanish version, which dates back to medieval times, is spiced with cinnamon and citrus zest, which are not present in the brulée, and the Catalana preparation sets by chilling, while in France theirs is finished in a bain-marie, or water bath. In modern times it is served year-round in Spain, but in the past it was a tradition set aside for St. Joseph's Day, March 19th. It is still sometimes referred to as "Crema St. Josep".

Many recipes call for caramelizing sugar on the tops of these desserts, as they do with crème brulée. However, I've taken that step out and instead crown the custards with a compote of apricots. These fruits were introduced to the Americas by Spanish settlers in the eighteenth century, and I find that these two Iberian traditional foods make an excellent pairing.

Crema Catalana with Apricot Compote

Ingredients
Crema Catalana
2 tablespoons cornstarch
2 tablespoons plus 1 quart whole milk
8 large egg yolks
1 scant cup of sugar
2 cinnamon sticks
½ teaspoon finely grated orange zest
¼ teaspoon vanilla extract
Apricot Compote (recipe follows)
Sprigs of mint for garnish

Instructions
1. Dissolve the cornstarch in the 2 tablespoons of milk in a small container.
2. In a large bowl, beat the egg yolks, sugar, and dissolved cornstarch with an electric mixer until well incorporated; it should be a light yellow color and frothy.
3. In a large saucepan, add the quart of milk, cinnamon sticks, zest, and vanilla. Place over medium-high heat and cook, stirring, until it comes *just* to a boil. Remove from heat immediately and discard the cinnamon sticks.
4. Pour the heated milk, in a steady, slow stream, into the egg mixture, whisking the whole time.
5. When fully incorporated, pour the mixture back into the saucepan and return to the stove over medium-low heat. Whisk until the custard *just* begins to simmer; reduce heat to low and whisk

constantly for 2 to 3 minutes, or until the custard is thick enough to cover the back of a spoon.

6. Pour the custard into six 6-ounce ramekins and allow to cool slightly.
7. Place the ramekins in the refrigerator, and when chilled, cover with plastic wrap.
8. When ready to serve, top each Crema with a couple of tablespoons of apricot compote and garnish with a sprig of spearmint.

Apricot Compote

Ingredients
2 cups fresh, peeled apricot halves, coarsely chopped (if fresh are not available, use frozen, jarred, or canned)
3 tablespoons sugar
2 tablespoons fresh lime juice

Instructions
Add all ingredients together in a medium-sized saucepan; cook over medium to medium-high heat, stirring, until the apricots become soft and the sugar makes a slight syrup, about 5 minutes. Chill 2 to 4 hours before serving.

Servings
Serves 6

* * *

A few years after Tom and I met, we took a trip to France and spent almost three weeks in Paris, touring the City of Lights and enjoying all the magnificent things that make Paris the wonder that it is. On our way over, we made a stop in London for a few days. While for the most part the first leg of our vacation was lovely, I had an unfortunate battle with some distilled juniper berries and required a full day of recuperation and bed rest.

Before I met my foe, we started our first full day with a wonderful lunch at the five-star St. James Hotel and Club near Buckingham Palace. Tom and I were members of a club that had a reciprocal agreement with the St. James and decided to experience this venerable institution, which had been founded in 1857 by Earl Granville. The service and food were impeccable, and I was thoroughly impressed with the entire setting, and even got a good chuckle in the midst of all this finery.

While reading the menu, I noticed that all items were a la carte, as well as expensive. As Mama would have said "They certainly are proud of their food." Tom, though, can sometimes be impatient and did not read the obvious print of how things were priced.

When the waiter offered the side dish selection of vegetables, Tom, who does not really care for them, preferring meat and potatoes, pointed to the platter and said "I'll have one petit carrot, and two of the green beans."

Trying to get Tom's attention can sometimes turn into a situation of "no good deed goes unpunished." I had learned over the years that my dear friend is the type who, when you try to discreetly send a signal of caution about potentially disquieting topics or situations, will either simply ignore your efforts, or give you a bewildered look along with a loud, "What? What are you saying?" So oftentimes I just leave him to his own devices and que sera sera.

One such incident happened at a restaurant in Savannah years ago. The two of us were having dinner with a couple we had recently met. The husband was a graduate of the Citadel in Charleston, and their two sons were also alums of that Southern bastion of military training and education. It was just at the time when the discussion of allowing female cadets into the college was becoming serious, and somehow, in the course of conversation, the topic sprang up its controversial head. I realized from prior comments our fellow tablemates were more than likely archconservative on the subject, and at the same time knew Mr. Thomas Eugene held very forward-thinking views. I could sense immediately the good chance of a disastrous end to our evening out. Rather than trying to get his attention with a cut of the eyes or a "cough-cough look-at-me-and-shut-your-mouth expression," I opted to give him a swift kick in the shin. Instead of hitting him, though, my size-12 dress shoe struck of one of the dining table's legs, hard. Over toppled the four large goblets of red zinfandel we were drinking, and that blackberry colored wine spilled all across the table and, of course, poured right into our laps.

As you can imagine, the conversation was diverted. Fortunately the lady in our company had on a black dress, and the gentleman a dark suit. Nothing else was spoken of young ladies and the Citadel, but at the cost of utmost embarrassment to me.

So from lessons learned, I allowed Tom to order as he pleased that day in London.

When the bill came, his eyes widened, and clearly annoyed, he said in a loud whisper "Did you see they charged me *ten* pounds for that forkful of vegetables? That's almost twenty dollars for a carrot and couple of peas! I didn't want them to start with!"

Oh, well. Que sera sera, m'dear. I would have tried to tell you, but...

While Tom's lunch was an experience for him in terms of being too picky about eating his vegetables, that night proved to me that I should always and at all times stay away from gin.

Before we left the states, Tom had contacted some of his International Society of Interior Designer (ISID) colleagues to let them know we'd be in London for a few days. One of his fellow officers in the society, Jacqueline Duncan, extended the gracious offer to throw a party for us while on our visit. A decorator of worldwide renown, Jacqueline is the founder of the acclaimed Inchbald School of Design. While Tom knew her well, I had only met her on one occasion when she was in Savannah for an ISID conference, and was very appreciative of this kind and generous gesture of hospitality. The party was to be a black-tie affair and would be held in Jacqueline's stately, multistoried townhome on London's fashionable Eccleston Square.

The party was in British timing "seven for seven-fifteen," and we arrived promptly at midpoint. The house soon filled with about two dozen people, and through the evening I was introduced to an Earl, a few Lords, and an Honorable. Our hostess herself was an OBE, or Officer of the Most Excellent Order of the British Empire. The guests were impeccably dressed and richly bejeweled. I recall one lady especially for her triple strand of pearls adorned with an enormous, diamond-encrusted clasp; it was as large as a demitasse saucer.

I am gregarious by nature and not generally shy, but I was still young enough at twenty-eight to be a little intimidated by such sophisticated people who were of a different social strata than myself. That said, I was so relieved to find that all Jacqueline's guests were extremely nice, very solicitous, and kept me engaged in conversation throughout the evening. I was made to feel most welcome.

To alleviate some of my apprehension when I first arrived, I gladly accepted the offer of a cocktail from one of the waiters. "I'd like a bourbon on the rocks, thank you."

"I'm sorry, sir. We are offering either gin or champagne. Which would you prefer?" he answered, pronouncing the word "eye-ther."

I enjoy a glass of champagne, but generally for lunch or as an accompaniment to dessert, so I opted for gin, something I rarely drank.

The waiter brought me a handsome cut-crystal tumbler, filled to the brim and with one lonely piece of ice in it. I came to learn that Europeans don't have the same craving for ice that I have from all those years of drinking tall glasses of cold tea. I took a sip of the gin and gave an involuntary shudder. "Good Lord, this tastes like pine needles. How do people drink this stuff?" I thought to myself.

The more I sipped, though, the more tolerable the libation became, and after a bit, I offered an empty glass back to a waiter. "I'll have another gin, please, and if you don't mind, may I have a little extra ice with it?"

A moment or two later the server was back with my drink, and it held 300 percent more ice than the first glass. Yes, there were now three cubes cooling down about 8 ounces of alcohol. But as it happens sometimes, the more I drank, the easier it was to have a little more.

And the more I sipped, the easier it was to talk. I remember at one point trying to explain to someone about what was and what was not "Southern." It seems that many of the guests were of the polo set and very familiar with Palm Beach, with more than one of them making comments along the lines of how they "very much enjoyed visiting the American South in Palm Beach. I daresay Palm Beach is one of the most hospitable cities I've visited; but I suppose that is only fair, since it is such a Southern city."

There are many towns and places in Florida that epitomize Southern life, especially in the panhandle and down through the middle heart of the state that is home to magnificent, moss-strewn oaks, rolling pastures, and people who still say "yes, ma'am" and "yes, sir." However, Southern is not universal in the Sunshine State. Even when sober, it is not an easy task to try to describe how some spots, such as Palm Beach or Miami, aren't really "Southern" cities. The fact that they are located in the most extreme part of the region does indeed make them "southern," but not *"Southern."* The differences in accents, attitudes, lifestyles, and all things cultural go into the explanation, but I just wasn't up to the task of articulating those nuances, not with several tumblers of gin under my belt. So by the end of the evening, if anyone spoke of Palm Beach, I readily agreed that it was, in addition to polo, the land of grand plantations, mint juleps, demure debutantes, and fried chicken.

Dinner that night was a lovely offering plated on exquisite bone china, but not a seated affair. I vaguely recall looking at the delicious meal in front of me through a cloud of Beefeater and thinking, "If I stand up and try to eat, I'm going to spill these tiny little peas all over Jacqueline's Aubusson." So instead of having dinner, I had another gin.

By the time we left, I was in a wonderful humor and found that I had enjoyed myself enormously in all this convivial British upper-crust elegance. That changed dramatically when I got back to our rented flat and I lay across the bed. Yes, the room started spinning, and I went from happiness to misery in about the time you could say "Queen Elizabeth." The next morning I sent Tom to the pharmacy, and along with aspirin, I had him get me a bottle of Nyquil. I figured if I was going to stay the day in bed—I was in no condition to greet the greater London public—then I'd do it sleeping.

Fortunately I recovered after a day of bed rest and was able to take in a few of the sites of London. I plan to return sometime soon to see more of the city. I'd also like to spend a few weeks in a thatched cottage in the Cotswolds and make an excursion down to visit the coast of Cornwall when I am back.

Before we left for France, another of Tom's designer friends in London provided us with a long list of recommended restaurants to visit while in Paris. An unabashed Francophile, which is rather an anomaly in Great Britain, this gentleman knew all of the best out-of-the-way *mere-et-pere* bistros in several of the *arrondissements* throughout the city. It was to be our go-to guide for dinner on many evenings.

Paris was a marvelous and beautiful encounter with so many astounding things to do, see, and experience. So much has been written about this center of culture and history that it would be hard for me to add anything else to showcase its appeal. Although we were in the city for three full weeks, we still did not see and do all that we'd hoped. However, we made a gallant effort.

We started with the Louvre, where we spent almost two days taking in such magnificent masterpieces as the *Mona Lisa*, which is a surprisingly small painting, and the immense and powerful marble statue of Winged Victory. This Hellenistic sculpture dates to the second century BC, and is of Nike, the Greek Goddess of Victory. I was so entranced by the beauty of those powerful stone wings and the dramatic billowing drapery, which was so lifelike, that I stood in place in awe for more than an hour.

Another cultural excursion was to the Rodin museum, and I have a great photo of Tom posed at the base of the artist's most well-known sculpture, *The Thinker*. While at the museum, we also saw *The Gates of Hell*, which actually was a bit disturbing to me and not something I'd want welcoming people into my home. While it took the artist over thirty-five years to create, and is an incredible piece of artistry, it made me uncomfortable viewing the multitude of chaotic humanity carved into the design.

And while I have a very good picture of me in front of the phenomenal Beaux-Arts building of the d'Orsay museum, we did not get to venture in to see its world-famous collection of impressionist and postimpressionist works. I had saved this museum, which I believed would be my favorite because of my fascination with the impressionist period, for our last day in Paris. But it was a Monday, the only day of the week the museum was not open. Merde! Oh well, something for another trip.

We took an evening boat ride on the Seine, said our Hail Marys and lit candles at Notre Dame Cathedral, strolled through Catherine de Medici's Tuileries Gardens, shopped along the Champs-Elysees, poured through antique stores, and admired the paintings by Parisian artists at Montmartre and along the Pont Neuf. We also saw a cabaret at the famous Folies Bergere, watching lithe young women, all dressed in exotic but entirely revealing costumes, dance across the stage. While this exquisite show was spectacular, I would not recommend it to any visiting members of the "Hosanna in the Highest" adult Sunday school class from your local First Baptist Church.

Now many people in the States believe that Parisians are arrogant and unfriendly, but I found this to be far from the truth. They do not throw their arms up in the air and squeal, "Bonjour, Sucre!" (Hello, Sugar!) whenever they run into an old friend, like we are prone to do in Dixie, but I felt that the French were hospitable and kind, and I did not encounter any form of rudeness at all while there. When a waiter or shopkeeper saw that I was trying to use a few words of their language, such as a simple "merci" or "s'il vous plait," I always received a smile and, on most occasions, an answer in English in return.

You can find rude anywhere, even at the grocery store back home. One afternoon a few years back, I'd taken Mama out to do a little shopping. We were turning our buggy into a checkout line when this perky soccer mom, who was talking away on her cell phone, pulled in front of us and broke in line without so much as an "excuse me."

Mama, particularly as she got older, did not suffer fools, or rudeness, well. She reached right up and tapped the gibbering young lady on the shoulder. The line-cutter turned around with an impatient look and raised eyebrows. "Yes?"

Mama, with deadpan delivery, asked her, "I don't suppose you'd jump in my grave that fast, now would you, honey?"

The young lady, whom I had already recognized, turned scarlet when she realized who we were and started apologizing with, "Oh, Johnathon, Mrs. Barrett, I am so sorry, I just didn't see you!" which was a big ol' lie. Mr. Young Successful Stockbroker's wife had looked right at the two of us when she whipped her buggy ahead of ours.

Mama gave her an "It's all fine, sugar," smile. "That's okay, honey, just don't do a lot of driving until you get yourself to the eye doctor."

Besides being known for her fishing and jellies, my mother was also great with the one-liners. So rudeness is universal, and it can even happen back home in such friendly places as the Piggly Wiggly.

Parisians were kind to me, and I had an especially nice time in their bistros and restaurants. We went to both the famous spots, as well as to the out-of-the-way places that were recommended, and fully immersed ourselves in all the fabulous dishes the French are known for.

One lunch was at the renowned Le Jules Verne restaurant midway up the Eiffel Tower, which provided a spectacular view of Paris and was a true fine-dining experience. I recall a marvelous main course of veal loin with an orange sauce; I also recall getting bug-eyed when I got the bill. While Tom treated at the St. Jame's, Le Jules Verne was on my tab. I had never paid that much for a meal in my life for two people, and this was just lunch. But it is not every day you get to dine in the Eiffel Tower, overlooking one of the most beautiful cities in the world. It was worth every franc.

Another meal was at Maxim's, which has been known as the world's most famous and fashionable restaurant. Because we had our tuxedos with us for Jacqueline's party, we chose to make reservations there for a Friday night, as the restaurant required formal dress for those evenings. Beautifully appointed in the rich, flowing lines of the Art Nouveau style, it is a stunning setting harkening back to more glamorous times. Tom and I both ordered their wonderful onion soup au gratin, and he feasted on lobster and steak while I had roast duck for a main course. We finished this celebration with a bottle of Madame Clicquot and a signature soufflé.

The most unusual meal we had was at La Boule Rouge, just near the Folies Bergere. The food at "The Red Ball" is Jewish Tunisian. It was the first time I had experienced this cuisine, and I found it to be a nice change from some of the other standards we'd been dining upon during our visit. It also seemed like an incredibly popular destination, as it was filled to capacity with people waiting to dine when we finished our meal. I thought a lot about my father that night; he spent a great deal of time in Tunis while serving in WWII. In his letters, he wrote about how very hot it was in Africa, and that while a July day in Georgia could be scorching, it did not compare to Tunisia. Besides being hot, he also was under the threat of warfare, and told my aunts how he was ready to get back home. Knowing Daddy's tastes, too, I can't imagine he would have liked the local food. While I enjoyed my couscous and lamb, I knew my father would have not liked partaking of anything that had once bleated or came with spices other than black pepper and onion (yes, onion is a spice down South).

Other dining experiences were at smaller, family-owned bistros and cafes. It was astounding how inexpensively and well you could dine in Paris if you just knew where to go. The food was always freshly prepared, full of wonderful flavors, and served in generous portions. And the wine! It was not uncommon to find a splendid house wine for three or four dollars a bottle. I wrote in my journal of one outing to a restaurant on the Left Bank that included three courses and two full bottles of wine. With tip, it was less than $50 for the two of us. Being creatures of habit, we found our favorite French offerings during the course of our stay. Most evenings found Tom eating a bowl of onion soup followed by a grilled strip steak and pomme frites, and I habitually ordered some sort of paté or cheeses, along with duck cooked whichever way the chef thought best. The trip was, as a whole, a wonderful twenty-one-day gastronomical journey.

We sampled a number of different dishes while in Paris, and many I have prepared at home. To create a menu that can be cooked beforehand and needs little assembly just before serving somewhat limits your choices. As in my previous selections, I have found that working with some of the classics, such as the buco, paella, or lobster roll, allows you to serve a true representation of the cuisine all while allowing yourself the needed time to enjoy a relaxed evening with your guests.

I have two entrée selections chosen, either of which will make a great French presentation. For the hors d'oeuvres, I suggest creating a large, impressive charcuterie. Provide some small plates and forks for your guests, and allow them to prepare their own sampling of the pate, cheeses, and other ingredients found under the Ossabaw Buco menu on pages 174-76.

When your guests arrive, have Edith Piaf playing softly in the background, the charcuterie on display, a variety of wonderful champagnes and wines for sampling, and voila! You have set the stage for a lovely night in the Republique Francaise.

Menu

~Charcuterie Platter
~Onion Soup Gratinée
~Salade Nicoise *or* Grouper Cheek Meuniere with Rice Mirepoix and Roasted Carrots
~Pear and Plum Tart Rustique

Onion soup is one of Tom's and my favorites, and it can be a wonderful main course with a salad on a cold, wintry night. It is not a difficult dish to create, but you have to make certain you follow a few important steps, such as caramelizing the onions, adding in a splash of cognac or dry sherry, and using Gruyere cheese for the topping.

The cheese is an important factor, and if you substitute other varieties, the quality of your course will be subpar. I had an unfortunate incident with the dish many years ago in a downtown Atlanta restaurant. When the server brought out the soup and placed the bubbling crock in front of me, I could tell instantly that the cheese was mozzarella. It was a thick, white melted mass without any of the nutty aroma of toasted Gruyere. I cut the topping and with some of the soup placed a spoonful in my mouth. After a moment of chewing, I tried to swallow, but part of the cheese would not all go down properly; it formed a sinewy rope that caught in my throat and I could not get it to move. Regardless of how much I chewed or tried to swallow, it stayed stuck, from mouth to stomach. I did not want to embarrass myself in this crowded restaurant, but finally had to ask for help as I was gasping for air and I literally thought I was going to die. The Heimlich maneuver was administered by a waiter to no luck *because you can't cough up a four-inch string of rubbery cheese.* While I know this sounds rather unpleasant, I had to reach into my mouth and literally yank on this tenacious rope of mozzarella until it came all the way out, intact, onto the table. So important point here: if you want to serve proper onion soup gratinee, and not put the lives of your guests in mortal danger, use Gruyere!

Onion Soup Gratinée

Ingredients
1 wide baguette or other French-style bread, about 4 inches in diameter
2 tablespoons olive oil
2 cloves of garlic, crushed
½ cup unsalted butter
4 pounds thinly sliced white or yellow onions (not Vidalia or other sweet varieties)
1 teaspoon sugar
3 tablespoons all-purpose flour
1½ teaspoons minced, fresh thyme
2 bay leaves
¼ teaspoon freshly ground black pepper
1 cup dry vermouth
2 quarts less one cup homemade beef broth, or a good low-sodium commercial brand
¼ cup dry sherry or cognac
2 cups grated Gruyere cheese (done with a box grater on the large holes), about 6 ounces

Instructions
1. Preheat your oven to 350 degrees F.

2. Cut out six ½-inch thick slices of the bread, and remove crusts. Brush each slice with olive oil and rub with the crushed garlic.
3. Place each slice of the bread directly on an oven rack; bake until toasted, turning once, about 8 minutes. Set aside and do not cover.
4. In a large stockpot or Dutch oven, melt the butter over medium-high heat.
5. Add the onions and spread out in a layer; sprinkle with sugar.
6. Stir well to mix, and reduce heat to medium low. Cover and cook for 5 minutes, allowing the onions to sweat.
7. Remove cover and stir. Keep uncovered, and stir occasionally, until the onions are a nutty brown color and fully caramelized, about 30 to 40 minutes. The timing will depend on the circumference of your pan.
8. When caramelized, add the flour to the onions and mix; cook for 2 minutes, stirring occasionally.
9. Add the thyme, bay leaves, and black pepper. Stir.
10. Pour in the vermouth and stock and return the heat to medium-high. Cook, stirring occasionally, until the mixture begins to thicken, about 5 minutes.
11. Reduce the heat down to low and allow the soup to cook at a slow simmer for 20 minutes; while simmering, turn your oven on broil at 450 degrees F.
12. Add the dry sherry or cognac; stir to mix. Remove and discard the bay leaves.*
13. Place 6 oven-proof bowls on a cookie sheet. Pour equal parts soup into each of the bowls, lay a slice of the toasted bread on the soup, and top with equal amounts of the cheese.
14. Place the bowls under the oven broiler and allow the cheese to melt and start to brown slightly around the edges, about 2 minutes, watching carefully so as not to burn. Serve immediately.

*If making ahead of time, you can refrigerate the soup in an airtight container until ready to serve; reheat the soup in a pot and follow steps 13 and 14.

Servings
Serves 6

* * *

The salade Nicoise is a French classic and a popular dish here in the States. The wonderful thing about this entrée is that it is a small buffet unto itself, a veritable one-dish meal. Served slightly chilled, it is perfect for a summer supper.

The dish gets its name from the nutty-flavored Nicoise olive, which grows in the Cote d'Azur region of southern France near Nice. It actually is a low food crop, and most true Nicoise olives are used domestically. Many of the ones we purchase in the United States are Nicoise *style* olives.

Traditional salade Nicoise is served with canned tuna in France. Not the watery, fishy-tasting little shavings that we Americans use when making a sandwich, but rather packaged pieces of filet stored in flavorful extra-virgin olive oil. The taste difference is as vast as comparing skim milk to heavy cream. Some chefs create their own cured tuna, cooking the yellowfin in a court-bouillon, packing it in airtight containers with some fruity olive oil, and then storing it in the refrigerator for a couple of weeks or more so the flavor and texture fully develop.

Two very good oil-packed commercial brands available here in the states include Genova and Cento. I've used them both and found that they have a nice texture and full flavor. However, if you have some hesitation serving your guests canned tuna (I'd say get over it, but my true Southern gentleman self will not allow me to be so straightforward), purchase some fresh tuna and cook it as you would like, either on the grill or sautéed, and substitute it instead.

Salade Nicoise

Ingredients
3 cups Boston lettuce, gently packed
1½ cups arugula, gently packed
1½ cups watercress, gently packed
1/8 teaspoon kosher salt
Several grinds of fresh black pepper
1 teaspoon minced fresh thyme
1 teaspoon minced fresh tarragon
1 teaspoon minced fresh parsley
1 tablespoon lemon juice
2 tablespoons olive oil

18 small new red potatoes boiled in salted water until just done (about
   10 to 12 minutes), drained and chilled
8 ounces blanched and chilled haricot verts*
6 5-ounce cans solid light tuna packed in olive oil
2 cups Nicoise olives
1 14 ounce can hearts of palm, drained and sliced into 1-inch rounds
1½ cups thinly sliced red onion
3 ripe tomatoes, about 1 pound, cut into 18 wedges
6 large sprigs of parsley for garnish
*Bring two quarts of water and 2 tablespoons kosher salt to a boil. Add
green beans and allow to cook for 1 minute. Drain and immediately plunge
into a bowl of ice water. Drain again, dry with paper towels, and cover and
chill until ready to serve.

Instructions
1. Toss the lettuces in a bowl with the salt and black pepper.
2. Sprinkle the fresh herbs over the leaves and then sprinkle on the
   lemon juice and olive oil. Toss lightly.
3. Place the greens on a large plate or charger and arrange the potatoes,
   green beans, tuna, olives, hearts of palm, onion, and tomatoes
   decoratively alongside. This placement can be done grouping items
   together, separating them out in parts, or however you'd like the
   visual effect to be. Garnish with the parsley sprigs. Serve
   immediately.

Servings
Serves 6

* * *

My favorite way to eat fish is to have it prepared a la meuniere. Meuniere
translates to mean "in the style of the miller's wife," as it is dusted in flour.
With just a few simple ingredients, it is easy to prepare and results in a truly
delicious way to serve a good piece of fish. The seasonings, besides a bit of
kosher salt, include only a little olive oil, butter, lemon juice, and fresh
parsley. I also like to throw in just a sprinkling of capers to add an extra
touch to the finale. The sauce, which is made by deglazing the pan with the
lemon juice and butter, provides a tart, velvety coating for the sautéed fish.

You'll notice that in many of my recipes I use a good bit of fresh parsley. I think that this herb is an incredible complement for a number of dishes, particularly those where you are combining the subtle flavors and tastes of a course that does not need over-spicing. It has a wonderful crisp, fresh taste that can be the gilding agent for simple foods that need only a little extra spirit to become outstanding. The fresh parsley here beautifully underscores the zing of the lemon and creaminess of the butter.

My choice of fish is grouper, specifically, grouper cheeks. This portion of the fish is sliced from the front of the fish on the head and comes out in thick, round circles. I use these for three reasons: first, they share the same solid, white consistency and taste as other cuts of grouper, secondly, they are usually priced at half of what the grouper filets costs, and lastly because I can cook several of these at a time in a pan. Since they are thicker and more compact than a long filet, I can sauté six at a time, perfect for a dinner party.

If you cannot find the cheeks, substitute any other firm-bodied white fish, such as halibut, trout, or flounder.

This dish will require you to utilize your practice of *mise en place* so that you will not spend an inordinate amount of time in the kitchen. If you have all things laid out and measured in advance, the actual cooking time is less than 15 minutes.

Grouper Cheek Meuniere

Ingredients
1½ pounds grouper cheeks, or other solid white fish cut in 6 equal-sized portions
½ teaspoon kosher salt
1/8 teaspoon freshly ground black pepper
½ cup olive oil
6 tablespoons clarified unsalted butter
½ cup all-purpose flour
2 tablespoons capers, drained
3 tablespoons lemon juice
3 tablespoons unsalted butter
3 tablespoons packed, chopped fresh parsley

Instructions

1. Rinse the fish and allow to drain in colander, but do not dry.
2. Sprinkle the fish with the salt and pepper.
3. Using a large sauté pan, heat the olive oil and clarified butter over medium-high heat.
4. Dredge each piece of fish in the flour, shaking off excess, and add to pan. If the pan is not large enough to hold all the pieces *without touching*, cook in 2 separate batches. If cooking in two batches, you may need to add a little additional olive oil for the second batch.
5. Cook each piece about 2 to 3 minutes or more per side, depending on their thickness, allowing to slightly brown and cook through.
6. Remove from the pan, and place fish on a platter or cookie sheet.
7. When all filets are finished, drain off all but 3 tablespoons or so of the oil/clarified butter.
8. Return the pan to the stove, add the capers, and stir.
9. Continuing on medium-high heat, add the lemon juice and butter. Stir well, scraping up the browned bits of fish and flour on the bottom. Cook for about 1 to 1½ minutes until hot and thickened.
10. To serve, spoon a serving of the Rice Mirepoix (recipe follows) on each plate and with a spatula, gently rest a piece of the fish to cover a portion of the rice; pour the lemon caper sauce over the fish and garnish with the fresh parsley.

Servings

Serves 6

* * *

A number of chefs pair their fish dishes with potatoes. While I love a roasted *pomme de terre* almost as much as my aunt Bea did, I don't care for the contrast of a heavy potato with that of delicately sautéed fish. When you take a bite of fish and then potato, the fish can be lost beside the density of its pairing.

For this dish, I prefer rice, which does not battle with the fragility of the fish. Rice is also perfect for absorbing the wonderful lemon sauce and the moist drippings that come from the sautéed fish. Here I've chosen to do a recipe that mixes rice with the aromatic French accompaniment of mirepoix, which in its basic form is sautéed carrots, onions, and celery. In the South, particularly with Creole cooking, we call this mixture of vegetables "The Holy Trinity," as it is the basis for many recipes.

Rice Mirepoix

Ingredients
5 tablespoons unsalted butter, divided
½ cup each finely diced celery, carrots, and onion
Dash of kosher salt
½ teaspoon minced fresh thyme
1½ cups long-grain rice
1 bay leaf
3 cups low-sodium chicken stock

Instructions
1. In a saucepan, melt 3 tablespoons of the butter over medium heat. Add the vegetables and stir. Cover for about 1 minute.
2. Remove cover and continue cooking, stirring occasionally, for another 4 minutes.
3. Add the salt and thyme. Stir and continue cooking until the vegetables are soft but not browned. Set aside.
4. In a medium-sized pot, melt the remaining 2 tablespoons butter over medium-high heat.
5. Add the rice and bay leaf, and stir to coat.
6. Pour in the stock, and add the mirepoix from step 3.
7. Bring to a boil, stir once more, and cover.
8. Reduce the heat to low and allow to cook 20 minutes, or until just done and all the moisture is absorbed. Small holes should appear across the flat surface of the rice.
9. Remove from heat and keep covered until ready to serve. This dish can be made ahead of time; add a couple of tablespoons of stock or water when reheating.

Servings
Serves 6

* * *

When modestly prepared and roasted, the carrots will surprise you with their abundance of fresh taste. Oftentimes you find these vegetables so overcooked they are just a semi-orange pulp, or so highly sweetened that they serve only as the vehicle for the syrup in which they are buried. This recipe combines a few simple ingredients that result in a naturally sweet and flavorful dish.

Roasted Carrots

Ingredients
2 pounds fresh carrots, peeled and cut on a crosswise slant into 3-inch slices*
½ teaspoon kosher salt
½ teaspoon freshly ground black pepper
½ teaspoon sugar
2 teaspoons chopped fresh rosemary
2 tablespoons olive oil
*If possible, choose carrots of the same size

Instructions
1. Preheat oven to 400 degrees F.
2. Place carrots in a large mixing bowl.
3. Sprinkle the salt, black pepper, sugar, and rosemary over the carrots and drizzle in the olive oil.
4. Gently toss to coat.
5. Place carrots on a nonstick cookie sheet or baking pan and bake for 10 minutes. Remove from the oven and stir the carrots. Return to the oven and cook for 10 additional minutes or more, depending on thickness of the vegetables, until just done.
6. Remove from the oven and serve immediately. If making ahead of time, reheat, covered, in a 350-degree F oven until hot. (I do not suggest using the microwave oven as they will lose the nice gloss that occurred while baking.)

Servings
Serves 6

* * *

A fan of subtle tastes, I love this pear and plum tart rustique. It combines the gentle flavors of these two fruits with just a hint of brown sugar, cinnamon, and nutmeg to create a delicious and wonderful dessert that is easy to make and not heavy on the palate. Gild this French fleur de lis with a spoonful of lightly sweetened cream and offer a cordial of Frangelico to go along side. Bon. Tres bon.

Pear and Plum Tart Rustique

Ingredients
1 sheet unbaked prepared piecrust
2 teaspoons all-purpose flour, divided
2 cups (about 1 pound) ripe pears, cored, peeled, and sliced ¼-inch thick lengthwise
2 cups (about 1 pound) ripe red or purple plums, *unpeeled*, seeds removed, sliced ½-inch thick
¼ cup packed dark brown sugar
¼ cup granulated sugar
¼ teaspoon cinnamon
¼ teaspoon finely ground whole nutmeg
Pinch of kosher salt
1½ tablespoons unsalted butter, melted
1 egg, beaten with 1 tablespoon of water
Whipped cream for garnish

Instructions
1. Preheat oven to 350 degrees F.
2. Dust one side of the piecrust with ½ teaspoon of the flour; shake off excess and lay crust, flour side down, on a nonstick pizza pan or cookie sheet.
3. Place the fruit in a large bowl. Add the sugars, spices, salt, and remaining 1½ teaspoon of the flour. Toss gently and coat the fruit well.
4. Drizzle the butter over the fruit and toss again to thoroughly coat all the fruit.

5. Mold the fruit and sugar juices in the middle of the piecrust and spread out evenly in a circle, leaving 2 to 3 inches of the edge of piecrust exposed.
6. Fold the piecrust over the edge of the fruit to form the tart. Crimp every few inches. The result will be a filling of exposed fruit, held in place by a short layer of pie shell.
7. Brush the folded shell circumference of the tart with the egg wash. You will not need to use the entire egg, just enough to lightly coat the crust.
8. Bake for 40 minutes, until the crust is browned and the fruit cooked.
9. Allow the tart to cool for 8 to 10 minutes before serving; garnish each slice with fresh whipped cream.

Servings
Serves 6

* * *

Traveling is one of my joys in life, and I am not back in Savannah from one trip before I start planning another. There is so much to see and do, and I take every opportunity available to visit new places and experience the great selections of food offered up wherever I go.

That said, it sure is nice to return home, too. Being able to come back to loved ones, and their welcoming embraces, especially done in the Southern manner of greeting you with a warm and delicious meal, is a real gift in life. I have learned that, no matter how far I roam, the red clay of Georgia has a mighty pull on my soul, and I miss it when I'm gone.

Eugene Walter, in the 1971 Time-Life Books *American Cooking: Southern Style*, relays this story:

On a summer's evening some years ago, two of the South's most celebrated writers, William Faulkner and Katherine Anne Porter, were dining together at a plush restaurant in Paris. Everything had been laid on to perfection; a splendid meal had been consumed, a bottle of fine Burgundy emptied, and thimble-sized glasses of an expensive liqueur drained. The maître d' and an entourage of waiters hovered close by, ready to satisfy any final whim. "Back home the butter beans are in," said Faulkner, peering into the distance, "the speckled ones." Miss Porter fiddled with her glass and stared into space. "Blackberries," she said, wistfully.

While I am not by any means trying to put myself into a writing category with either the renowned Porter or Faulkner, I share this passage rather to associate the commonality of how we Southerner's place such store in our food traditions and meals. It is, to those of us from this region, a birthright.

When I had graduated from college and was off working, I'd return often to spend the weekends with my parents. I'd pull up in the driveway, and Daddy and Missy would be waiting on the wooden swing under the shade of an old oak tree in our yard. My father would walk on up to greet me, and Missy would be running around in circles, all excited and happy. While my father would help me grab my bags from the car, I could already breathe in the smell of fried pork chops wafting in the air from the box fan in the kitchen window, blowing out the smell of home onto the side porch. Mama knew my favorite food, one that I could not cook well or get in just any restaurant, was fried pork chops. They'd be prepared in one of Ninnie's old cast-iron skillets, and it was Mama's way of saying I love you with food.

After Daddy passed away and I moved Mama down to Savannah to live near me, I knew whenever I returned from a trip without her, she'd have supper waiting for Tom and me. We'd have disembarked from a cruise, and I'd call home to tell her I was back on terra firma safely. "Honey, I'll cook you all something to eat, so you don't have to worry about going out or fixing something when you get home tonight" would always be her ending to the call. That night there might be a platter of fried chicken and potato salad made, or a pot roast with the green beans and potatoes and carrots, or maybe a platter of some country-style barbecued ribs and coleslaw spread out on the dining table.

I can relate to you that those last two paragraphs were the most difficult and poignant that I've written, because, of course, Daddy isn't here to greet me at the gate with little Missy, and Mama isn't around to fry something for me when I get home. It is, and I say it unashamedly, very sad to me. I miss them so, so much. I do indeed love to travel, but I sure did love coming home to my parents, too.

But my mother and father would not want me to be unhappy, and Mama even told me so. A few weeks after she passed away, I had a dream so realistic I could swear that it was an actual event.

It was in the middle of the night, and the phone rang. I distinctly remember sitting up in bed and picking up the receiver. On the line was Mama, and the following conversation ensued.

"Hey, honey, it's Mama."

Not understanding and totally confused at what I had just heard, I answered back, "Mama, this can't be you. You died."

"Honey, I am *fine*. Don't worry about me." It was the sound of her voice, and her inflection, as plain as day, and she did sound just fine, like her old self.

"But Mama, you died. I don't understand. Are you sure that you are okay?"

Patiently she said again, "John, honey, I am fine."

"Okay, I just can't believe I am talking to you.... I'm glad to know you're alright. But Mama, tell me. I have been worried sick over this and it has haunted me every day. Did you suffer while you were in ICU for all that time?"

Mama always had a low chuckle, which she gave through the line to me, and then answered in typical humor, "Well, John, what do you think? *I was in ICU.* But now I am fine and you have to quit worrying about me."

"Okay, if you're sure you're fine.... I love you, Mama."

"I love you, too, honey." And with that, she hung up.

I woke at that point, sitting upright in the bed, believing, as I still do, that my mother had, in a very real way, reached out to me to let me know that she was at peace and at rest.

So coming home is a little bittersweet now, but fortunately I have a bevy of good friends to help say "welcome back," and most of the time it is with a warm meal.

My dear friends Barbara and Carter, our neighbors, are always so good about inviting us over for dinner the day we get back home from an excursion. Barbara will call us and sing into the phone, "We're glad you're hoooome!" And then she'll ask us down for a wonderful Savannah supper.

Over the years, she knows now what I'd like to have. After any extended trip away, such as the last one we took to St. Thomas for a wedding, where I had my fill of jerk fish, coconut, and plantains, Barbara had prepared some of my old time favorites: roasted pork, spiced apples, mashed potatoes, and a big green-bean casserole. It was good Southern comfort food, cooked the best way, with love.

So this old hound dog will, without hesitation, jump on the back of the pickup and take off to whatever destination it might lead. But his tail wags just as hard and fast when he gets back home.

My fortieth birthday party tablemates; the night included a cocktail party, seated dinner for forty, and a five-piece disco band!

Closing

"Friends are relatives you make for yourself."
—Eustache Deschamps

As I noted before, 2012 was a painful year for me. So many in our family passed away, and losing Mama was especially hard. She had been my link to the past, the one who kept the memories of all those loved ones alive through her stories, her cooking, and her strong sense of family and self.

Her cooking and close relationship with food in particular was always a reminder of our kin. She associated some sort of dish or meal with everyone within our circle, and her conversations and observations were constantly peppered with those thoughts.

Whenever she prepared roast beef for dinner, she'd reminisce, "The very first meal your aunt Lil cooked for me after I married your daddy was a chuck roast, and she served it with fresh green beans, coleslaw, and sticks of cornbread. I had no idea at the time why she had slaw with beef; I guessed they ate a lot of cabbage up in North Georgia. But it was so good together I've served it the same way ever since."

If something was said in a conversation about tomatoes, she might remark, "Dr. Hendrix would drive all the way from Perry to Clinchfield each week in the summer for a basket of Daddy's Big Boys. Everybody in town knew he grew the best ones in the county."

Someone would mention quail hunting, and she would bring up memories of Uncle Telford and Aunt Martha. "Telford had some of the best hunting dogs in South Georgia, and those quail Martha cooked were the best you ever put in your mouth. She'd fry them with gravy, and the meat would be so tender it just fell off the bone. The best breakfast I've ever had was sitting at their table, dining on smothered quail, scrambled eggs, and biscuits."

We could be at a restaurant having a steak, and while she would be putting the sour cream and butter on her baked potato, she'd make some remark about Aunt Bea's affinity and love of starches. "Bless that girl. Beatrice can *straight* put away a potato." (Note to folks not from below the Mason-Dixon Line: the phrase "put away" in Southern food talk means "to eat a lot of something" and/or "to eat something quickly.")

If we were having the ubiquitous bowl of squash, she never failed to comment about my father's love of the yellow-neck vegetable. "I think your daddy could've been served stewed squash every day of his life and never gotten tired of eating it. If there wasn't but a tablespoon of it left after supper, he'd get me or Carrie to wrap it up and save it for the next day."

And Aunt Hazel was known in Mama's cooking memories for her home-jarred pickles. "There was not another woman in Houston County who could put up a better jar of bread-and-butter pickles than Hazel Grace. I could make a meal off a bowl of her pickles and a couple of fried chicken wings."

These are just a few of the dozens of food stories and inferences Mama had and would always share. In her mind, just like that of so many Southerners, people and food are interrelated in a way that goes far beyond simple sustenance. The bond and affiliation is such that you can easily name off the foods your loved ones like or dislike and the tales behind them, just as simply as you can recall the color of their hair or the sound of their voice.

Mama's recollections helped keep our relatives in the forefront of everyday life. And I sorely miss that comforting, ongoing exchange of familial history.

To my great benefit and good fortune, though, my very close group of friends constantly surrounded me during these burdensome days. They were a continuous source of compassion, empathy, and sympathy, and, of course, food.

From the time my mother entered the ICU, through the months that ensued, and until well after her funeral, I never had to cook or worry about going to the grocery store. Friends provided all of my meals. They coordinated together so that each day was covered, whether it was something special from one of their kitchens, a catered dinner, or someone taking me out to eat.

They even went as so far as to plan the wake. With my sweet friend Carolyn as the chief coordinator, they orchestrated an incredible meal that was both delicious and beautiful. Silver platters and crystal bowls of all sorts of Southern and coastal delicacies arrived by the armful, as well as cases of wines and other spirits. When you walked into the house, it was as if you'd stepped into a one of the Cloister's celebrated buffet feasts. Also delivered were warm embraces, soft kisses, and murmurings of affection by the ladies, along with bear hugs, meaningful shoulder crunches across the back, and firm handshakes from the fellows where they would grab you by the forearm and pull you close to say how sorry they were.

Serving all this magnificent food was my favorite caterer, Becca. She arrived at the house along with two of her staff to tend bar, wait on the guests, and clean up afterwards. When the evening was at an end, I came into the kitchen to thank them and pulled out my wallet to pay for their efforts. They had been at the house, tending to well over one hundred people, for more than four hours, and given up a Friday night to do so. But much to my aggravation, and then complete affection, they would not be paid. Despite my protests, they refused all my offers and filed out the back door, got into the catering van, and drove off without accepting anything but a hug from me.

Other kindnesses flowed freely as well. One of my dearest friends, Cathy, is an incredible florist and interior designer (as well as a former Miss Savannah). Her sense of decor is incredibly rich but at the same time elegantly understated. The morning after my mother passed away, on our door was a magnificent wreath made of pittosporum, white roses, forest-green baby magnolia, and English ivy, all laced through with a black, silk ribbon that was tied at the top in a large bow that she'd made. Cathy also took charge of the flowers for the church. She spent two days creating a magnificent masterpiece that spanned the length of the high altar at St. Paul's Episcopal, as well as making a stunning arrangement that graced the table where Mama's ashes were held. Cathy would not accept any payment for her services, but said it was a gesture of love and friendship and the respect she had for my mom.

This book is a tribute, as you have seen, in so many ways to my mother and father and the family members I miss so much. I'd like this closing, though, to be a thanks to my loving friends, who have been so good to me over the years, and who took such special care of me during the times when I needed them by my side. I appreciate the laughter, tears, jokes, trips, meals, dances, parties, and camaraderie we've had over the years. My family has expanded with each and every one of these caring and kind souls.

The final menu I have is one that is inspired by those comforting friends, and several of the recipes are ones shared by some of them who enjoy their time in the kitchen as much as I do. These dishes are what you might find on a typical Savannah cocktail buffet, complete with hors d'oeuvres, entrées, side dishes, and desserts so that your friends can happily nosh and nibble in a fashion befitting the Hostess City of the South. And staying true to my efforts, these can all be prepared in advance of whatever type soiree you're throwing, allowing you time to mix, mingle, share some sports scores, and gossip.

I have been so fully blessed in life, and while I miss my folks each and every day, I'll always have, along with their wonderful memories, the promise of God's grace, good friends, and, of course, good food. I'd like to close by sharing some of the words of my most favorite hymn. We ended Mom's funeral Mass with an uplifting and stirring rendition of "Ode to Joy," and this stanza makes me smile. I fully realize that I've been fortunate to have sung many sweet verses in the "song of life," and I find incredible comfort in knowing that there is still much to look forward to and oh, so much to be grateful for.

Mortals, join the happy chorus, which the morning stars began;
Father love is reigning o'er us, brother love binds man to man.
Ever singing, march we onward, victors in the midst of strife,
Joyful music leads us Sunward in the triumph song of life.
Amen.

Mama and Daddy, their last photo together, on our front porch
on Ball Street, Perry, Georgia, Thanksgiving afternoon, 1997

Menu of Items for a Savannah Soiree

~Tomato Sandwiches (recipe found on page 142)
~Baked Crab and Artichoke Spread
~Crudité with Curried Mayonnaise
~Terrine of Chevre and Rosemary
~Low-Country Pickled Shrimp
~Pimento Cheese Biscuits with Ham Butter
~Barbara's Perfect Beef Tenderloin with Horseradish Cream Sauce
~Grilled Filet of Salmon
~Savannah Spinach Squares
~Lemon Bars
~Pecan Tassies

Baked Crab and Artichoke Spread

The following is a variation on two favorites that you find at Savannah parties, combining the main ingredients of luscious coastal Georgia blue crab and the slightly tart and equally soft-textured artichoke. Blended and baked with Vidalia onions, Parmesan cheese, and mayonnaise, it is a stellar appetizer for any occasion.

Ingredients
3 tablespoons olive oil
2 cups chopped Vidalia onions
2 14-ounce cans of baby artichokes, drained
1 4-ounce jar of diced pimento, drained
1¼ cup to 1½ cup real mayonnaise
3 tablespoons Dijon mustard
Dash of hot sauce
8 ounces of freshly grated Parmesan cheese
1 pound claw crabmeat, picked over for shells
Toast points or water crackers

Instructions
1. Preheat oven to 350 degrees F.
2. Heat the oil in a large skillet over medium-high heat. Add the onions and cook, stirring often, until they are tender but not browned, about 5 minutes. Remove from heat.
3. Squeeze the excess moisture from the artichokes by taking 3 to 4 into your hand and firmly pressing the water out over the sink. When all are finished, chop the artichokes into 1-inch pieces.
4. In a mixing bowl, add the onions, artichoke hearts, pimento, mayonnaise, mustard, hot sauce, and Parmesan cheese; mix until thoroughly incorporated.
5. With a spatula, fold in the crab, being careful not to tear the larger pieces.
6. Spread in a 9-x-13 baking dish and cook for about 30 minutes, or until the top starts to lightly brown.
7. Remove from heat and allow to cool for 10 minutes. Serve with toast points or water crackers.

Servings
Serves 16 to 20

* * *

Crudité with Curried Mayonnaise

We need some veggies on our buffet to balance out the menu, and to keep our vegetarian friends happy and fed. Of course you may use any items you choose, I just like the combination of colors and tastes of the listing below. The curried mayo adds a somewhat sweet and soft finish to the dish.

Ingredients
1 gallon of water
¼ cup kosher salt
3 pounds fresh asparagus
3 red bell peppers, seeded and sliced thinly into strips
3 14-ounce cans hearts of palm, sliced into ½-inch rings

2 cups real mayonnaise
1 tablespoon curry powder
2 tablespoons minced fresh chives

Instructions
1. In a large pot, bring the water and salt to a boil. Add asparagus. For pencil-thin sizes, cook for 30 seconds and drain. For larger pieces, cook 60 to 90 seconds until just blanched through. Drain immediately.
2. Place drained asparagus in a sink full of iced water, or in a very large bowl containing enough ice water to submerge the vegetables. The asparagus must be totally chilled and cooled or it will lose its bright-green color. Drain, and dry the spears in batches on paper towels. Place in a container, cover tightly, and keep cold until ready to serve.
3. To make the curried dip, combine the mayonnaise, curry, and chives. Cover and chill for 2 hours.
4. Arrange the vegetables on a platter and serve with a bowl of the dip alongside.

Servings
Serves 16 to 20

* * *

Terrine of Chevre and Rosemary

My friend Erica has a keen ability of combining a variety of tastes, whether using an old Southern keepsake recipe or trying out a fusion-style dish that shouts "new order." Here, she has an elegant presentation that looks and tastes very rich but is simple to make. I like to serve this terrine atop a footed cake stand. As this recipe needs to be refrigerated overnight, make sure you begin the preparation the day before you plan to serve it.

Ingredients
2 pounds chevre (or any soft, mild goat cheese)
1 pound cream cheese

1/8 teaspoon kosher salt
3 tablespoons fresh rosemary, minced
1/3 cup half-and-half
3 tablespoons plum jam (or other tart jam)
3 tablespoons honey
1½ teaspoons water
1 cup shelled pistachios, chopped
Crackers or toast points
Sprigs of rosemary for garnish

Instructions
1. Allow the cheeses to come to room temperature.
2. Place the cheeses and salt into a mixing bowl; beat over medium speed until thoroughly mixed and softened.
3. Add the rosemary and half-and-half to the cheese spread; beat for a moment until fully incorporated.
4. Line a springform pan with plastic wrap; place the cheese mixture into the pan and pat down with a spatula until it is evenly and firmly distributed. Cover tightly and refrigerate overnight.
5. In a mixing bowl, whisk the jam, honey, and water together until fully mixed. Set aside.
6. Unmold the terrine onto a platter or cake stand. Drizzle the top and overlap the sides with the jam and honey mixture and finish by sprinkling the pistachios on top.
7. Serve with rice crackers, water crackers, or toast points and garnish with sprigs of fresh rosemary.

Servings
Serves 16 to 20

* * *

Low-Country Pickled Shrimp

This dish is a fixture on Savannah buffet tables and sideboards. Usually served in large cut-glass bowls, it makes a beautiful presentation. There are a number of variations on the dish—some with capers, maybe green bell pepper, some spice it up with red pepper flakes. Tom likes to throw in cherry tomatoes and fresh bay leaves to give it a bold splash of color, particularly at a Christmas party. But the basics are always the same: lightly poached shrimp, oil, vinegar, onions, and celery. I enjoy the taste of fresh dill with shrimp and include it in this recipe.

Ingredients
3 quarts of water
¼ cup Old Bay seasoning
3 pounds large US wild-caught shrimp, peeled and deveined, tails removed
3 stalks of celery, sliced into thin 2-inch long julienne strips
1 medium-sized Vidalia or red onion, very thinly sliced into rings
1 4-ounce jar sliced pimento, drained
6 to 8 fresh bay leaves
3 tablespoons capers, drained
¼ cup packed minced fresh dill weed
1½ cups good-quality vegetable oil
¾ cup apple cider vinegar
½ teaspoon Dijon mustard
1 teaspoon salt
¼ teaspoon freshly ground black pepper
3 to 4 large sprigs of fresh parsley for garnish

Instructions
1. Bring 3 quarts of water and the Old Bay seasoning to a boil in a large pot; add shrimp, stir, cover, remove from heat, and set aside for 5 minutes. The shrimp are done when the tail section curves up and almost touches the head area. Thoroughly drain in a colander; do not rinse.
2. Place the shrimp into a large airtight container along with the celery, onion, pimento, bay leaves, capers, and dill. Toss to mix.
3. In a bowl, whisk together the oil and remaining ingredients except for the parsley. Pour over the shrimp mixture and toss to coat. Cover the container and refrigerate 8 hours or overnight. Stir once or twice during the chilling process.

4. Before serving, drain the shrimp in a colander and discard the juice. Place the shrimp mixture in a decorative crystal or cut glass bowl and garnish with the parsley.

Servings
Serves 16 to 20

* * *

Pimento Cheese Biscuits with Ham Butter

Our good friend and neighbor Cathy brought a platter of these delicacies to the house a while back, and they were gone before you could say Boo Radley. Pimento cheese and biscuits are both staples in the South, and when cooked together, with a little spice to warm the palate, you have a beautiful mini-food portrait of Savannah. Gild these lilies with a bowl of rich, sweet ham butter as an accompanying spread, and you won't be able to keep the fellows away from the sideboard.

Ingredients
Pimento Cheese Biscuits
2 cups White Lily self-rising flour
2 tablespoons sugar
1 teaspoon ground black pepper
¼ teaspoon cayenne pepper
¼ cup Crisco shortening
¾ cup whole-milk buttermilk (don't use the low-fat buttermilk or the
  biscuits won't be as moist)
1 cup shredded sharp cheddar cheese
1 4-ounce jar pimentos, drained

Ham Butter
2 cups good-quality ham, such as Honey Baked
1 cup unsalted butter, at room temperature
2 tablespoons minced fresh chives

Instructions

Pimento Cheese Biscuits:

1. Preheat oven to 475 F.
2. Sift flour and dry ingredients into a large mixing bowl.
3. Add shortening.
4. With your fingers, very gently rub together the flour and shortening until thoroughly incorporated, about 2 minutes.
5. Drizzle the buttermilk over the mixture.
6. With a large fork, gently mix the buttermilk and flour/shortening, folding over and over until just mixed together well. This step is crucial for light biscuits: if you are too heavy-handed with the mixing, the biscuits won't rise and will be hard.
7. Add in the cheese and pimentos; mix lightly until just incorporated.
8. With a spatula, fold the mixture out onto a floured surface.
9. Flour your hands and gently knead together a few times.
10. Gently spread the dough out until it is a disc about 6 inches wide, and fold over onto itself.
11. With your hands, push down on the dough until you get a flat surface that is roughly an inch- or an inch-and-a-half thick. You can use a rolling pin, just don't press too hard.
12. Using a floured 2-inch disc, cut the biscuits out and place on a nonstick cookie sheet or a well-seasoned cast-iron skillet.
13. Place biscuits in oven and reduce heat to 400 degrees F.
14. Bake 8 to 10 minutes until done and just beginning to brown on top.
15. Remove from the stove; allow to cool to room temperature. Serve with Ham Butter.

Servings

Makes 18 to 20 2-inch biscuits

Ham Butter:

1. In a food processor, finely grind the ham.
2. Add the butter, and pulse several times to thoroughly mix.
3. Place mixture in a bowl, stir in the chives, and cover tightly. Chill for 4 hours or overnight. Serve with Pimento Cheese Biscuits.

Servings

Serves 16-20

* * *

Barbara's Perfect Beef Tenderloin with Horseradish Cream Sauce

Our dear friend Barbara has a recipe for beef tenderloin that is fail-proof; follow the directions exactly, and you'll be rewarded with a perfectly roasted piece of prime meat that has a luscious crust and a deep-pink, medium-rare center. The medallions will be fork-tender, so no need for a knife. The meat is excellent for a buffet served on small rolls or slider buns.

Ingredients
Beef Tenderloin
1 6- to 7-pound beef tenderloin, trimmed (trimming instructions are found at the end of the recipe)
2 tablespoons Worcestershire sauce
3 tablespoons olive oil
2 tablespoons each kosher salt, freshly ground black pepper, garlic powder, and onion powder
Small rolls or slider buns

Horseradish Cream Sauce
2 scant cups good-quality, real mayonnaise
2/3 cup sour cream
1/3 cup (plus more if needed) finely ground horseradish

Instructions
Beef Tenderloin:
1. Preheat oven to 500 degrees F.
2. Coat the tenderloin on all sides, first with the Worcestershire and then the olive oil.
3. Sprinkle the seasonings on the meat evenly on all sides.
4. Place the tenderloin in a large, shallow roasting pan, uncovered. Roast, uncovered, 5 minutes for each pound of beef (if the roast is 5 pounds, then 25 minutes; if 6, then 30, and so forth.) After this step, turn the heat off and leave the roast in the oven *exactly* 1 hour. *Do not open the oven door during any point of the cooking process.*

5. Remove the meat from the oven and set aside; allow it to rest 20 minutes before carving. Slice into ¼-inch thick medallions for a buffet (or into eight equally sized steaks for a main course.) This dish is easily made ahead and can be refrigerated; simply allow the meat to cool, cover tightly, and keep until ready to slice and serve.

6. Serve at room temperature with small, soft rolls and the following Horseradish Cream Sauce.

Trimming a beef tenderloin: Some people do not dress the meat before cooking it; however, I highly recommend doing so. By removing the excess fat, silver skin, flat tail-end, and the loose side muscle, called "the chain," which runs the length of the roast, you will have a uniform piece of meat that can be carved into slices of equal size. An important reason for removing the silver skin is that, left unpeeled, this pearlescent-colored membrane will restrict the roast while cooking, making it curl instead of staying in a straight shape. Save the tail-end and chain, which you can freeze, and use later for a stir-fry or other dish. Discard the skin and fat.

If you attempt this yourself, the main thing to remember is to take your time when removing the membrane, which is the hardest part. Using a sharp paring or boning knife, make an inch-long cut into the skin at the top of the meat. Keeping your knife pointed upward away from the roast, slowly and carefully saw the membrane until you can remove it. Continue until all the roast is unpeeled. I suggest asking your butcher, an expert, to complete these steps for you, though. It saves time and you'll be assured of getting exactly what you need.

Horseradish Cream Sauce:

Mix ingredients; taste and add additional horseradish if you would like a spicier sauce. Cover and allow to chill for 2 hours. Serve with prime rib or beef tenderloin.

Servings
Serves 24 for a buffet, 8 as a main course
* * *

Grilled Filet of Salmon

I've recently acquired two new friends who moved to Savannah from Washington, DC, Ray Hrabec and Anne Tyree. He is a bon vivant and she a sweet beauty, and they love to entertain. Whenever we have a neighborhood party, we always ask them to bring this very simple but incredibly delicious dish. Dusted with spices and grilled until just done, it is perfect for an hors d'oeuvre, or you may prepare it in larger portions as an entrée.

Ingredients
1 3-pound filet of fresh, wild-caught salmon, skin on
1½ tablespoons olive oil
½ teaspoon kosher salt
½ teaspoon sweet paprika
½ teaspoon dried thyme
¼ teaspoon freshly ground black pepper
¼ teaspoon onion powder
¼ teaspoon garlic powder
1/8 teaspoon cayenne or red pepper
8 ounces chevre cheese, at room temperature (may substitute cream cheese)
1 teaspoon each finely minced fresh basil, thyme, and parsley
3 tablespoons capers, along with slices of lemon and parsley sprigs for garnish

Instructions
1. Heat your gas grill to 400 degrees F (or prepare a charcoal grill according to bag instructions).
2. Rub the salmon filet with olive oil.
3. In a small bowl, mix together the kosher salt, paprika, thyme, black pepper, onion powder, garlic powder, and cayenne pepper. Sprinkle this on top of the salmon.
4. Cook the salmon on a greased grill, skin side down—do not turn— with the lid of the grill closed, for 10 minutes. Check for doneness: the meat in the middle should be easy to test-flake with a fork. The timing will depend on thickness.

5. Remove from heat onto a plate and tent with aluminum foil. Allow to sit for 10 minutes.
6. Take off foil and carefully remove the skin from the salmon on the bottom (save the skin for your cat). Place salmon on a serving platter.
7. Place chevre in a small bowl; stir and press with a spoon until soft and creamy. Divide the chevre in two equal portions and form two small patties of the cheese. Place the two servings on either side of your salmon, and sprinkle the cheese with the basil, thyme, and parsley.
8. Garnish the platter with the lemon, parsley, and capers, and serve with crackers or toast points.

Servings
Serves 16 for a buffet

* * *

Savannah Spinach Squares

I love alliteration, and since our city is laid out in squares, this is a fitting title for a vegetable-and-cheese side dish. My friend Gayle Morris, a wonderful buddy and a Bulldog fan of the highest order, shared this recipe with me. Gayle is one of the best Southern cooks I've encountered over the years. She once made me a chicken pot pie with a homemade biscuit topping, and it was so good, I ate three helpings...and literally gained two pounds overnight. Was just fabulous.

This casserole is perfect for a buffet dinner—you can cook it ahead of time and serve it sliced into bite-sized squares. The fresh spinach, along with a burst of garlic and hint of nutmeg, make for a really tasty side dish, or can be a main event for our vegetarian friends.

Ingredients
3 tablespoons olive oil
2 tablespoons freshly minced garlic
16 ounces (1 pound) fresh spinach, chopped
1 15-ounce container ricotta cheese

3 large eggs, slightly beaten
6 tablespoons unsalted butter, melted
2 cups shredded Italian cheese blend (Parmesan, mozzarella, Romano)
2/3 cup self-rising flour
1 teaspoon salt
¼ teaspoon freshly ground black pepper
¼ teaspoon freshly grated nutmeg

Instructions
1. Preheat oven to 350 degrees F.
2. Butter or lightly grease a 9-x-13 baking dish and set aside.
3. In a large skillet, heat oil over medium. Add garlic and stir for about 30 seconds, being careful not to let the garlic brown.
4. Add the spinach. Stir well and cover. Wait about 1 minute, remove cover and stir. Continue to lightly sauté the spinach until just wilted, about 3 to 4 minutes total. Remove from heat, and pour the spinach mixture in a colander to drain.
5. In a large mixing bowl, whisk the ricotta until spreadable.
6. Add the eggs, butter, and cheese blend to the ricotta. Stir well to mix.
7. Gently squeeze out excess moisture from the spinach and add spinach to the mixing bowl.
8. Add the flour, salt, pepper, and nutmeg and stir well until fully mixed together.
9. Pour into the buttered baking dish and spread out evenly. Bake for 40 minutes or so, until the top starts to brown and the casserole is set.
10. Remove from oven. May be served hot, or allow to cool to room temperature. You may also chill the dish overnight, and, while cold, cut into 2-inch squares for a buffet dinner.

Servings
Serves 16 to 20

* * *

Desserts for a stand-up cocktail buffet, at least in my opinion, should be uncomplicated and easy to serve so you don't worry about a balancing act with the food and the glass of Veuve Clicquot you have in hand. These recipes are served bite-sized, and all are a delicious way to end a night of culinary repast.

Lemon Bars

This dessert dish is incredibly popular in our hot coastal city; the zesty taste of the citrus is a very nice way to finish off a heavy meal, particularly in the middle of our humid summers. You'll find recipes for these squares in most Savannah cookbooks, including those by local culinary icons Damon Lee Fowler, Susan Mason, and Martha Nesbit. The basics for this simple but utterly delicious dish are the same: a shortbread crust that you prebake and a sweet but "suck-your-cheeks-in" tart filling of lemon zest and juice.

Ingredients
Crust
1 cup plus 1 tablespoon unsalted butter, at room temperature, divided
2 cups all-purpose flour
¾ cup confectioner's sugar
Pinch of salt

Filling
4 large eggs
2 cups sugar
1/3 cup freshly squeezed lemon juice
2 teaspoons finely grated lemon zest
1 teaspoon baking powder
¼ teaspoon salt
¼ cup all-purpose flour
2 or 3 tablespoons superfine or confectioner's sugar for decoration

Instructions
Crust
1. Preheat oven to 350 degrees F.
2. Grease a 9-x-13 baking dish with 1 tablespoon of butter.

3. Mix the 1 cup of butter, flour, sugar, and salt in a bowl; stir well until thoroughly mixed.
4. Place dough in the baking dish, and pat down the mixture into the bottom of the dish with your hands until evenly distributed.
5. Bake for 15 to 20 minutes until the crust is a golden color. Remove from oven and allow to cool.

Filling
1. Beat the eggs and sugar until smooth.
2. Add the juice, zest, powder, salt, and flour; stir until well incorporated. Pour the filling over the crust.
3. Bake for 25 to 30 minutes until the filling is set.
4. Allow to cool to room temperature. Sprinkle with sugar and cut into bars. Can be stored for several days in an airtight container.

Servings
Serves 16 to 20

* * *

Pecan Tassies

This is another dessert popularly served in Savannah and throughout the South. They are basically miniature pecan pies, and the recipes for this classic are all very similar. Usually made with a cream-cheese pastry dough, I bypass that route and use a commercially made piecrust that you can unroll, cut, and you're ready.

Ingredients
1 16-ounce package rolled piecrusts
1 egg
¾ cup dark brown sugar
2 tablespoons unsalted butter, melted
1 teaspoon vanilla extract
1 cup finely chopped pecans

Instructions
1. Lightly grease a 24-count mini-muffin pan.

2. Preheat oven to 350 degrees F.
3. Unroll the piecrust dough and lightly dust one side of each crust with flour.
4. With a 2½" –3"cookie cutter, slice out 24 discs. Place one disc into each tin, flour side down.
5. In a mixing bowl, beat together the egg, sugar, butter, and vanilla until smooth.
6. Equally measure out the pecans, placing some in the bottom of each of the pastry shells.
7. Pour the egg mixture over the pecans so that each tin is about 2/3 to ¾ of the way full.
8. Bake for 25 minutes, or until the filling is set.
9. Remove from the oven, and allow to cool for 5 minutes or so. Remove the pies from the pan and place them on a wire rack to cool. Refrigerate in an airtight container until ready to serve.

Note: you can dress up these tarts up with a bit of sweetened cream cheese and top with a glazed pecan.

Servings
Makes 24 mini-tarts

Acknowledgments

My biggest thanks go first and foremost to Janis Owens and Joyce Dixon. Just out of college, Joyce was my high school literature teacher, bringing to Westfield High School a fresh approach to academics and introducing me to the magic of Southern literature. For her continued belief in me and my efforts, I am forever grateful. Janis, my Cracker "cousin," lovingly critiqued, guided, and counseled me throughout this journey; I would not be writing these acknowledgements today were it not for her. A bushel and a peck, Janis.

To Monique: I knew when we met, sipping cocktails on that gorgeous veranda overlooking downtown Savannah and talking about books and food, that we'd be lifelong friends. Thanks for being the catalyst for *Rise and Shine!* and for providing that mustard seed.

Deep appreciation is extended to Alphus Christopher Spears and Lisa Lacy White for lending their time and extensive knowledge of the Queen's English; your editing and encouragement helped get the book on Mercer's desk...cheers and lots of Middle Georgia love to you both.

And to the folks at Mercer University Press: thank you for putting your name behind my work and for the faith you have in this Georgia son. I hope to do you proud.

Tom, thanks for the staunch support for lo these many months and for being my taste-tester in the kitchen and stand-in cook. Aren't you glad my piddling came to fruition?

Gaye Smith (Missy!), many thanks for the judicious ear, sage advice, and for accompanying me on so many food expeditions across the state. Here's to the Colonnade and fried chicken livers!

Thanks to my first cousins, Andrea Tucker, Ann Miller, Bucky and Patti Barrett, and Joyce Giles, as well as to my sister, for helping me bring together family recipes and making certain what I had in my memory and from Mama's notecards was accurate.

For my cousin Linda Michelle...what a few years it has been. Mama and Aunt Bea brought us together and gave us so much, and, luckily, we had each other to hold on to when we had to tell them goodbye. I know that they are so happy in the bond we share. Love you.

Levy, Elodie, Tommy, and Logan, each time I look at you I can imagine the smile on Mama's face, hear Daddy whooping when he landed a big one, or see Aunt Bea patting her foot along to a Rascal Flatts song. I hope this book helps keep their memories alive for you in a special way as you grow into adulthood and beyond. I love each of you from the bottom of my heart.

Index of Recipes

Entrees

Jams, Jellies and Preserves

Salads

Author

Johnathon Barrett is a seventh-generation Georgian, who grew up amongst a family that placed high value on fresh, farm-to-table food. He held on to those roots and became a renowned cook and host in culinary-rich Savannah. A nonprofit executive and CPA, Johnathon is also an avid reader, fisherman, and gardener. This is his first book.